Longman H

**Ronald Carter
and Michael N. Long**

Tea

Liter

Longman

Longman Group UK Limited,
Longman House, Burnt Mill, Harlow,
Essex CM20 2JE, England
and Associated Companies throughout the world.

Published in the United States of America
by Longman Inc., New York

First published 1991

British Library Cataloguing in Publication Data
Carter, R. A. (Ronald A.)
    Teaching literature – (Longman handbooks for
    language teachers)
    1. Great Britain. Secondary schools. Curriculum
    subjects: English literature. Teaching.
    I. Title   II. Long, M. N.
    820.71241

ISBN 0582 74628 0

Library of Congress Cataloging in Publication Data
Carter, R. A.
    Teaching literature / R.A. Carter and M.N. Long.
        p.   cm.--(Longman handbooks for language
teachers)
    Includes bibliographical references.
    ISBN 0-582-74628-0
    1. Literature--Study and teaching (Higher)   I. Long,
M.N.
    II. Title.   III. Series.
PN59.C29   1991
807'.1'1--dc20   90-42580
                                                           CIP

Set in 10/12pt Linotronic 202 Times Roman

Produced by Longman Group (FE) Ltd
Printed in Hong Kong

Contents

ACKNOWLEDGEMENTS

We are grateful to the following for permission to reproduce copyright material:

Cambridge University Press for an extract from *The Web of Words* by R Carter & M Long & questions from past 'Cambridge First Certificate' & 'Cambridge Proficiency' examination papers; Carcanet Press Ltd & New Directions Publishing Corporation for the poem 'The Red Wheelbarrow' by William Carlos Williams from *Collected Poems of William Carlos Williams, 1909–1939, Vol I.* Copyright 1938 by New Directions Publishing Corporation; the author, Nissim Ezekiel & Oxford University Press, India, for an extract from the poem 'The Patriot' from *Collected Poems* (pub 1989); Faber & Faber Ltd & New Directions Publishing Corporation for the poem 'In a Station of the Metro' from *Collected Shorter Poems* by Erza Pound, US title *Personae* by Ezra Pound, copyright 1926 by Erza Pound; Faber & Faber Ltd & The Putnam Publishing Group for an extract form *Lord of the Flies* by William Golding, copyright © 1954 by William Gerald Golding; Grafton Books, a division of Harper Collins Publishers Ltd, & Liveright Publishing Corporation for an extract from the poem 'Yes, is a pleasant country' from *Complete Poems, 1913–1962* by E E Cummings. Copyright © 1923, 1925, 1932, 1935, 1938, 1939, 1940, 1944, 1945, 1947, 1948, 1949, 1950, 1951, 1952, 1953, 1954, 1955, 1956, 1957, 1958, 1959, 1960, 1961, 1962 by the Trustees for the E E Cummings Trust. Copyright © 1961, 1963, 1968 by Marion Morehouse Cummings; Heinemann Publishers (Oxford) Ltd for an extract from *A Man of the People* by C Achebe (pub Heinemann Educational Books Ltd); the author's agent & Faber & Faber Ltd for the poem 'The Warm & The Cold' from *Season Songs* by Ted Hughes; Longman Group UK Ltd for extracts from *Adam Bede* by George Eliot, simplified by G Horsley (pub Longman Simplified English Series, 1964), an extract from *Openings* by Brian Tomlinson (pub Lingual House, 1986); the author's agent for the poem 'Owl' from *Collected Poems 1958–82* by George MacBeth (pub Hutchinson Books Ltd), copyright © George MacBeth 1965; Macmillan Ltd, London & Basingstoke, for an adapted bibliography from *Literature & the Language Learner: Methodological Approaches* edited by R Carter et al (pub 1989); Ewan MacNaughton Associates for the article '80 dead 100 hurt in Spanish hotel fire' by Timothy Brown from *The Daily Telegraph* 13.7.79, © The Daily Telegraph plc; the author's agent for the poem '40 Love' from *After the Merrymaking* by Rober McGough (pub Jonathan Cape Ltd); Methuen, an imprint of Octopus Publishing Group Ltd, for extracts from *Golden Girls* by Louise Page (pub Methuen Drama); John Murray (Publishers) Ltd for the poems 'Meditation on the A30' & 'Harvest Hymn' by John Betjeman from *Collected Poems*; Northern Songs for lyrics of the song 'And I love her' by John Lennon & Paul McCartney, copyright © 1964; Oxford University Press for an extract from *The Oxford Companion to English Literature* (4th Edition, 1978); Random Century Group, on behalf of the Estate of Robert Frost, & Henry Holt & Co, Inc, for the poems 'The Road Not Taken' & 'The Hill Wife' by Robert Frost from *The Poetry of Robert Frost* edited by Edward Connery Lathem (pub Jonathan Cape Ltd). Copyright 1916, © 1969 by Holt, Rinehart & Winston. Copyright 1944 by Robert Frost; Reuters Ltd for a report by Kathleen Callo from *Bangkok Post* 10.4.87; George T Sassoon for the poem 'The General' by Siegfried Sassoon; the author, Vernon Scannell for an extract from his poem 'Autumn' from *New & Collected Poems* (pub Robson Books Ltd); The Statesman & Nation Publishing Co Ltd for the poem 'High Wood' by Philip Johnstone from *Nation* 16.2.18.

We have been unable to trace the copyright holders in the following & would appreciate any information that would enable us to do so;

the poem 'Song of Lawino' by Okot p'Bitek; the poem 'Neighbours' by Kit Wright; a report in *The Daily Telegraph* 17.3.87.

We are grateful to the following for permission to use copyright material and photographs.

Barnaby's Picture Library for page 63 (top left). The Bath Hotel, for page 104. Robert Bosch Domestic Appliances Limited for pages 34 and 35. Mary Evans Picture Library for page 63 (top right). Caroline Hands/Canns Down Press for page 14. Trustees of The Imperial War Museum, London for page 32. London Weekend Television Limited for page 63 (bottom right). Lynx Cars Limited for page 14. Mercury Asset Management for page 109. THAI Airways International/Formula Communications for page 40.

Authors' note

Many people have contributed to this book. The authors would like to offer particular thanks to: Neville Grant, for helpful comments on earlier drafts of the book; Jean Greenwood, John McRae, Mavis Hawkey and Luke Prodromou for some inspiring teaching ideas on which we have drawn in parts of the book, especially in Chapters 3 and 4; Damien Tunnacliffe and Helena Gomm for exemplary editorial support and high degrees of patience.

Preface: The organisation of the book

Our rationale is closely related to how we envisage the book might be *used*, for this is a book which we hope will be read by individual teachers and which may help to meet the demand for course-books for the ever increasing numbers of training courses for the teaching of literature in a second or foreign language.

We have chosen to begin by raising some key issues in the classroom treatment of literature within the context of language teaching, elaborating in the second chapter our view that literature must be treated in such a way as to engage with the experience of students. Unless literary texts are discovered to be meaningful and relevant to personal experience then there is little point to their treatment in the classroom. The approaches described in the following three chapters are designed to try to prepare the way for a contact between literature and experience.

The second section of the book (comprising the next three chapters) is principally concerned with classroom procedures with a range of different strategies being illustrated and discussed. The emphasis is on language-based approaches for it is our main argument here that attention to language provides a 'way-in' to the text, creating an access to textual meaning and a set of heuristic devices and strategies for working in a collaborative learner-centred and activity-based manner to discover for oneself what and how literary texts mean. We also argue that such approaches can usefully augment language development in English thus creating a degree of integration in the usually divided language and literature curriculum. The approaches become increasingly advanced and draw continuously on well-tried language teaching strategies which we hope to have adapted sensitively to the needs of the non-native student of literature in English. In order to underline the importance of an integrated approach, Chapter 5 links a number of language-based approaches to a single text.

In Section III we return to some key general issues and introduce questions of a more theoretical nature, which are designed to take us beyond the limits of the previous sections. In particular, we explore the possible relevance of recent work in literary and cultural theory to the design and development of the literature curriculum in different parts of the world in which English is studied.

Throughout the book there are regular opportunities for reflecting on or exploring beyond our discussion. We pose a number of questions at the end of each section and create tasks for individual or collective exploration. We hope that these opportunities allow examination and evaluation of approaches as well as further discussion of issues which relate to the many different contexts in which readers/users of the book will find themselves. The teaching of literature is an important and complex business and is always relative to different cultural, experiential and pedagogic concerns. We certainly do not claim in this book to have all the answers, but we do at least hope to have helped you to explore some relevant questions.

SECTION 1
LITERATURE IN THE CLASSROOM

1

Why literature?

1.0
Introduction

Until relatively recent times the teaching of literature in foreign-language classes was an activity whose justification was assumed to be obvious. In many places this is still true: the study of certain classic pieces of English literature is considered a *sine qua non* for the truly educated person.

More recently – and especially in the last fifteen years or so – the emphasis on the study of English for specific practical purposes, technical or otherwise, as well as, more broadly, an emphasis on the spoken more than on the written language, has severely challenged the place of literature in the teaching of English as a second or foreign language. Looking through TEFL/TESL writings in the seventies or early eighties, we find surprisingly little about the teaching of literature, and hardly anything controversial. Perhaps this is partly due to the fact that in places where literature continued to be taught for the 'old' reasons there seemed no need for justification, and in other places it tended not to come into the picture at all – or at least not to any significant degree. Certainly, there was little or no extended discussion of the role of literature teaching in a second or foreign language or even of the relationship between language and literature teaching.

During the 1980s the situation has changed quite radically and literature is undergoing an extensive reconsideration within the language teaching profession, provoking a series of articles in professional journals, books, conferences and curricular reviews. This book aims to contribute further to such discussion and debate.

1.1
Why teach literature?

One important outcome of a relative neglect followed by a re-introduction of literature in the language classroom has been the prompting of a fundamental question: *why* teach literature? It is a question which has to be answered before any meaningful discussion can take place concerning either the place of literature in the EFL/ESL classroom or the interface of literature and language

1

teaching. The *reasons* for teaching literature necessarily transcend the particular circumstances, places and contexts in which literature is taught.

Three main reasons for the teaching of literature have been consistently advanced. Each embraces a particular set of learning objectives for the student of literature. These are:

- The cultural model
- The language model
- The personal growth model

The three models are not of course mutually exclusive and should preferably be viewed as tendencies; but they do represent distinct models which are embraced by teachers as reasons or purposes for the teaching of literature and they are related to specific pedagogic practices. The models may be summarised as follows:

The cultural model
Teachers working within such an orientation stress the value of literature in encapsulating the accumulated wisdom, the best that has been thought and felt within a culture. Literature expresses the most significant ideas and sentiments of human beings and teaching literature represents a means by which students can be put in touch with a range of expression – often of universal value and validity – over an historical period or periods. Teaching literature within a cultural model enables students to understand and appreciate cultures and ideologies different from their own in time and space and to come to perceive tradition of thought, feeling, and artistic form within the heritage the literature of such cultures endows. It is this particular 'human' sense that gives literature a central place in the study and teaching of the humanities in many parts of the world.

The language model
It is sometimes argued that a justification for the teaching of literature is its value in promoting language development. This is taken by some teachers to mean that literature can be an instrument for use in connection with the teaching of specific vocabulary or structures or for language manipulation. Such an argument misunderstands the nature of language in literature and may even result in mechanistic and demotivating teaching practices which substitute language activities in place of a genuine engagement with the work as literature and will probably have the detrimental effect of spoiling any pleasure the poem or story might have given. One of the main reasons for a teacher's orientation towards a language model for teaching literature is to demonstrate what 'oft was thought but ne'er so well expressed', that is, to put students in touch with some of the more subtle and varied creative uses of the language. There is much to be gained in terms of language development, too, from exposure to such language but a main impulse of language-centred literature teaching is to help students find ways into a text in a methodical way and for themselves. The proponents of this model argue that language is the literary medium, that literature is *made* from language and that the more students can read in and through language the better able they will be to come to terms with a literary text as literature.

The personal growth model

One of the main goals for teachers who are primarily committed to a personal growth model of literature teaching is to try to help students to achieve an *engagement* with the reading of literary texts. This engagement cannot really be measured in terms of passing examinations in literature; the test of the teacher's success in teaching literature is the extent to which students carry with them *beyond* the classroom an enjoyment and love for literature which is renewed as they continue to engage with literature throughout their lives. What the teacher will have imparted in such cases is a lasting pleasure in reading and a deep satisfaction in a continuing growth of understanding. This *personal growth* is rewarding because it results from learning how to appreciate and evaluate complex cultural artefacts; it is fulfilling because it is stimulated by an understanding of our society and culture and of ourselves as we function within that society and culture. Helping students to read literature more effectively is helping them to grow as individuals as well as in their relationships with the people and institutions around them. To encourage personal growth the teacher has to stimulate and enliven students in the literature class by selecting texts to which students can respond and in which they can participate imaginatively, by promoting the kind of conditions for learning in the classroom which will make the reading of literature a memorable, individual and collective experience and, above all, by enthusiasm for and commitment to the teaching of literature as literature.

1.2 Literature for study: literature as a resource

In the context of the above discussion, it is clear that there has to be a distinction between the *study* of literature and the use of literature as a *resource*.

The study of literature involves reading literature within an academic, institutionalised setting for purposes of obtaining qualifications in literary studies. It involves a considerable baggage of critical concepts, literary conventions and metalanguage and the requirement is often that students should show an ability to use such terms and concepts in talking and writing about literature. Such study can also involve analysis of particular literary texts, often by means of a method or methods of reading which may be Marxist or feminist or linguistic or semiotic or whatever. The study of literary texts can also, and regularly does, involve acquiring a compendious store of information about the history of the target literature, its traditions and conventions, its particular heritage, the nature of the influences and relationships between the authors, texts and contexts which make up that literary culture. One distinct advantage of such an approach is that it fosters an understanding of literature as a body of texts, and a view of literary texts as belonging to a 'background' of specific historical, social, and ideological contexts.

Using literature as a resource suggests a less academic though no less serious approach to the reading of literature. As we have seen, literature can be a special resource for personal development and growth, an aim being to encourage greater sensitivity and self-awareness and greater understanding of the world around us. It can also supply many linguistic opportunities to the language teacher and allow many of the most valuable exercises of language learning to be based on material capable of stimulating greater interest and involvement than can be the case with many language teaching texts. Literature is a legitimate and valuable resource for language teaching.

One potential disadvantage of the *study* of literature is that it can hinder the use of literature as a resource. This is especially likely to happen if the teaching and examining approaches focus more on knowledge *about* literature than knowledge *of* literature. Knowledge *about* literature means accumulating facts about literary contexts, dates, authors, titles of texts, names of conventions, literary terms, etc. It can easily become knowledge for its own sake and does not automatically lead to a more responsive reading or to a fuller interpretation of a text. Courses which involve extensive *surveys* of literary history, and teaching methods which rely substantially on lectures, may help students to pass the required examinations but they do little to develop literature for the resources of the majority of individual students.

Such methods of presenting literature are information-based and transmissive in operation with the facts or information transmitted to the student in a form to be remembered and conveniently recalled when required (usually for purposes of examination). There is usually little concern with how to use such information to read literature for oneself and to learn how to make one's own meanings. The outcome for students is that they come to rely on authorities *outside* themselves, whether in the form of the teacher or in the form of histories of literature or books of literary criticism. Students with good memories do well under such a system. The more successful students are also probably those who would develop in any case the necessary literary competence whether they had a teacher or not. Needless to say, such presentational methods do not bear any systematic relation to the development of language skills in students, and those teaching literature in this way would probably deny that literature and language study could be successfully integrated.

Knowledge *of* literature is perhaps better expressed in terms of pleasure and enjoyment rather than in terms of the accumulation of facts, however valuable those facts may sometimes be. The teacher who wishes to impart knowledge *of* literature aims to impart personal pleasure in reading literary texts and is likely to select teaching methods which lead to active involvement in reading particular texts rather than to a passive reception of information about the texts. The Victorian poet and critic Matthew Arnold asserted that he knew when he had encountered great literature because the hair at the back of his head stood up. It is that kind of emotional and experiential involvement which constitutes a knowledge *of* literature. This kind of knowledge is not normally conveyed by survey lecture courses about literature; it is more likely to be conveyed by activity-based, student-centered approaches which aim to lead to a high level of personal response and involvement. In this book there is a focus on exploring ways of fostering this kind of knowledge *of* literature.

1.3
Breadth v. depth

In this section we raise a basic but very important question. The question relates to the design of a literature curriculum and to whether it is better to have a syllabus in which a broad range of texts is studied or one in which students develop the capacity for reading a more limited number of texts *in depth*. Those in favour of a breadth approach argue that reading literature effectively depends on a wide experience of different kinds of literary texts, all of which describe different situations in different styles and conventions. The breadth approach allows students to accumulate a varied range of responses and so to be able to relate their reading of one text to their reading of other texts.

Those in favour of a depth approach argue that it is always better to know one text well rather than several texts more superficially and that learning to read effectively depends on a detailed, close engagement with the thematic and linguistic particularities of a text. Methods of teaching literature which adopt this approach are taking a predominantly language model for literature teaching but believe it to be essential for the development of necessary capacities of close reading, analysis and detailed, language-based interpretation. The strong version of the argument is that once one text has been read *accurately* then greater fluency will ensue; the strong version of the opposing argument is that only greater reading *fluency* – from learning to read in breadth – will provide the basis from which more accurate reading can be encouraged and practised.

A decision such as whether to adopt an essentially in-breadth or in-depth approach influences both syllabus design and broader curricular objectives; for example, it will affect whether a number of different kinds of literary texts are read and studied extensively in the early part of a literature curriculum; whether there should be intensive reading of a limited number and type of texts; or whether there should be a combination of both main approaches. A combination might be general reading of several texts alongside intensive, detailed scrutiny of, say, two short stories and two or three poems. (See Chapter 7 for further consideration of these and related issues.) The debate between accuracy and fluency is particularly concentrated on the early stages of the curriculum and it must be said very clearly that our ultimate goal is to produce accurate *and* fluent readers and to synthesise in-breadth and in-depth approaches to reading literature. The aim is to bring students to a point where, as Christopher Brumfit puts it, 'The process of reading is a process of meaning creation by integrating one's own needs, understanding and expectations with a written text'. (Brumfit, 1985 p. 119). Such a process of 'meaning creation' leads into questions of literary competence.

1.4 Language competence and literary competence

In the previous section we discussed some pros and cons of reading in breadth and in depth. In doing so we begged two important questions: How much language competence is required before a literary text can be read whether in breadth or in depth? What exactly is meant by literary competence, and what kind of literary competence do we wish to develop in our students?

An answer to the first question is not easy to provide and it is in any case further connected with the question of what is a suitable literary text for second language learners. Of course, language difficulty has to be considered because access is restricted if students cannot attain a basic level of comprehension and as a general rule it is better to choose for teaching literary texts which are not too far beyond the students' normal reading comprehension.

More important, however, is access on an experiential level. That is, students need to be able to identify and identify *with* the experiences, thoughts

5

and situations which are depicted in the text. They need to be able to discover the kind of pleasure and enjoyment which comes from making the text their own, and interpreting it in relation to their *own* knowledge of themselves and of the world they inhabit. 'The fundamental ability of a good reader of literature is the ability to generalise from the given text to either other aspects of the literary tradition or personal or social significances outside literature.' (Brumfit, 1985 p. 108) This kind of experience and enjoyment need not always be inhibited by linguistic difficulty since an exciting or moving text can itself be an incentive to overcome some of the linguistic or cultural barriers in the text. A reader who is genuinely involved with a text which is relevant to them will be one who is willing to work at reading. A further point to bear in mind here is that a reader who is involved with the text is likely to gain most benefit from exposure to the language of literature. In this way the literary text can be a vital support and stimulus for language development.

Some teachers believe in the value of simplified texts or readers, either in themselves or as preparation for reading the authentic text. The issues here are examined in some detail in 7.2, but we can observe now that facilitating greater linguistic access does not guarantee that a text will be made more enjoyable. Much depends on how well the simplification is done. There are good, bad and indifferent simplified texts and a crucial factor will be the extent to which sufficient stimulus can be given both to read a story for itself and then to proceed to the original story from which the simplified version is derived.

Simplified readers can also help to promote literary competence by introducing to students well-constructed and interesting material which demands some kind of inference from the reader. It is hard to define what is involved in literary competence but it includes the ability to infer a message. The student who declares that Shakespeare's *Macbeth* is not about royalty in feudal Scotland but about ambition may be developing the rudiments of a literary competence.

In the case of second or foreign language learners, that competence may or may not be developed, depending on the degree of exposure to literature in the first language. But it can be fostered by a teacher who selects material to read which is motivating and which produces in the reader a desire to read, to read on, to read more and to read more into (i.e. interpret) the particular text. Such motivation may not always be best encouraged by classic, canonical literary texts; any text which stimulates a sufficient interest to read between the lines will be a good choice.

To some extent literary and language competence cannot be easily separated for one will always be dependent on the other. We have already said that an appropriate level of proficiency is required before a text is read, but beyond that the process of reading will be augmented by a recognition of *patterns* of language. In many respects literary language may be best defined as language which is patterned for particular expressive purposes. Of course, patterned language occurs in many contexts, and this suggests that starting points can be varied. Advertisements, for example, frequently contain fascinating examples of play between words, related metaphors and formal patterns which can be creative and entertaining, and some teachers believe more can be made of reading advertisements in the target language as a way of encouraging linguistic-literary competence and of creating better access to texts. In this way a kind of cline or continuum is established which leads to the especially dense and aesthetically organised patterns normally associated with canonical literary texts.

These issues of literariness in language and of using clines for purposes of arranging the texts to be read in a literature curriculum are discussed in greater detail at 6.2 and elsewhere in the book. Our main point here is to stress the importance of creative uses of language in the making of literature and to note that literary competence is intimately connected with the ability to perceive how patterns of language reinforce the message. In the next section we discuss language-based approaches to literature which are designed to develop sensitivity to language and an ability to interpret the creative uses of that language in the establishment of meaning. But a final observation is that students may possess greater literary competence than we sometimes allow, especially as far as language is concerned. Literary language surrounds us in many different ways and is to be found in many daily practices; as children, students will have encountered examples of such use in nursery rhymes, children's stories and songs, playground rituals, verbal games and jokes and, growing into the adult world, will have encountered verbal experiences patterned to varying degrees of complexity. There has been little real research into the acquisition of literary competence, but it may be dangerous to assume that it all begins only in the literature classroom or to imagine that language does not have a central place in such competence.

1.5 Language-based approaches

There are many places in this book where language-based approaches to literature are discussed and illustrated and we shall therefore examine such approaches only briefly here.

Language in literature can, of course, be studied and linguistic analysis of literary texts undertaken in a systematic and methodical way. Such analysis is in our view often valuable, especially with advanced students, and we discuss the role in literature teaching of what is generally termed stylistics at 4.5 and 6.4. Stylistics still represents, however, an approach to the study of literary texts. Consequently, there is a tendency for such analysis to be teacher-centred and to view the text as a product even though an ultimate aim is to provide students with some analytical tools with which they can find a 'way-in' to texts for themselves.

Language-based approaches are normally less concerned with the literary text as a product and are more concerned with processes of reading. A process-centred, language-based pedagogy means that the teacher has to come 'down from the pedestal'. It means that the teacher becomes an *enabler*, working with students and creatively intervening to ensure a relevant and meaningful experience through a direct contact with the text. Such an approach involves a classroom treatment of literature which does *not* view the text as a sacrosanct object for reverential study. In fact, a basic principle of such approaches is that no hard and fast dividing line should be drawn between what is designated 'literary' and 'non-literary'.

The implications of this general philosophy are that a whole range of strategies drawn mainly from the language teaching classroom are applied to the teaching of reading literature in a second or foreign language. This means that standard EFL procedures such as cloze, prediction, creative writing, re-writing, role play, etc. are deployed for purposes of opening up the literary text and releasing its meanings. Such language-based, student-centred activities aim to involve students with a text, to develop their perceptions of it and to help them explore and express those perceptions. In such activities the channel of communication will cease to be exclusively one-way; there will be a proportion of group and pair work appropriate to the nature of the activities, and the selected activities will in turn be those appropriate to the particular text. These language-based approaches are examined in particular from Chapters 3–6 in this book, and it will be seen from this that we advocate such approaches as especially relevant to the teaching of literature in an ESL/EFL environment and that we believe in the integration of language and literature within the curriculum.

Earlier in this chapter, however, we have pointed out some of the real dangers in the treatment of literary texts as no more than further language teaching material, however interesting and motivating for learning such material may be. It is initially important that language-based approaches should service literary goals. In the next chapter (2.1) we discuss the extent to which literature *represents* experience. One feature of reading literature is that readers are normally required to suspend disbelief and participate imaginatively in the world created by the text. Such an experience is normally indirect, but this does not mean that readers cannot relate it to actual experience in a direct way. It is important that something of the nature of this representation of experience is conveyed in the lesson whether it be termed a literature or a language lesson. Otherwise, the essential *pleasure* in reading literature can easily be lost in the more instrumental manipulation of a text for language learning, and in such contexts a literary text is as good as any other text. For us literary texts are not just any text. We do not believe they are always best taught in a teacher-centred way, from the pedestal or lectern so to speak, or that they are best taught using product-centred methodologies, or that they should be seen as sacrosanct objects to be revered. But literary texts *are* special and bestow special enjoyment and fulfillment. If this special quality is lost, then much of the real purpose in teaching and reading literature is lost too.

1.6 Levels of reading: Conclusion

In section 1.1 above we discussed the question 'Why teach literature?' and in so doing described three main 'models' of literature teaching: a cultural model; a language model; a personal growth model. The models are associated, as we have seen, with particular pedagogic practices. For example:

The cultural model: is normally associated with a more teacher-centred, transmissive pedagogic mode which focuses on the text as a product about which students learn to acquire information. It is usually the model by which literature is *studied*, although there is not much attention given to individual works. Instead there is often what has been termed a 'flight from the text'.

The language model: is normally associated with language-based approaches. These aim to be learner-centred and activity-based and to proceed with particular attention to the way language is used. The importance of interpreting relations between linguistic forms and literary meanings and of learning to read between rather than in the lines of the text is paramount.

The personal growth model: is, like the language model, more student-centred, the overall aim being to motivate the student to read by relating the themes and topics depicted in a literary text to his or her own personal experience. The approach is mainly anti-analytic and does not equate easily with information-based, product-centred teaching. As long as the text is not subject to detailed linguistic study, it is more closely related to a language model for reading literature in order to make the text one's own. There is also probably a greater impulse to encourage students to *evaluate* what they read so that they learn to distinguish for themselves great literature from less successful examples.

We must reiterate that these models are necessarily abstractions. In reality there is a greater overlap between the language and personal growth models. However, since the language model is the model which is to receive the most prominent treatment and advocacy in *Teaching Literature*, it may be useful to underline briefly the points at which language-based approaches *converge* with the teaching methods and orientation of the other models.

Language-based approaches are more closely related to personal growth models than to models of culture and heritage, particularly as far as methodology is concerned. This is not to deny the importance of historical and cultural traditions, for fuller interpretations of texts can only be realised by examining them in relation to the contexts in which they were produced and these contexts necessarily determine the kind of shape they have. In Chapter 6 (6.6) we devote particular attention to developing students' awareness and understanding of how texts relate to their backgrounds. However, it is probably clear by now that language-based approaches have more in common with personal growth models. Language-based approaches are less concerned with evaluating relative aesthetic merits and generally view literature with a small 'l' (rather than see literature with a capital 'L'), preferring to work with a cline of texts from the 'literary' to the 'non-literary'. Such approaches also probably more regularly seek a 'way-in' to texts through language and responses to language. However, these language-based approaches share a lot with approaches like the personal growth model which foster individual responses to texts by flexible student-centred and process-based methodologies. In many respects, too, language-based approaches are not sufficient in themselves and are only of real value if they embrace the personal growth approach, and are thus utilised as a means to a richer end of fuller personal development.

In conclusion, we have to recognise that much depends on *approaches to reading*, that is, on how and for what particular purposes we are reading literature, especially reading literature in a non-native language. If we are studying literature for examinations, then a syllabus has to be followed and skills acquired which will ultimately be tested. Normally, this is the accumulation of knowledge about literature and its cultural and socio-historical background. If we are studying literature for cultural knowledge about societies different from our own and which we wish to understand better, then there are advantages to this. The approach to reading here can embrace complex cultural interpretation. However, if we are reading literature for personal enrichment we are likely to read it more closely, particularly in so far as it relates to our own lives. (And the closest and most direct engagement with literary texts is likely to ensue as a result of language-based approaches. A focus on language is designed to facilitate a more systematic approach and is more frequently based on familiar strategies from the language teaching classroom. Language-based approaches develop a view of literature as a resource for personal and linguistic development. These approaches do not necessarily deliver a full interpretation, but they provide a secure basis for one and are therefore useful in the initial stages of reading literature. Fuller intepretation is a higher level of reading and normally demands reference to a cultural or intertextual heritage, but we would argue that it is only through process-oriented teaching rather than through product-based or transmissive teaching that such goals of fuller individual interpretation can be reached.)

1.7 Summary

At the end of each chapter of this book and sometimes at the end of sections we supply some tasks and questions for discussion. At the end of this first chapter, however, it may be more practical simply to list again some of the main points we have raised and some of the points we have particularly argued for:

1 There are three main models of literature teaching (cultural; language; personal growth). Although they do not exclude each other, each represents different tendencies in methodology and in classroom practice.

2 There needs to be a distinction made between studying literature and the use of literature as a resource. Studying literature for examinations and reading literature for responsive enjoyment normally involve different approaches and result in different outcomes for the student.

3 There is a difference between knowledge about literature and knowledge of literature.

4 Reading literature in breadth or in depth (accurately or fluently) similarly requires different approaches and raises some complex questions of curriculum and syllabus design.

5 Literary competence is complex to define, but it is connected with different levels of linguistic competence.

6 In the teaching of literature it is important to distinguish teacher-centred, transmissive, product-centred pedagogies from student-centred, language-based and process-oriented pedagogies.

7 Language-based approaches provide a secure and systematic set of procedures for beginning to talk about and interpret a literary text. Our strong view is that such approaches enable students to secure an initial 'way-in' or *access* to literary texts. They represent a very necessary and important stage on the way to personal growth.)

8 Reading literature should be a source of pleasure and a stimulus to personal development.)

As we have indicated, many of these points are developed further in ensuing chapters.

2

Literature and experience

**2.0
Introduction**

In this second chapter we ask readers to consider the following questions under these general headings:

Literature and life
Do literary texts directly reflect experience of what happens in the world? If they don't, should they? Would you say that most literary texts reflect the world we live in and our experience of it *indirectly* rather than directly?

Relevance
Clearly, our reading of literary texts is enhanced and enriched if it can be related to our own experience of the world. How often does the literature read by our students do this?

The role of the teacher
It is probably the case that the less the literature is directly relevant to the students, the more the teacher has to find ways of linking the two, that is, of building bridges between the experiences of the students and the experiences described in the work of literature. What are the best ways of achieving this?

In this chapter we focus on ways of motivating students to read literature and we explore the role of student-centred, activity-based processes in developing the student's interest in and experiences of different literary texts.

**2.1
Representing
experience**

In this section we discuss the relation between your own experience and the way experience is conveyed by the cultural products which surround you. The following questions aim to prompt the discussion.

Question A
A man wakes up one morning to find he has turned into a beetle. His family are not surprised by this and continue to treat him in the way they have always treated him.

What would be your reaction if you were to read a novel about this situation?

Question B

Look at the advertisement in Figure 1 on page 14. What kind of experience does the advertisement appeal to?

Would you be likely to have such an experience?

Question C

Is the picture in Figure 2 on page 15 a realistic one? If so, why? If not, why not?

Commentary

Question A: The situation is depicted in a novella by the German writer Franz Kafka. The novella is called *The Metamorphosis* and was published in 1914. On one level, the situation is impossible; on another level, Kafka could be saying that the family had always treated him as if he were an insect. Kafka is not depicting the situation directly or realistically. But *indirectly* he could be said to be representing the truth of the situation.

Question B: The advertisement works by appealing to an experience that many people would like to have. Maybe it is an experience we all aspire to have, even if we do not want to admit it openly. However, is it likely that such an experience will ever come true? Is it only a dream with no real relation to life as we know it?

Question C: The reality which is depicted is not one we see everyday. Perhaps we see it only in dreams, or nightmares. How easy is it to explain or interpret what is being represented here? Is it too far from experiences we can identify with? Is it more or less realistic than the story narrated in *The Metamorphosis*? Is the reality depicted here more or less realistic than that depicted in the advertisement in Figure 1?

2.1.1
Literature: fact or fiction?

Does literature represent events which are true to life or to a reader's experience? The question is a complex one and has attracted numerous commentaries over many centuries. To answer the question we must also first ask: What is meant by literary representation? How is a literary representation different from a non-literary one?

The answer is complicated because several established literary texts deal with events which really happened. Tolstoy's *War and Peace* contains reference to the French invasion of Russia by Napoleon in 1812. Truman Capote's novel *In Cold Blood* (1962) contains direct reference to characters awaiting execution by electric chair for murders they committed. The author bases his novel on interviews he conducted personally with men facing the death penalty and on data he gathered from research in the prisons prior to the execution of the prisoners. In Alexander Solzhenitsyn's novel *The First Circle* one of the main characters is the Soviet leader Joseph Stalin (1879–1953).

However, the existence of real-life events or characters does not guarantee a true-to-life literary representation. The main criterion here is the capacity of the author to create contexts with which readers can identify. If readers can identify with events or characters and project themselves into them *imaginatively* then a certain truth to experience can have been created: It is this imaginative, truthful re-creation of experience which is often taken to be a distinguishing characteristic of established literary texts. Writers can hold a mirror up to experience or can ensure that their works contain numerous accurate facts; but the result may be that the work is no more than a

Figure 1

Figure 2   Conversation with a Bird
                                            Caroline Hands ©
                        Published by CDP 14B CANNS DOWN PRESS

documentary. A *direct* reflection of the world or of experiences of the world does not automatically guarantee that the work has a literary character.

On the other hand, writers can exaggerate the picture they draw. The work can contain information which cannot be true. (Take for example, the plot of *The Metamorphosis* outlined in 2.1.) But readers can still read it as if it were true. The actions or events can even sufficiently imitate those we might identify as true and readers can make the imaginative leap necessary to re-create it as true. Critics use the term *fiction* to describe literary texts such as novels. But if the fictional world has its own internal coherence then it can achieve a unique truth of its own.

It is important that teachers and students of literature should recognise that a balance between fact and fiction is necessary in literary texts. Experience which is fictionalised is not necessarily experience which is untrue or unrecognisable. Readers need to be able to identify it as true and to recognise it as belonging, even if *indirectly,* to a recognisable world.

2.2 Processes of reading

When we read we are usually sitting down. We are usually inactive and the surroundings in which we read are quiet. We do not seem to be *doing* anything. Yet reading is probably not the passive process we take it to be. It involves us in several ways.

Reading involves us in:

1 sharing in the world the writer has created. This occurs as a result of the imaginative leaps we make in order to fit the created world with the world we know.

2 relating the experience of the text to experiences we ourselves have undergone or can imagine ourselves undergoing. This occurs as a result of an active shuttling back and forth between the 'fictional' world and the 'real' world.

3 interpreting what the texts might mean. The literary representation of experience is not a direct one; it is frequently indirect. This forces the reader to make connections, to read between the lines, to seek for explanations and meanings. In literary texts such meanings are rarely stated directly.

Reading may be more active a process than we think. Teaching approaches which reinforce the activity of reading and which *activate* the reader in different ways may be appropriate approaches.

2.3 Motivating the student

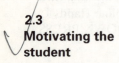

Students need to see a point to reading, particularly to reading extended texts. Many school pupils have grown up in a world dominated by television, magazines, comics, and pulp romantic or adventure stories. These media tend to provide immediate short-term satisfaction, they switch topic or scene rapidly and do not demand sustained concentration; they are invariably of a short time span. Reading literary texts requires concentration over a period of time, it requires hard work from the reader (often the text will need to be read more than once), and it requires considerable patience. Many teachers rightly see the task of encouraging students to read literature as a difficult and demanding one. In several places in this book we discuss the question of motivating students to read.

One important principle is that students will be motivated to read if the process of reading is related to them as individuals. A good starting point may, therefore, be to elicit from students as many of their *own* ideas, feelings and attitudes as possible before they begin reading. One activity here may be especially useful. It is called 'vote a quote'.

A class is given a list of quotations from established literary authors, or proverbs or well-known sayings. They have to choose two from the list:

- One which they would like to have framed in a place of honour in their own home. It should express a thought or idea of which they approve.
- One which would be engraved on their tombstone. It should express a key feature of their own personality.

No man, but a blockhead, ever wrote for money.
(Dr. Johnson)

Human kind cannot bear very much reality.
(T.S. Eliot)

I have spread my dreams under your feet.
Tread softly for you tread on my dreams.
(W.B. Yeats)

And forgive us our trespasses
as we forgive those who trespass against us.
(*The Lord's Prayer*)

Words are, of course, the most powerful drug used by mankind.
(Rudyard Kipling)

But at my back I always hear Time's winged chariot hurrying near.
(Andrew Marvell)

Beware that you do not lose the substance by grasping at the shadow.
(Aesop)

Those who can do; those who can't teach.
(G.B. Shaw)

A classic is something everyone wants to have read
and no one wants to read.
(Mark Twain)

All men are created equal.
But some are more equal than others.
(George Orwell)

The aim here is to show students that literature is something we can relate to as individuals. It represents our experience and can, effectively and economically, put into words what we feel about things.

Another 'pre-reading' activity which can be more specifically targeted towards a particular text is called 'pyramid discussion'. In this activity students are invited to select from a list of statements on a particular theme those with which they most agree. Here the statements relate to the themes of 'war' and 'neighbourliness' which are the topics of the poems we discuss at 2.4.1 and 2.4.2. Students should select three on war and three on neighbours. They should then work in pairs and agree on two for each topic. They should then work in groups of five or six and agree one quotation for each topic which they would accept as a member of the whole group. The whole class might then vote on one statement for each topic. The vote will probably involve class discussion of pros and cons and will draw on ideas which will have been exchanged in pairs and in groups. The 'pyramid' idea reflects the move from a broad base to a single point at the top.

NEIGHBOURS

A Do unto others as you would have them do unto you.

B Never be friends with your neighbour.

C You can choose your friends but you can't choose your neighbours.

D Everyone should mind their own business.

E Neighbourliness is next to godliness.

F You should always have *one* neighbour you can rely on.

WAR

A War is nothing more than the continuation of politics by other means.

B War is futile.

C National Service should be abolished.

D War is a game played by old men who have lost interest in life.

E Children should not be allowed toy guns or toy soldiers.

F We should go to war in defence of our country.

G War is another form of patriotism.

In this section one main principle has emerged. This principle is that students will be better motivated to read a literary text if they can relate it to their own experience. In the first instance this means that they should be able to relate it to themselves *as individuals,* that is, to their own ideas, feelings, opinions and perceptions; then they should be able to relate it to their own experience of the world and, in particular, of the society in which they live. 'Vote a quote' and 'pyramid discussion' and other preparatory activities are important in giving students an appropriate orientation and a motivation to read a particular text in some depth.

We have benefited from suggestions given to us by Jean Greenwood in connection with 'vote a quote' and 'pyramid discussion' activities. For further elaboration, see Jean Greenwood, 1989 *Class Readers* OUP.

2.4
Preparing the student

2.4.1 'Neighbours'

The poem which follows is by the contemporary British poet, Kit Wright. It is entitled 'Neighbours' and explores indirectly some of the attitudes we have towards our neighbours. The theme of 'neighbours' or 'neighbourliness' is an accessible one. Everyone has a neighbour. This can be the person we live next to, or the person we sit next to at work or in the classroom. We can even think of the people who live in an adjacent village or town or country as our neighbours. Thus, we all probably have experience of neighbours. In preparing students for reading this poem, a starting point may be to try to *activate* this experience. This can ensure that they approach the poem with the right mental set. In particular, it can be useful to concentrate on sensitising students to problems that can occur with neighbours and to prompt them to think about their experiences and to project themselves imaginatively into situations which might occur and which would involve them with the *issue* of neighbours.

Examples of situations involving neighbours which appropriately prepare students could be:

1 Your neighbour's television is on every night, late into the night. It is also at a high volume. You find it very difficult to sleep at night. Do you
   a) sleep with your head under the pillow?
   b) keep your own T.V. on very loudly every morning?
   c) speak to your neighbour and ask him to be more considerate?

2 You do not usually see much of the family who live in the flat next door to yours. They are very private and keep themselves to themselves. They have three children. One of their children is suddenly taken very ill. It is obvious to you that the family cannot cope with the other children. Do you offer to help to look after the other two children
   a) occasionally?
   b) every day for a couple of hours?
   c) not at all?

3 Your neighbour, whom you never speak to, comes home one evening covered in bandages and with two walking sticks. Should you ask what is wrong or keep quiet?

You can probably think of other similar dilemmas which would stimulate discussion and interest with your own students.

Now read the following poem:

Neighbours

I first noticed the neighbours were getting smaller
When driving away, he had to stand
To put his foot on the clutch.
She leant on tiptoe,
Getting the rubbish into the garbage bin.

That evening, returning from work,
He set his shoulder to his briefcase.
Scraping it up the garden path
And reached to the heavens with his house-key.

Later we heard through the kitchen wall
Their quarrels like kittens mewing for milk.

Later we heard them through the bedroom wall
Their tiny cries of love like cries for help.

Soon we'd be putting out birdseed for them:
But who was I to interfere?
For I was growing longer, day by night.

When I shaved
In the nude
In the morning,
The mirror reflected the wrong hair.
Soon I slept with my head up the chimney,
Feet out the window,
And outfaced the treetops, tip to tip.

And when it changed and I grew lower,
My chin on the basin, chest at the toilet top,
And my voice grew slower and weaker
And lesser as theirs grew louder
In sudden authority with their new-found height.

I prayed they would do me no harm
As I had done them no harm,
Nor tread on a neighbour in or out of sight.

Kit Wright

What questions would you put to your students after they have read this poem? How can you relate the poem to their own experiences of 'neighbours'? Which of the preparatory questions would be the most successful in sensitising students to the way the subject is represented in the poem? How can a student's experience be extended as a result of reading the poem?

Ways in which students' experience could be extended might include:

1 They should be invited to consider how their country would react if a neighbouring country were invaded.
2 They should discuss in groups whether one country should go to war on behalf of another neighbouring country.

3 They should consider whether they would offer help to a neighbour whom they did not know and to whom they had not been introduced.

4 They should discuss whether they feel greater obligations to a neighbour at school (e.g. someone they sit next to and work with every day) or a neighbour whom they live next to at their home.

The aim of these explorations is to discuss neighbours in a *literal* sense (someone we live next door to) and to extend the understanding of the concept in a more *metaphorical* sense of, for example, neighbouring countries. Readers might like to consider other alternatives which are more relevant to their own students' experiences.

2.4.2
'Futility'

The next poem we examine for preparatory teaching is 'Futility' by the First World War poet, Wilfred Owen. Teaching the poem raises a number of issues of appropriate preparation and relevant pre-reading activities. Read the poem first.

Futility

Move him into the sun –
Gently its touch awoke him once,
At home, whispering of fields unsown.
Always it woke him, even in France,
Until this morning and this snow.
If anything might rouse him now
The kind old sun will know.

Think how it wakes the seeds, –
Woke, once, the clays of a cold star.
Are limbs, so dear-achieved, are sides,
Full-nerved – still warm – too hard to stir?
Was it for this the clay grew tall?
– O what made fatuous sunbeams toil
To break earth's sleep at all?

Wilfred Owen

If you were preparing to teach this poem, consider the four approaches listed below and decide which one would be the most suitable with your students. Would one approach be more suitable with one group of students than with another? What are the relevant factors?

1 Teachers may consider that the poem cannot be adequately taught without students having knowledge of the First World War. Relevant factual knowledge includes: the conditions of battle in the trenches in northern France and Belgium during the period 1914–1918; the numbers of soldiers, especially young men, killed during these years; Wilfred Owen's own involvement as an artillery captain; the fact of Owen's own death in battle four days before the Armistice was signed in 1918.

2 Teachers may consider that pictures of First World War battles or even of slaughtered soldiers would stimulate students to participate imaginatively in the situation depicted in the poem.

3 Teachers may consider that students should be prepared for the treatment of individual death in the poem. This is a much more sensitive subject; but consideration might be given to the futility of life in a world where death is frequent and where life is in any case tragically short.

4 Teachers may consider that the students should be prepared by being asked to consider the futility of death at an early age. They can be asked if the death of a young person is more or less futile if it takes place during a war.

Of these four starting points number 4 is the most immediate and possibly closest to most students' own experiences. It is the preparatory context which is also most similar to that suggested for preparing students 'experientially' for reading the poem 'Neighbours'. But approaches 1–3 locate the poem more directly in relation to its historical background.

2.5
Relating pre-reading activities to text

Pre-reading activities of the kind we have discussed above should be coherent as activities and consistent with one another. But they are not designed to be self-contained. Their purpose is to direct attention to a text. The pyramid discussion activities and preparatory questions examined in 2.4 were principally selected in order to sensitise students to ideas and themes embodied in the two texts and to encourage students to relate them to their own experience. In the case of 'Futility' for example, the attitude of the narrator in the poem is significant. Here questions are raised not simply about the death of an individual soldier; the questions concern a perceived universal futility, a pointlessness in everything. This is especially marked in the second stanza and in the three questions which conclude the poem but to which no answers are given or appear to be available.

Of course, not all pre-reading activities need to be related to theme. They can reinforce perceptions of language and style, the particular point of view from which a text is written or the cultural factors embedded in the text. In the case of cultural factors there may be particular difficulties which pre-reading activities can ease. For example, different conditions and perceptions of neighbourliness obtain in different countries and cultures. The attitudes explored in Wright's poem may be markedly British and may need demystifying by preliminary statements about the British character or by contrasting photographs of different kinds of proximity in different types of housing in Britain and other countries. More basically, pre-reading activities for 'Futility' could be oriented to the winter setting of the poem, the weakness of the sun at that time of the year as well as the appropriate symbolic connotations of winter with death, or of 'sleep' with death, which may not be shared intercultural associations.

In a related way connections can and should be established with follow-up reading which students might undertake. For example, Robert Frost's poem 'Mending Wall' (which contains the line 'good fences make good neighbours') would make an interesting point of extension from Kit Wright's 'Neighbours'.

There are many ways in which individual experiences can be utilised by teachers for reading literary works though the process does not, of course, apply to all texts. Some texts represent the world in such a way that it is difficult to find appropriate links between the reader's experience and the writer's representation. (For example, Kafka's *The Metamorphosis* (above), or the kinds of supernatural events which occur in folk tales or in some children's stories.) Some literary texts deal with abstract and philosophical issues which students may not have encountered; or they may raise political issues which it is difficult to experience, even imaginatively. (For example, imprisonment in a Soviet labour camp.)

The above points lead on to questions other than how to prepare students for reading a particular text. For example, one question is that of the criteria teachers should use when selecting texts for their students). Questioning strategies are discussed in more detail in sections 3.1–3.4. However, the basic point we want to make in this introductory chapter is this:

Students need to be *prepared* for reading a literary text. The initial preparation should be as concrete and specific as possible. Teachers should try, where possible, to help students to use their own actual experiences.

2.6 Teacher-centred literature classes

In many parts of the world the teaching of literature has traditionally been a teacher-centred process. By this we mean that much of the classroom time is taken up by the teacher talking to the learners. At its best this process has worked well, because clearly no learners received *all* their literature in this fashion. It probably stimulated pupils to go and read more widely, and subsequently develop their own judgements and opinions from the initial stimulus of the wise and learned teacher. Of course, at the opposite extreme, there must indeed have been teachers who created a real aversion to literature among learners who might otherwise have enjoyed it, even if not as an academic subject. This was not necessarily because the teachers themselves were without knowledge of their subject. The two most likely faults were a dreary manner of presentation, and a selection of texts, whether externally imposed or not, which failed to arouse the interest and motivation of the students.

2.6.1 Classroom presentation of literature

You may have noticed in the last paragraph that we used the phrase 'manner of presentation'. This was a deliberate attempt to avoid the words 'method' and 'methodology', which have acquired very specific meaning in the teaching of English as a foreign language. There are, clearly, many important links between the teaching of the language and the teaching of literature but the assumed orthodoxy of language teaching methodology is not one of them. The greater the invention and enthusiasm of the literature teacher, the greater the likelihood that learners will like, or come to like, the literary text which has been presented, and from there proceed to look at further texts and teach themselves to like them too.

In the teaching of literature the infectious enthusiasm of a teacher can be crucial. We can enthuse about a literary text in a way few other subject teachers have an opportunity to do. (The teacher of engineering may enthuse about an engine/bridge, etc., the archaeologist about a 'dig', the chemist about an original experiment, but none of these is likely to be presented in the classroom as part of their normal and everyday material.)

The other issue is the selection of texts, which is a complex and difficult topic, to be addressed further in 7.1. One obvious difficulty here is that decision-taking is not always the province of the teacher. The selection has probably been determined by a higher authority, often regardless of its suitability for the learners themselves, and reflects a taste, or preference, which might be quite inappropriate to either the language competence or the literary sophistication of the learners. This is why the phrase 'set texts' has come to have sinister overtones, and also explains, in part, the lines above where we said that the teaching of literature had not been a very student-centred process.

2.6.2 Developing learner response

Lt

A common variation of the teacher-centred literature class involves the teacher in 'working through' the text, and asking a long series of questions, usually related to the meanings of words or phrases, the incidence of metaphors, etc., or even slightly higher order questions of the type 'Why does (a character) do/ say that?' This is almost certainly a common process in the literature classroom, and is perhaps broadly associated with 'explaining' the text. At first sight the process may be quite unobjectionable. It is clearly some way removed from a lecture and there is a dialogue of sorts between the teacher and the learners. However, there are dangers.

The first of these is that the process constantly focuses on the small unit, the discrete point; at its worst the class spends a lot of time worrying or agonising about a single word which may have no great significance in an appreciation of the whole work. Secondly, it can become as teacher-centred as the lecture; all decision-taking is in the hands of the teacher, and the questioning seldom relates the text to the learners' wider experience outside the classroom. Thirdly, if such a process is the regular, or frequent mode of presentation it seems designed rather for what we might call the 'short-term pay-off' than the longer term growth of the literary text as a 'treasured object'. In short, *language* learners, expect a pay-off from what they are learning; they hope to be able to put it to use in the short term, and learn better if they see this as a prospect. No such pay-off is likely or possible in the literature class. It is better perhaps that the text should 'stay with the learners' for a long period, and that they remember it as one of their favourite poems, plays or novels. The teacher for whom the text is also a favourite will be aiming for a sharing of interest, with possible additional long-term benefits in words acquired, and language skills. This seldom happens instantly. Over-detailed explanation in the interests of an instant pay-off may obscure the more lengthy process by which a hard-earned text is remembered and enjoyed well after the learner has finished his or her literature classes.

2.7 **Student-centred literature classes**

2.7.1 Engaging with the text

Lt

Teacher-centred literature classes imply, at least, that learners are allowed too little opportunity to formulate their own feelings about a literary text and that too much of the formulation comes directly from the teacher, who also does most of the talking. We should not assume from this that in student-centred literature classes the teacher is phased out, and the learners do most of the talking. A student-centred literature class is one which allows *more exploration of the literary text by the learners* and invites learners to develop their own

Trs note should allow

responses and sensitivities. It leads learners to make their own judgements and to refine and develop their techniques for doing this so that they can apply them to a wider range of texts for their own benefit) This means, first and foremost, a careful and preferably uninterrupted reading. Learners submit their individual or collective judgements for approval either to their peers or to the teacher. But, first of all, the learners must be very clear about what they have to do, and a large part of this book is devoted to this topic.

The big difference here, of course, is that learners have been able to make judgements in the first place instead of merely accepting the judgements of the teacher. This in no way implies that any viewpoint presented by the teacher is wrong. But there is always a danger that a viewpoint (or judgement) presented by an authority becomes more important than the text itself. If learners develop their own viewpoints then they must most certainly have read the text, and the reading should have been in itself a literary experience.)

2.7.2 Finding your way into poetry

The teacher is by no means superceded. She or he will have set up the process, and possibly indicate features to look for or to note, and 'teaching' will continue to be necessary to develop procedures for exploring texts more thoroughly. An example might be useful at this point. In 1987 Inspectors of Schools in England issued a report which criticised the present 'superficial' approach to poetry teaching and urged that pupils should be encouraged to 'read and experience' poetry for themselves. This, of course, was for native speakers, but the concern of the inspectors was with the 'approach' or mode of presentation. This was reported in the press item quoted as follows:

Schools, the inspectors say, should be encouraging children to explore their own 'feel' for poems. Instead, there is a continual effort to fill them with paraphrasable chunks that are intended to help them pass exams. Too many school libraries are crammed with exam-orientated 'crib' booklets. What children need is a good range of anthologies that they can discover and peruse independently.

Poetry *can* be revived, the inspectors say, and they spell out how: abolish rote-learning of selected stanzas; bring in group discussion. They cite the discussion (*see below*) of a Ted Hughes poem, 'The Warm and The Cold', between 13- and 14-year-olds at an Oxfordshire school as an example of how it should be done. The pupils start by interpreting a phrase in the third stanza . . .

THE POEM

Freezing dusk is closing
Like a slow trap of steel
On trees and roads and hills and
all
That can no longer feel.
But the carp is in its depth
Like a planet in its heaven.
And the badger in its bedding
Like a loaf in the oven.
And the butterfly in its mummy
Like a viol in its case.
And the owl in its feathers
Like a doll in its lace.

Freezing dusk has tightened
Like a nut screwed tight
On the starry aeroplane
Of the soaring night.
But the trout is in its hole
Like a chuckle in a sleeper.
The hare strays down the
highway
Like a root going deeper.
The snail is dry in the outhouse
Like a seed in a sunflower.
The owl is pale on the gatepost
Like a clock on its tower.

Moonlight freezes the shaggy
world
Like a mammoth of ice –
The past and the future
Are the jaws of a steel vice.
But the cod is in the tide-rip
Like a key in a purse.
The deer are on the bare-blown
hill
Like smiles on a nurse.
The flies are behind the plaster
Like the lost score of a jig.
Sparrows are in the ivy-clump
Like money in a pig.

Such a frost
The flimsy moon
Has lost her wits.

A star falls.

The sweating farmers
Turn in their sleep
Like oxen on spits.

THE DISCUSSION

Graham: So the lost score, the score is what it's written on – it's the music.

Zoe: So they lost it, nobody knows what it is.

Tom: Eh?

Nick: Everything's coming to an end at the end of the day.

Tom: Oh yes sort of –

Nick: Everything's sort of slowing down till it stops.

Tom: Yeah!

Graham: The day, the day's sort of a dance.

Tom: and dusk's the last bit of it.

Graham: 'The deer on the . . .' What about 'the deer on the bare-blown hill/like smiles on a nurse'?

Zoe: I don't get that.

Graham: No, it doesn't seem like all this. The others kind of relate – the cod, and the key in the purse, kind of relate more than 'the deer on . . .'.

Tom: Yeah, What is . . . I mean it's got fish in all three here – 'the carp's in its depth/like a planet in its heaven' then 'the trout's in its hole/like a chuckle in a sleeper' . . . erm, and 'the cod's in the tide-rip/like a key in a purse'. It must all relate somehow.

Graham: The first verse is always fish.

Tom: You know, the first bit of it.

Graham: Yes, the first line, up here you've got the first four lines then you've got fish.

Zoe: The last one's always – a bird.

Tom: Yeah, and then you've got . . .

Zoe: Badger and all the mammals.

Tom: Yeah and you've got a lot about steel in there as well – 'the slow trap of steel' . . . erm
You got badger
'jaws of a steel vice'.

Graham: Badger.

Zoe: Hare.

Lucy: and deer.

Tom: We're paying a lot of attention to what he's said.

Nick: and music as well. (Inaudible) . . . things 'cos you've got a clock in its tower –

Graham: It's all natural.

Nick: – and sparrows in the key clump.

Tom: Yeah, what about.

Nick: – then it's got 'doll in its lace'.

Zoe: It's sort of all relating.

Tom: Yeah and music as well 'like a viol in its case' . . . erm –

Graham: It all matches as if –

Tom: and . . . erm – 'lost score of a jig'.

Graham: Apart from the flies behind the plaster, that sounds quite different.

Tom: Yeah, I can't understand that.

Zoe: and the smiles on the nurse, I don't understand.

Graham: 'The flies are behind the plaster' is different, the rest of them are –

Tom: Yeah, I don't understand things like 'The deer on the bare blown hill/like smiles on a nurse'. I mean what are they?

(from a report in the *Daily Telegraph*, March 17th 1987)

2.7.3
The role of
the teacher

In spite of the difference in situation for most readers of this book, this report is of great interest for 'student-centred literature classes'. It will be observed at once that the four speakers are unsophisticated students of literature, and that all they succeed in doing is imposing some elementary order on a poem in which a large number of apparently heterogenous items are arbitrarily linked together. In this, they are relatively successful. This suggests some possible first principles for the student-centred literature class: it is exploratory, it is simple, it is text-based, and it uses a limited range of technical terms. These principles should remain the same for classes with non-native speakers.

The second point about the above discussion is that it is largely unstructured. It need not be so and many parts of this book are devoted to suggesting frames, some easy and some more complex, within which learners can 'discuss' and so avoid any silences caused by the open endedness of the task or the limitation of the learners' language competence. But the pupils here do not require any supporting structure at this stage.

Thirdly, the learning is entrusted largely to the learners themselves. The teacher has to decide on *the process which is most appropriate to making the text more accessible* and the teacher will certainly not try to impose his or her own interpretation of the text on the learners as being 'correct'. It is the responsibility of the teacher however, to ensure that the interpretations, which are produced, are *valid*.

We are not providing a recipe for removing the teacher from the classroom. Things do not always develop in the ways illustrated in the above report, and, in order to underline basic points of principle, we are conscious of begging some questions. For example, there are times where technical terms are helpful and enabling. Later in the book there is discussion of *how* limited a critical metalanguage can or should be in classroom explorations of literature and in teaching literature for examinations. There are also times when a teacher needs to intervene in a group discussion to provide further prompts and further stimulus. (These questions are also examined further in sections 3.1–3.4.)

2.7.4
The teacher, the
student and the text:
some preliminary
conclusions

The discussion so far has pointed to differences between teacher-centred and student-centred approaches to teaching literary texts. We should remind ourselves, of course, that although the approaches are different, they are not mutually exclusive. There is a continuum between the poles which allows for a mixing of approaches. Similarly, even so-called student-centred classes require the active involvement of the teacher. We need to remember also that the acceptability of teacher-centred and student-centred presentation of literature varies from one culture to another. In some countries, for example, teachers and students may feel that the teacher loses respect and authority if student-centred teaching becomes a norm. Most important of all, such methods of presentation have to be related to the purposes of the literature classes. As noted above, the short-term needs of passing examinations which may require *knowledge about* literature in the form of facts, dates, or an ability to name literary tropes, may have to conflict with a longer-term pay-off for students in the form of personal engagement with literature and a lasting enjoyment in reading and interpreting for oneself. Of course, some examinations can involve both overall aims at the same time: context questions which demand knowledge about literature *and* more general questions which demand an overall response to a text from students. Further discussion of these issues is undertaken at 7.5.

We need to stress the following:

1 Teacher-centred and student-centred approaches are convenient descriptions of particular pedagogic orientations. They are not necessarily incompatible.

2 There are occasions where such approaches should be combined; and there are cultures and situations where such combinations are necessary.

3 We reiterate our belief, however, that *student-centred* approaches, appropriately controlled and monitored by the teacher, are more likely to deliver a lasting enjoyment of literature and a competence to read literature for oneself.

4 However, in the literature class one component underlies successful engagement with the literature: this is a teacher's enthusiasm for literature and his or her ability to convey this enthusiasm to the students and to help them respond with the same enjoyment and pleasure.

5 It is also important to stress that teacher-centredness should *not* be confused with occasional teacher intervention. There are many occasions in the literature class where the teacher needs to intervene relevantly and creatively in order to augment the students' experience and to help them to respond appropriately to a text.

2.8 Experiencing language: elementary stylistics

We have suggested that students should, where feasible and appropriate, be *prepared* for reading literary texts by questions or activities which put them in the right frame of mind for exploring the text. The kinds of preparation we have suggested focus on the themes of the text and aim to prepare students for further engagement with the writer's representation of his or her subject matter.

However, the principle of pre-reading cannot be confined to the reading of literary texts. The principle can be applied to reading *all* texts, though we feel it is especially important in the case of literature.

One of the differences between literary and non-literary material lies in the *way* in which material is represented in literary texts. Frequently, this involves the writer deploying form and language in such a way that the reader is able to establish an organic relation between *what* is said and *how* it is said. Form and style can help to underscore or reinforce a message. A good example is the poem 'Forty-Love' by Roger McGough (see practical task below p. 33). *Formally,* the poem is divided on the page by two lines which serve to represent a tennis court, with a net dividing the court into two halves. The reader reads across either side of the net in a way parallel to the movement of a tennis ball across the net from one partner to another. A kind of tennis dialogue is established which is reinforced *linguistically* by the poem's title which belongs to the register of scoring in tennis; this is also a pun on the words 'love' and '40' (middle age), love in middle age being the specific subject matter represented in the poem.

This approach does not exclude taking canonical lines from English literature and discussing how they create particular metaphoric or musical effects: 'The slings and arrows of outrageous fortune' (Shakespeare: *Hamlet*) and 'Season of mists and mellow fruitfulness' (Keats: 'Ode to Autumn') are now well-known lines. The former line sets up an analogy between being attacked by weapons and being pursued by considerable misfortune. The second line aims to produce a feeling of autumn in the long, slow and replete movement of the line. The latter example also demonstrates that the relation between language and experience is necessarily a close one; for the experience of the language here may be difficult for, say, a student in Singapore who may not have experienced an English autumn. The line may have a verbal impact, but it may not have a simultaneous *experiential* impact.

The discussion here is of what we might term 'elementary stylistics'. However, it would be a mistake to assume that the practice is valuable only in relation to canonical literary texts. Advertisements, jokes and puns are a rich source for analysis of properties of language use which are literary in character. Such exploration lays an important foundation for subsequent appreciation of how language works for literary purposes and of how language serves to overlay and reinforce a particular message. Here are some well-known examples which, we suggest, might make rich starting points for this elementary work in promoting fuller language awareness and interpretation. Such activity, we should note, also helps to develop initial interpretive skills.

1 *Advertisements for British Food Marketing Boards*

Drinka pinta milka day	– visual and sound patterns reinforce message
Go to work on an egg	– double meaning: eat an egg heartily; start work having had an egg for breakfast
Say cheese – and smile!	– 'Say cheese' is frequently said to people whose photograph is being taken so that they look 'smiling'; this suggests cheese is enjoyable

2 *General advertisements*

How to get to Hollywood via a brief appearance in Dallas (American Airlines)	– The effect here depends on lexical knowledge (i.e. appearance = acting) and cultural knowledge (i.e. Dallas is a T.V. series; Hollywood is the centre of the international film industry) – the overlap here between content and context is a significant one for much literary appreciation.
Thai Airlines – Smooth as Silk	– a 'smooth' flight; 'smooth' organisation; silk is a world-renowned product of Thailand

3 *Jokes*

a) Waiter Jokes

How long will the pizza be?	– play on the word 'long'
We don't do long ones, Sir, only round.	

b) Book jokes

At the North Pole by I.C. Blast	– visual, aural and semantic effects
Jungle Fever by Amos Quito	interconnect
The Unknown Author by Ann Onymous	

There are many more variants . . . .

Readers might like now to re-read the poem 'Futility' and select two lines which might be used to develop linguistic sensitivity prior to or during a classroom exploration of the poem. Would you select the following?

Was it for this the clay grew tall?

If so, why? If not, why not?

(A key word here is *clay*. It is polysemic, carrying reference to the earth and the human body (human clay: a biblical usage). The line fuses a sense of the universal *and* individual futility which the poem conveys.)

Unlike a car owner's service manual or a weather forecast, the formal and linguistic organisation of literary texts is regularly *polysemic* rather than monosemic. It generates more than one meaning; part of the pleasure a reader derives from reading a literary text lies in activating these multiple meanings. We believe that students need to be prepared *linguistically* for reading literature. We also believe this is especially so in the case of reading literature in a second or foreign language. This topic of the methods and the procedures of literary stylistics is discussed further at 6.4. where its application at more advanced levels is explored.

2.9 Conclusion

Throughout this chapter we have underlined that effective, and confident reading of literature is closely connected with a reader's ability to relate a text to his or her own experience. We have also stressed that approaches to literary texts, whether to individual lines or groups of words or to whole texts, should lead to greater *involvement* with and *access* to literary texts. We have suggested that this can be best effected by students engaging in activity-centred reading. A further point of emphasis has been that working with the language of a literary text is necessary for effective reading and for developing skills of interpretation and sensitivity to literary effects. Above all, however, we have tried to underline that a focus on language should be *integrated* with a focus on the student's experience and that the various pre- and post-reading activities need to be integrated with a student-centred development of response to a text. Such integration is unlikely to occur and the experiences of most students are unlikely to be engaged if the literature class is a wholly teacher-centred one.

2.10 Practical tasks and points for discussion

1 Make up a series of statements for a pyramid discussion which prepares your students for reading the following text. Ask a colleague to do the same and then compare your statements. Justify your respective choices to each other.

When you have completed this task, you may like to compare your statements with those suggested in Chapter 5 (pp. 94–100) where the story is examined in more detail.

At Denver, a great many passengers joined the coaches on the east-bound Boston and Maine train. In one coach, there sat a very pretty young woman. She was beautifully and richly dressed. Among the new-comers were two men. The younger one was good-looking with a bold, honest face and manner. The other was a large, sad-faced person, roughly dressed. The two were handcuffed together.

As they passed down the aisle of the coach, the only empty seat was one facing the young woman. Here the linked pair seated themselves. The woman quickly glanced at them with disinterest. Then with a lovely smile, she held out a little gray-gloved hand. When she spoke, her voice showed that she was used to speaking and being heard.

"Well, Mr Easton, if you *will* make me speak first, I suppose I must. Don't you ever say hello to old friends when you meet them in the West?"

The younger man pulled himself up sharply at the sound of her voice. He seemed to struggle with a little embarrassment, which he threw off instantly. Then he held her fingers with his left hand.

"It's Miss Fairchild," he said, with a smile. "I'll ask you to excuse the other hand, I'm not able to use it just at present."

He slightly raised his right hand, which was bound at the wrist by the shining bracelet to the left one of his partner. The happy look in the woman's eyes slowly changed to one of puzzled horror. The glow passed from her cheeks. Easton, with a little laugh, as if amused, was about to speak again when the other stopped him. The sad-faced man had been watching the young woman's face with his sharp, searching eyes.

"You'll excuse me for speaking, miss. But I see you know the marshal here. If you'll ask him to speak a word for me when we get to the pen, he'll do it. It'll make things easier for me there. He's taking me to Leavenworth Prison. It's seven years for counterfeiting."

"Oh!" she said, with a deep breath and returning color. "So that is what you are doing out here. A marshal!"

"My dear Miss Fairchild," said Easton calmly, "I had to do something. Money has a way of taking wings. You know it takes money to keep in step with our crowd in Washington. I saw this opening in the West, and . . . Well, a marshal isn't quite as high a position as that of an ambassador, but . . ."

"The ambassador," she said warmly, "doesn't call anymore. He needn't ever have done so. You ought to know that. So now you are one of these dashing western heroes. And you ride and shoot and go into all kinds of dangers. That's different from the Washington life. You have been missed by the old crowd."

The woman's eyes, interested, went back, widening a little, to rest upon the shiny handcuffs.

"Don't you worry about them, miss," said the other man. "All marshals handcuff themselves to their prisoners to keep them from getting away. Mr Easton knows his business."

"Will we see you again soon in Washington?" asked Miss Fairchild.

"Not soon, I think," said Easton. "My carefree days are over, I fear."

"I love the West," she said. Her eyes were shining softly. She looked away and out the train window. She began to speak truly and simply, forgetting about style and manner. "Mamma and I spent the summer in Denver. She went home a week ago because Father was ill. I could live and be happy in the West. I think the air here agrees with me. Money isn't everything. But people always misunderstand things and remain stupid –"

"Say, Mr. Marshal," growled the sad-faced man. "This isn't quite fair. I'm needin' a drink of water. Haven't you talked long enough? Take me into the dining car now, won't you?"

The bound travelers rose to their feet. Easton still had the same slow smile on his face.

"I can't say no to a need for water," he said lightly. "It's the one friend of the unfortunate. Good-bye, Miss Fairchild. Duty calls, you know.'' He held out his hand for a farewell.

"It's too bad you are not going East," she said, remembering again her manner and style. "But you must go on to Leavenworth, I suppose?"

"Yes," said Easton. "I must go on to Leavenworth."

The two men made their way down the aisle into the dining car.

The two passengers in a seat nearby heard most of the conversation. Said one of them, "That marshal is a good sort of chap. Some of these Westerners are all right."

"Pretty young to hold an office like that, isn't he?" asked the other.

"Young!" exclaimed the first speaker. "Why . . . Oh! . . . Didn't you catch on? Say, did you ever know an officer to handcuff a prisoner to his *right* hand?"

2 What other preparatory, pre-reading activities would be suitable for your students prior to reading the above text? Would there be some questions you would put to your students before others?

3 Examine carefully the following picture (Figure 3). It is a painting by Eric Kennington entitled *The Kensingtons at Laventie, Winter, 1914.*

Figure 3

('The Kensingtons' is the name of a London regiment of soldiers.) The contrast in the picture between the young man lying in the snow and the men standing almost indifferently around him is a marked one. There is also a contrast between this painting which depicts an incident and Wilfred Owen's poem 'Futility' which explores a response to an incident and does so in an overt and direct manner. Either choose a war poem yourself or take 'Futility' as an example. How would you use this painting in your teaching as

a) a pre-reading task

b) a while-reading task

c) a post-reading task

What questions would you ask, or what kind of activities would you devise to further motivate your students' reading of the poem?

4 Choose a picture which contrasts with Kit Wright's depiction in 'Neighbours', *or* take a text which you teach frequently yourself and choose a picture which contrasts with it. How would you use the picture in the classroom?

5 Write the following poem on the blackboard:

40		Love
middle		aged
couple		playing
ten		nis
when		the
game		ends
and		they
go		home
the		net
will		still
be		be
tween		them

Roger McGough

Begin:
'Well you can see immediately that this poem has some unusual features. What do you notice about its punctuation? Perhaps more important is its shape . . .'

Limit yourself strictly to *two* minutes to introduce the poem, including reading it aloud.

Then:
'Now I want you to discuss this poem in groups of five. What other unusual features are there? What effect do they have? How many levels of meaning can you find in the title?'

If possible record the discussion of *one* group. On playback consider to what extent the discussion is 'exploratory, simple, text-based and uses no specialised terminology'. (see p. 27 above)

A further interesting strategy with this poem is to write it out as a piece of prose. Students are told the text is a poem, supplied with the title and invited to reconstruct it. This is another, perhaps even more activity-based way of discovering some answers posed to the above questions.

Middle-aged couple playing tennis when the game ends and they go home the net will still be between them.

6 Look again at the poem 'Futility' (p. 21). Prepare a fifteen minute lesson on this poem. You may make brief references to a) the poetry of the First World War and b) biographical data about Wilfred Owen. Continue by making a list of questions which you might ask on the second stanza. Begin by asking:
   a) What do you understand by 'dear-achieved'? 'full-nerved'?
   b) What does the 'cold star' refer to?

As a final question ask:

What connection can you make between the 'creation' theme of the stanza and the war?

Consider what answers you might get to each question and what answers you would accept as being most nearly 'correct'. Where practicable teach the lesson, but only if the students have not previously met this poem. In a follow-up lesson ask learners to say whether they liked or disliked the poem.

To what extent do you regard this process as 'teacher-centred'? How many learners showed an inclination to look up other poems by Wilfred Owen?

7 Discuss how you would draw attention to and help students experience the language of the following advertising slogan. What is 'literary' about its language? To what extent do you think experiencing the language of advertisement helps create further *access* to the language of literary texts? After you have completed this task read the complete advertisement on page 35 in which the different meanings of the slogan are explained.

A dishwasher for those who'd like to tuck away dinner for six and still stay slim.

Discussion

1 What are the features which you would say make a good literature teacher? Rank the first three of these in order of importance.

2 Why is it important that the literature lesson should not be completely 'teacher-centred' or 'teacher-dominated'?

3 What are the implications for 'individual development' in the teaching of literature? To what extent do you consider such development feasible?

4 What are the advantages and disadvantages of working through a text, with the teacher asking questions on lexical items, figures of speech, rhyme schemes, metre or historical facts, etc.? What is the frequency of this 'method' in the educational system in which you are working?

5 Do you consider it too idealistic to say that a text should become a 'treasured object' *for a non-native speaker?* Do you think more practical objectives should be established? If so, what are those objectives?

6 Are there cultural barriers in your country to 'student-centred' approaches to literature teaching? Are student-centred and teacher-centred methods of presentation compatible or incompatible in your teaching context?

7 In the report quoted (p. 25 above) why do you think the inspectors are so concerned with poetry? Do you think that prose should play an almost equal part in language development, or indeed, for non-native speakers, a larger part as being closer to normal written discourse and therefore having wider application? What is the situation in your own teaching environment?

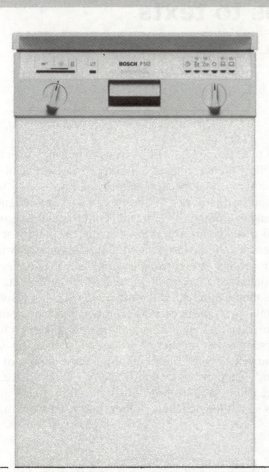

8   What are the implications of saying that the student-centred literature class is a) exploratory and b) text-based? What changes in approach will be required of the teacher who conventionally works through a text line by line to establish comprehension?

9   In Chapter 1 we posed the question 'Why literature?' List your own reasons why you consider the teaching of literature to be important and to be relevant to your students.

3

Approaches to texts

**3.0
Introduction**

The aim of this chapter is to examine the various types of question which may precede, accompany or follow the teaching of a literary text. The use of questions does not necessarily mean a teacher-centred activity, as it is clearly possible to work from a book with a series of questions which are designed to lead learners to a better understanding of theme and content, and to promote discussion. Such questions could be answered individually, as a group activity, or interactively with the teacher. In the latter case the teacher may reformulate the answers of learners, or prompt alternative answers. Collectively the questions may lead from details of content, at one end of the process, to individual response to the theme of a text at the other. In yet other activities the learners might undertake procedures such as exercises in summary or prediction, which would involve them in asking and answering their own questions, without recourse to either teacher or pre-set questions. The way in which this questioning is arranged constitutes one of the most important approaches to the text, and, whether tightly controlled or relatively free, is an important feature in the teaching of literature. Which questions to ask at what point and in what order is something teachers of literature need to continue to explore.

**3.1
A preliminary
taxonomy of
questions**

Let us begin with some preliminary and provisional classification of the kinds of questions which may occur in a literature class, as well as some description of their purpose. Our starting points are as follows:

1 The ultimate end of questioning strategies in the classroom treatment of literature is to help lead students to greater *understanding* of particular literary texts and of the nature of literature in general.

2 A useful division can be made into *low-order* and *high-order* questions. Low-order questions are questions which attempt to retrieve factual information,

literal meanings or the basic propositions or content of a text. They are useful in assisting with preliminary orientation to a text. High-order questions are less to do with literal meanings or factual content and rather more to do with involving the learner's own responses, inferences, knowledge and experience of the world. They are of a 'higher' interpretive order and seldom have a 'right' answer.

3 Another related classification of questions is into categories of *open* and *closed* questions. Open questions will tend to be open to exploration and probing investigation; closed questions require above all an accurate, information-based response. Closed, lower-order questions focus on the factual content of a text; open, higher-order questions focus on the imaginative or symbolic content of a text or the context of meaning which it generates.

This preliminary taxonomy might be represented diagramatically as follows:

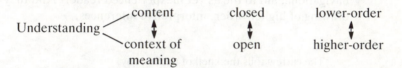

We shall now proceed to fuller examination of how such a description of questions and question types might work in practice.

3.1.1 Basic question types

The following is the opening paragraph of a short story (*A Fly in the Ointment*) by D. H. Lawrence:

> Muriel had sent me some mauve primroses, slightly weather beaten, and some honeysuckle – twine threaded with grey-green rosettes, and some timid hazel catkins. They had arrived in a forlorn little cardboard box just as I was rushing off to school.

These five lines contain a number of 'facts' or 'propositions' which combine to form the literal content of the text. This content is the sum of the information which the author gives to his readers. Content questions relate to the propositions or information of the text. Such questions would be:

Who sent the flowers?
How many types of flower were there?
When did they arrive?

It is possible to use such questions to check understanding at the time of reading, or recall at some later time, but there is otherwise little point in 'working through' a text with a long series of such low-order questions. Indeed to do so is likely to spoil one's enjoyment of the story.

Note that the question 'What are catkins?' is a different type of question. It is a language question rather than a content question, and might be used with non-native speakers if it was considered important that they should know what catkins are. A somewhat higher-order question, related to the literary or imaginative quality of the language, is 'Why does the author refer to the hazel catkins as "timid"?' Further questions, which are more open still, might be

'Why does Muriel send flowers?' and 'Why is the author/narrator "rushing off to school"?'

From a reading of only five lines we cannot answer these questions with complete certainty, but our knowledge of the world allows us to predict, or guess. This is, however, typical of how the wider external connections of a text are conveyed, namely by a series of increments. The text does not state the proposition 'Muriel was my girlfriend at that time', nor does it state that 'I was rushing off to school because I had to teach'. We do not expect that every detail of the world created by the text is stated explicitly in this way. It is not necessary, unless we stop at each contextual reference. If a teacher reveals only the first word of the above story, 'Muriel', that teacher cannot then ask 'Who is Muriel?' The reader, of course, does *not* stop; he or she reads on, expecting to establish fairly quickly who Muriel is. Expecting, that is, to establish the context. Questions which are designed to check that the context is properly recognised can be useful in the teaching of literature; they can serve as a sort of navigational aid to the as yet inexperienced reader. And they can lead to the drawing of higher-order, interpretive inferences.

3.1.2
Dealing with a
text: purpose of
the questions

The curfew tolls the knell of parting day,
The lowing herd winds slowly o'er the lea,
The plowman homeward plods his weary way,
And leaves the world to darkness, and to me.

These lines, the opening to Gray's 'Elegy Written in a Country Churchyard' are in one sense, clear: there are few of the problems associated, for example, with the Ted Hughes' poem in 2.7.2 above. They nevertheless present problems to the non-native speaker, in part because of some low frequency vocabulary (knell, lowing, lea).

The teacher may wish to make learners aware of one or more of these lexical items, though the impulse to 'know' every word is seldom a good thing in the teaching of literature. The teacher may thus ask the question 'What does "lowing" mean here?'. This invites the learner to provide either a translation or a word or phrase of similar meaning by looking at the other words in the sentence and then making a guess. The learner attempts to decode the word from the immediate textual environment. It is nevertheless a *content* question. The word is related to the other words with which it occurs. The purpose of the question above is to make learners attribute some meaning to a single lexical item which they do not know as it occurs in the text, without the teacher explaining it for them. The word may, of course, have connotations of its own in isolation – consider for example the word 'plods'.

Content may be investigated by a whole series of questions about discrete features of any part of the text. The question 'What are the poetic features of the line "The plowman homeward plods his weary way"?' might elicit that it has 'shape' (10 syllables), that it has rhythm (there is regular stress), that there are two repetitions of sounds (plowman plods/weary way), that the word order is deviant in 'homeward plods', and that 'weary way' is an unusual formation, it being the plowman who is weary, not the way. This is a rich haul from the mere seven words of the line. We do not of course recommend that every line is analysed in this way, but careful questioning (e.g. 'What is special about the phrase "weary way"?') can be itself a mode of interactive teaching, engaging the learner more effectively than simply by conveying information and leading to higher-order interpretive activity. At some point in a literature course such teaching is necessary.

Consider now the following questions:

How do we know that the setting is in the country? (ignoring for the moment the title of the poem)
What time of year is it?
What feeling is generated by the setting?
What sort of a person do you imagine the 'me' of line 4 to be?

The first of this series of questions can be directly related to propositions within the text itself (you wouldn't expect to find either a 'lea' or a herd of cattle in a city or town) and could therefore be a content question, in the sense that it is detail- and information-specific.

The other questions, however, ask the learners to try to establish a relationship between the author and themselves. Put in another way, the questions lead the reader into the ambience which the poet has attempted to create. They are 'open' questions, to which there is no single correct answer. The purpose of the questions is not to establish the discrete propositions about a bell, cattle and a plowman, but to share the feelings and perhaps also some of the knowledge of the poet. It is frequently this shared knowledge which it is difficult for the non-native speaker to detect. To use a common metaphor, author and reader are 'not on the same wavelength'. This in turn makes for only partial understanding of a text.

Context of meaning questions may be used less frequently than other questions, and there may be no single correct answer to them, but they establish the wider social setting of the text, without which the reader/learner can make very few assumptions about what is in the author's mind.

3.1.3
More about
context of meaning
questions

Look at the advertisement on page 40, which is for Thai International Airlines:

Content questions (e.g. 'What do you see in this picture?') do not elicit very much. A more productive line might be 'With what country do you associate a) a bull (and why?) and b) this rugby player (and why?)'. These questions examine the connotations of 'bull' and 'rugby' respectively. Note that 'a rugby player' does not work. It could be any one of a number of countries. The *context* here, however, is quite different. It is *not* literature, and we are therefore not directly concerned with an author. But, as with literature, we are concerned with message and impact. We must relate the bull and the rugby player to our knowledge of the world. We might thus ask (and in normal circumstances ask ourselves) 'Why does this make an interesting and arresting design?' A possible answer is that the pictures conjure up visions of distant countries (from, in this case, Thailand) which offer exciting spectacles, represented here by two different activities, but which in their aggression – and even danger – have some similarity. In transferring this sort of procedure to literary texts we indicate that the context question has no single correct answer;

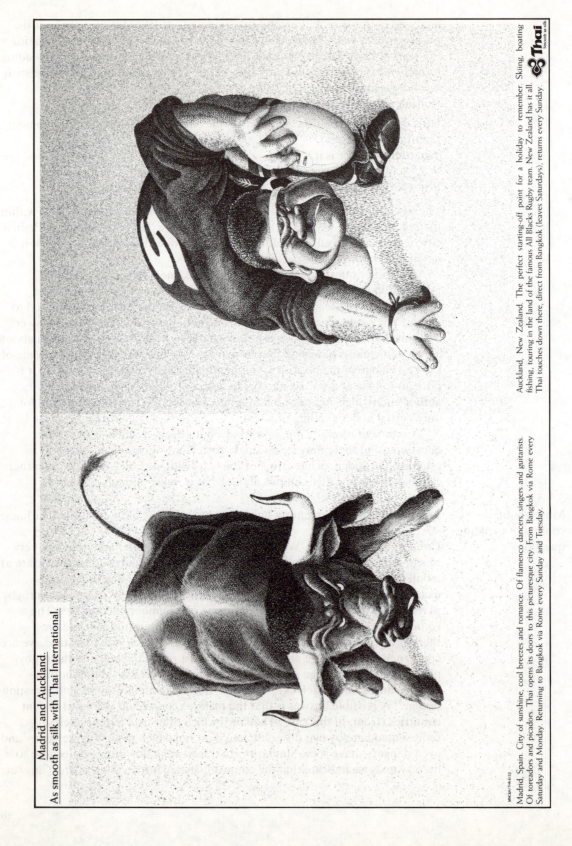

the context is 'broader' or 'narrower' for each person, according to how closely he or she is able to identify with the creator/author.

If we cannot establish a context of meaning we are going to have considerable difficulty in comprehending the text. This of course can happen (with native as well as with non-native speakers) in some modern poems, especially where the poet is seeking a greater intensity, and has deliberately omitted superfluous detail and connecting passages. Even prose can be quite 'sparse' or 'lean'. Consider the following extract from *The Killers* (the title is obviously significant) by Ernest Hemingway:

> 'I can hear you, all right,' Al said from the kitchen. He had propped open the slit that dishes passed through into the kitchen with a catsup bottle. 'Listen, bright boy,' he said from the kitchen to George. 'Stand a little farther along the bar. You move a little to the left, Max.' He was like a photographer arranging for a group picture.
>
> 'Talk to me, bright boy,' Max said. 'What do you think's going to happen?'
>
> George did not say anything.
>
> 'I'll tell you,' Max said. 'We're going to kill a Swede. Do you know a big Swede named Ole Andreson?'
>
> 'Yes.'
>
> 'He comes here to eat every night, don't he?'
>
> 'Sometimes he comes here.'
>
> 'He comes here at six o'clock, don't he?'
>
> 'If he comes.'
>
> 'We know all that, bright boy,' Max said. 'Talk about something else. Ever go the movies?'
>
> 'Once in a while.'
>
> 'You ought to go to the movies more. The movies are fine for a bright boy like you.'
>
> 'What are you going to kill Ole Andreson for? What did he ever do to you?'
>
> 'He never had a chance to do anything to us. He never even seen us.'
>
> 'And he's only going to see us once,' Al said from the kitchen.

Fairly low-order and *closed* questions would elicit that Al and Max are hired killers ('He never had a chance to do anything to us. He never even seen us'). A number of minor points could also be investigated by questioning, as for example why Max suddenly changes the subject, and asks George, the owner of the 'lunch room', if he ever goes to the movies. But what sort of people are these, and what are they involved in? These are *open* questions, and the only answer which the story provides, five pages on from the above extract, is that Ole Andreson 'must have got mixed up in something in Chicago'. The open questions are, however, important, whether we attempt to formulate answers to them or not. By asking them, or asking ourselves, we can feel the tension in the lunch room as the killers wait to see if Ole Andreson will arrive; we can imagine the two violent men, Al and Max, who joke while they wait for their victim; we can imagine a mysterious and sinister figure in the background who wants to have Andreson killed; we might even make a guess at what Andreson had been 'mixed up in'. All this is the context, without which the story has little meaning. Needless to say, few of us have ever met such characters, or been 'mixed up in' anything in Chicago; but our ability to create a context of meaning, or to help learners to do so by questioning, enables us to enjoy the story.

Setting and inference are also areas of questioning within a text. The following is from Malcolm Bradbury's novel *Rates of Exchange* (1983).

'Na, na,' says a voice by his ear; the heavy green stewardess is beside him once more. 'Na?' asks Petworth, staring at her; now she is small, and he big. 'Is not permitted . . ,' she begins; but then, her mouth open, she ceases utterance, her eyes staring, her brow furrowed. Petworth, who has taught many a seminar in language acquisition, knows these symptoms at once; the Babelian tragedy has struck, linguistic arrest, translator's block, has occurred. 'Yes, not permitted,' says Petworth patiently, 'Now, not permitted to do what?' 'Vistu ab stuli,' says the stewardess. 'Yes, well, try again, I don't understand,' says Petworth patiently. Big Petworth, little heavy green stewardess, they stare at each other for a moment, trapped together on the linguistic interface. Then two large green arms rise up from her body, and her big hands seize his shoulders in a tight grip. For a small woman, she is strong; she turns him a little, shoves him backward, pushes him down; this causes his knees to fold, his buttocks to smack heavily down into the foam-rubber aisle seat where he has been sitting, a pain to run up his spine, his overcoat to fly up over his face. But gesture is language too, indeed is probably language's very origin. 'Not permitted to get up from your seat?' suggests Petworth, removing the overcoat. 'Da, da,' says the stewardess, nodding vigorously, and putting the overcoat back onto the rack. 'Is not permitted to get up your seat.' And indeed, when Petworth looks round the cabin, he sees this is the universal understanding. For, though the doors are open, the steps ready, the blue buses moving toward them from the door marked INVAT, all his fellow-passengers have remained in their seats, strapped and silent, as if waiting for the next thing to happen.

The setting is an aeroplane, from which the passengers are about to disembark. But what airline treats its passenges like this? And, apart from being some sort of teacher, what sort of person is Petworth? We infer, from this extract alone, that it is a situation in which people do not argue with authority, or they do so at considerable risk. This, however, is the end product, the result of our reading. The teacher of literature still needs to generate the questions which will allow learners to comprehend, and to share those assumptions of the author which, collectively, make the context. Thus a low-order question might be 'What happens to Petworth when he fails to understand the stewardess?' A higher-order and inferential, question might be 'What does this incident tell us about Petworth, and about the society he is visiting?'. Once again it should be pointed out that context in extended prose is established through the fabric of the whole.

**3.2
Developing
responses:
approaches to
theme**

In the preceding section we have examined different types of question. The questions were aimed at different levels of understanding of a text, and ranged from low-order to high-order. All were designed to try to help students work out for themselves what a text might mean.

The academic study of literary texts has generated a vast ancillary 'literature', some of it concerned with spotting examination questions and generating answers which will satisfy the examiners. It is only fair to add that much of this material is well thought-out and can provide useful support to one's literary studies. It is all too easy, however, to let the ancillary literature take over so that one's own responses are stifled and the text itself given only an equal share with what other people, such as literary critics and commentators, have said about it. In this section and the next we explore ways of promoting fuller responses to literary texts on the part of students. One useful starting point can be in discussing themes, or getting learners to note how the themes of different texts are related. The role of the teacher in this lies in the careful selection of the texts, and then in questioning or prompting to establish comparisons or contrasts.

Themes, or subject matter, are familiar to all of us: either from personal experience, or from what is spoken or read about in daily life. Thus, though most learners may have no firsthand experience of war, it is familiar enough, in the present as in earlier times, and no special explanation of the theme will be required. 'Conflict' may be seen as a variation of the same theme, and there can be few people who have not experienced conflict in some form. In this sense the number of themes in literature is less diverse than may be imagined, however different the culture in which the learner is living, and however unusual the treatment given to that subject by the author. On the other hand, it would seem that learners get a greater sense of achievement out of reading a text if they are prompted to 'discover' the theme or subject matter for themselves. The point is, however, that theme, or subject matter, do not need to be stated in the teacher's opening words: 'This play/poem/story is about isolation frustration/anger'; but rather that the learners come to this awareness themselves *simultaneously with their reading of the text*. Incidentally, this is also a point at which to mention that a considerable number of books have appeared in recent years in which a block of texts are presented under headings like 'Love' or 'Society' or 'Environment'. There are potential dangers to this practice. The first is that the catch-all term seldom corresponds entirely with the text i.e. other words or phrases would express the theme equally well, though these are scarcely available when the heading to the chapter states the 'theme' in heavy black type. Secondly, the authors or compilers of the book frequently bend their text to a greater or lesser extent to fit the broad category.

3.2.1 Differentiating theme and plot: an initial example of comparison

This section illustrates how themes may be differentiated and compared in non-literary texts. The texts themselves would of course be given to students; the accompanying commentary is an outline of the teacher's 'approach'.

The following is a press release item relating to an incident in 1987 in which a ferry capsized near the Belgian port of Zeebrugge:

165 bodies recovered as ferry search continues

Zeebrugge (Reuter) – Divers yesterday resumed their grim search for more bodies in the wreck of the ill-fated British car ferry Herald of Free Enterprise with a total of 165 dead recovered so far.

Salvage experts completed work in the morning to steady the ship after it was judged too unstable for searching to continue, Belgian provincial authorities spokesman Roger Alleyn said.

Divers halted their search of the ship's upper decks around midnight on Wednesday night, after working for 30 hours with only a few breaks, to give salvagers time to stabilise the ship.

The crowded 7,951-tonne passenger and car ferry keeled over on March 6 minutes after leaving Zeebrugge for Dover in southeast England in the Channel's worst peacetime disaster.

The mud and water-filled wreck, lying a mile offshore, was winched off its side onto its keel on Tuesday in an eight-hour operation.

Workers have spotted many more corpses trapped in debris in the cavernous wreck and expect to recover 30 more bodies in the next few days. They said many more may be trapped below the waterline, indicating that the confirmed death toll could rise above 200.

Hans Walenkamp, chief salvage coordinator with the Dutch firm Smit Tak, told reporters on Wednesday night that search teams would have to stay off the vessel until noon.

Walenkamp said the Herald was only being held upright by the massive cables that were used to winch the ship off its side and that it could fall back again.

"If all goes well, the search parties can start up again at noon, but we must first stabilise the ship," Walenkamp said.

Search teams have scoured the upper decks, pulling rapidly decomposing corpses from mud and debris.

But shifting vehicles in the main car deck, which is still under water, have made it too dangerous for the divers to venture into the lower parts of the ship.

Peter Ford, chairman of ship's owners Townsend Thoresen, on Wednesday said it was expected that more bodies would be found deep in the ship's hull in engine rooms and sleeping quarters.

Commander Jack Birkett, leading a team of seven British navy divers, described conditions for search teams on the upper decks, dripping in oil and mud, as harrowing.

"It's horrific. It compares with nothing I've seen before," said Birkett, himself an experienced diver.

Investigators have yet to reach a conclusion on why the ship keeled over in under a minute in calm seas.

This item does not have a 'plot' because it is not an imaginative creation, but it is still possible to isolate the sequence of events. Thus

Beginning : March 6, 1987   Car ferry *Herald of Free Enterprise* capsized. At least 165 people drowned.

Middle : 'Tuesday' (refer to date of news items for time lapse).   Ferry salvaged. Many bodies recovered.

End : Date (?)   Final total of dead established. What were the consequences? Enquiry into reasons for the accident. Action taken (if any) with the ship itself.

Many other details can of course be inserted to give a more complete picture. For theme, or subject matter, we need not more detail but a distillation of the whole. This might be 'Disaster' (a word which actually occurs in this text) or 'Danger at Sea' or 'Horror at Sea' or 'Unpleasant Tasks' – according to the viewpoint which it is intended to take. This is the theme. Now ask students to read this extract from Joseph Conrad's short novel *Typhoon* (first published 1903).

Nobody – not even Captain MacWhirr, who alone on deck had caught sight of a white line of foam coming on at such a height that he couldn't believe his eyes – nobody was to know the steepness of that sea and the awful depth of the hollow the hurricane had scooped out behind the running wall of water.

It raced to meet the ship, and, with a pause, as of girding the loins, the *Nan-Shan* lifted her bows and leaped. The flames in all the lamps sank, darkening the engine-room. One went out. With a tearing crash and a swirling raving tumult, tons of water fell upon the deck, as though the ship had darted under the foot of a cataract.

Down there they looked at each other, stunned.

"Swept from end to end by God!" bawled Jukes.

She dipped into the hollow straight down, as if going over the edge of the world. The engine-room toppled forward menacingly, like the inside of a tower nodding in an earthquake. An awful racket, of iron things falling, came from the stokehold. She hung on this appalling slant long enough for Beale to drop on his hands and knees and begin to crawl as if he meant to fly on all fours out of the engine-room, and for Mr. Rout to turn his head slowly, rigid, cavernous, with the lower jaw dropping. Jukes had shut his eyes, and his face in a moment became hopelessly blank and gentle, like the face of a blind man.

At last she rose slowly, staggering, as if she had to lift a mountain with her bows.

Mr. Rout shut his mouth; Jukes blinked; and little Beale stood up hastily.

"Another one like this, and that's the last of her," cried the chief.

He and Jukes looked at each other, and the same thought came into their heads. The captain! Everything must have been swept away. Steering gear gone – ship like a log. All over directly.

To isolate the plot it is almost certainly necessary to look at the whole, and find out where the ship was going to, who was on it, and what the consequences were. However, the *theme* is similar to, but not exactly alike, the newspaper item: it is a danger at sea, interrelating with and inseparable from the actions of men, better, worse, or exactly as they are. The treatment of the theme is of course very different in the two samples, as can be seen from comparing just two sentences:

a) the crowded 7,951-tonne passenger car ferry keeled over on March 6 minutes after leaving Zeebrugge for Dover in southeast England.

b) She dipped into the hollow straight down, as if going over the edge of the world.

This difference may lead to a study of the features of literary (and non-literary) text. The themes, on the other hand, in their similarities and differences, remain the same. The fact that in the Conrad story the *Nan-Shan* did not capsize is a point of contrast with the *Herald of Free Enterprise*, which did. There are numerous points of contrast in the two texts. The teacher may use these contrasts in the content as a way out of pointing up, or 'marking', particular features in the literary text.

**3.3
Relating the
literary text to
the student's
personal world**

In 3.2 we indicated that the theme or subject matter of a literary text could be 'revealed' by asking questions which relate the theme(s) to appropriate areas of the student's knowledge and understanding. While this is a way of utilising the student's experience it is only a starting point in 'activating' experience and making the necessary links between 'what the text is about' and 'what this literary item means to me'. Without activating experience a vast amount of world literature becomes quite inaccessible.

3.3.1
The role of the teacher in activating experience

There are two primary considerations in linking experience with the study of literature. These are:

1 Many students have limited experience of literature as well as of the world in general, and this may make many texts puzzling, remote or inaccessible.
2 There is often something in the student's experience which has a connection with, or can be compared to the particular point in the literary text which seems remote. It needs the teacher to make the connection between the two, either by prompting or questioning. The student then suddenly discovers an insight into what was hitherto a 'difficult' text.

We shall exemplify (2) further before returning to (1). Suppose the students are required to study Thomas Hardy's novel *The Return of the Native*. The setting, Egdon Heath, is central to the novel as a whole, and exerts a total and fatal influence over the small group of characters who live on or near it. It is described at one point as 'a place perfectly accordant with man's nature . . . colossal and mysterious in its swarthy monotony . . . Twilight combined with the scenery of Egdon Heath to evolve a thing majestic without severity, impressive without showiness, emphatic in its admonitions, grand in its simplicity.'

We must now imagine the student reader who has no direct experience of a heath. The dictionary is of no help at all, at least for the headword. The teacher might ask:

Is the heath big or small? Are there any roads across it? What would you expect to find growing there? What does 'swarthy' mean? Why does Hardy say that it is 'swarthy'? In what way is it impressive? If you were looking out onto the heath on a wet day in November (implied question: What is the weather like in England in November?), what adjectives would you use to describe the heath? If you were looking out onto the heath on a fine summer's evening what adjectives would you use to describe it? What features would the heath have in common with a desert? How are they different? What would be the nearest equivalent to the heath in (our own country)?

If this particular example took ten to fifteen minutes, it would seem to be time well spent. For minor points the teacher may allow only a minute or two to 'activate' experience, but the significance of the topic in this case requires more time. Note that it is relatively student-centred, in that students are required to provide answers which cannot be lifted directly from the text, and which are neither 'right' nor 'wrong' – the teacher should avoid rejecting any answers totally, unless they are considered frivolous.

Answers add small increments to a mental picture, to which more can be added as the student a) reads more of the novel b) reads more of Hardy and c) learns more about the world generally. You could, of course, try to do it with a picture or a film, but that attempts to finalise it. That is not the intention here; to use a sort of pun, the intention is to give the learners enough 'landmarks' for them to develop a composite picture around Hardy's prose. Note that the questions themselves are simple, and make no excessive demands on learner experience, but in fact allow the learner to venture an answer for things actually *beyond* direct experience, as it is highly unlikely that most learners have been anywhere near Dorset on a November evening. The 'experience', on this particular point, is the recall of something from the sequence 'England – November – grey – miserable – bleak – forbidding – lonely – damp – etc.' The questions attempt to involve or generate an imaginative response to the text. They are *imagining* or *generative* questions. They are more likely to be framed linguistically in the following terms:

What or *How* would you feel if . . . . . . ?

(rather than in the more 'closed' literal or factual terms of 'have you ever . . . . . . ?')

It is not of course suggested that the above is the only series of questions, or the best, but it will be clear that the teaching process is interactive, and far removed from a teacher-centred lecture on some aspect of Hardy's fiction. The point is, however: does this appeal to experience have wider applications, or is this simply special pleading, with a carefully selected example which itself has a strong visual element? Can it be similarly applied to features of character, plot or 'theme'?

3.3.2
Relating a text to the world around us

The answer is of course that it can, as the two following and very diverse, examples should illustrate. The first is a stanza from Canto III of *Don Juan* by Byron:

> Haidée and Juan were not married, but
>   The fault was theirs, not mine: it is not fair
> Chaste reader, then, in any way to put
>   The blame on me, unless you wish they were;
> Then if you'd have them wedded, please to shut
>   The book which treats of this erroneous pair,
> Before the consequences grow too awful;
>   It's dangerous to read of loves unlawful.

This may be preceded by a question of the type 'What view does (our) society take of unmarried couples living together?' (The question to be adapted to the particular society.) This may be followed by questions about where this could/ could not occur at the present time, how people react to the situation, etc., leading to broader questions of public and private morality. Then introduce the stanza, and ask students to say what they think Byron's view was. In this procedure the teacher is using literature as a prompt for the student to express his/her view on a social issue.

The second is a poem by John Betjemen called 'Meditation on the A30':

> A man on his own in a car
>   Is revenging himself on his wife;
> He opens the throttle and bubbles with dottle
>   And puffs at his pitiful life.

> She's losing her looks very fast,
> She loses her temper all day;
> That lorry won't let me get past,
> This Mini is blocking my way.
>
> 'Why can't you step on it and shift her!
> I can't go on crawling like this!
> At breakfast she said that she wished I was dead –
> Thank heavens we don't have to kiss.
>
> 'I'd like a nice blonde on my knee
> And one who won't argue or nag.
> Who dares to come hooting at me?
> I only give way to a Jag.
>
> 'You're barmy or plastered, I'll pass you, you bastard –
> I will overtake you. I will!'
> As he clenches his pipe, his moment is ripe
> And the corner's accepting its kill.

Begin with a deliberately mundane question on the subject of how people drive. This is a central feature of this poem, and links 'experience' to 'plot'. Continue with questions like 'So why did he drive like that? What was upsetting him?' and 'What happened to him?', for which an element of prediction is required (but with related experience: 'Have you ever witnessed a road accident?'). There is no area of personal experience that may not have application to literary text; it just requires the appropriate text, and in many cases the appropriate prompt from the teacher, to activate it. In this particular example the subject of driving is only a prelude to discussion of marriage, why marriages go wrong, what is necessary to sustain a successful marriage, etc.

3.3.3
The background of the individual learner

It is now time to return to topic (1) above, and the limited experience of learners. There are at least three areas for consideration here, namely:
a) experience of mother tongue literature
b) experience of English literature
c) experience, or knowledge, of the world, life, people.

a) is an undoubted advantage and should be exploited wherever possible, however distant the conventions of the mother tongue literature may be from those of English. Learners who have read widely in their own literature will have learned, intuitively if not through formal training, to identify themes, and will recognise those themes again in the second literature.

   In the same way they will have learned to make a mental note of the pivotal points which carry the story forward. Unless we can assume they are absolutely fluent readers they will not do this so readily in the second literature, and could well find it necessary to search what they have already read to find why something has changed. They will nevertheless have a clearer idea of the structure of the whole. They will be able to make comparisons between different texts (usually in the same genre) which is one of the features of literary competence (see 1.4). As soon as they have read sufficiently in the second literature they will begin to do the same there. Whether they will make comparisons across the two literatures depends on a number of factors, not least the similarity of the conventions. Finally, they will know well enough what they find pleasurable in their own literature, and might thus be expected to look for something similar in the 'new' literature, rather than just waiting for it to come to them in a small number of set titles. Far from giving up the mother tongue literature, the learner of a second literature should be encouraged to read it further, and to use the experience to make comparisons and to mark contrasts.

3.3.4
The background of the individual learner in English literature

Experience of English literature (point (b) above) obviously helps in dealing with any further text in English. But, though local circumstances and individuals will vary widely, we have generally less expectation from utilising (b) and (c) than (a). Teachers tend to forget that their own literary competence is the acquisition of a number of years, and very few, if pressed, would claim that the sum of their experience was already complete when they finished their degree level studies. Thus, for many *students*, the amount of English literature which they have read is relatively small, and there is insufficient to draw upon to help in dealing with further texts. A very simple test will confirm or disprove this in the circumstances in which you are teaching. Try out the three short texts by Hardy (p. 46), Byron (p. 47) and Betjemen (p. 47). Ask learners what else they have read by these writers. If you do not favour an 'author' approach ask the following questions, with reference to the same texts:

What else have you read in English where the place or setting is important to the story as a whole?
What else have you read in English where the consequences of some illicit relationship were 'too awful'?
What else have you read in English where someone loses his temper, with serious consequences?

The third of these could, of course, be replaced by a question with a purely language focus:

What else have you read in English which uses modern idiomatic spoken language forms?

If the answers to these questions are promising – and the teacher may readily accept a wide range of answers – then by all means utilise the learner's experience. If the response is poor there is no need to be discouraged. It should be remembered that many native speaker students studying literature in an English speaking country do not have a wide experience of their own literature, beyond the texts which they have studied at school.

3.3.5
'Knowledge of the world'

Point (c) above – 'experience', or knowledge, of the world, life, people – is clearly so wide-ranging that valid comment is almost impossible. 'Experience' here does not mean quite the same thing as in 2.7. above, but refers to simple acquaintance with facts or names on any topic. There are clearly limitations. The following lines exemplify this:

> I am of Garth;
> Men call me Harapha, of stock renowned
> As Og, or Anak, and the Emims old
> That Kiriathaim held

Milton, *Samson Agonistes*
lines 1078–81

Here, for the vast majority of students, a footnote is necessary, if it is thought important to know the referent at all (consider also selection of texts (see 7.1)). But there is a vast and important range of items which it is certainly useful to know in tackling literature. If there is a large number of references related to one topic the difficulty, supposing there is a difficulty, merges into 'background' and 'background studies' (see 6.6).

3.3.6
Practical tasks

1 'Myself when young did eagerly frequent
   Doctor and Saint, and heard great argument
   About it and about, but evermore
   Come out by the same door as in I went

   'With them the seed of Wisdom did I sow,
   And with mine own hand wrought to make it grow;
   And this was all the Harvest that I reaped –
   "I came like Water, and like Wind I go"

The Rubaiyat of Omar Khayyam
stanzas 27 and 28

Make a series of content questions on the above two stanzas. These may be designed to 'translate' peculiarities of the syntax, etc., or to produce a paraphrase, but should also pick out the proposition (or propositions) contained in these eight lines.

Secondly, and separately, and without reference to source material, what do you consider to be the *context*? (Basically, who might have said this? To whom? For what purpose?). What question or questions would you use to elicit the context and what words/phrases/lines in the text would you particularly draw attention to?

2 If practicable, make an audio recording of an interactive lesson i.e. a lesson in which there is a great deal of questioning, with close reference to a text. The lesson should be prepared, but not scripted.

   Play back, and evaluate all the questions.

   How many questions may be classified as content questions and how many as context of meaning questions? How many learner answers lead to a further (unprepared) teacher question?

   Is this further question 'content' or 'context of meaning'?

   Is there any evidence that learners have more difficulty answering context of meaning questions than content questions?

3 Develop a set of questions on the poem 'Meditation on the A30' (p. 47 above). Divide into two clear sections, namely, those which relate to 'experience' and those which relate to knowledge of the world:

Experience

Have you ever driven a car/been alone on a journey by yourself?
What did you think about?
Have you ever lived with anyone who loses his/her temper very easily?
How did you feel towards this person?
(leading to questions which are directly applicable to the poem:)
Why was the man's life 'pitiful'? (line 4)
How did he relieve his anger and frustration?
Extend this list.

Knowledge of the world

What is the A30?
What age group does the driver belong to? How do you know?
What is 'a Jag'?
Who owns such a vehicle?
Why should the man in the poem 'give way' to it?
Extend this list.

Read the poem to a group of learners two or three times, explaining any words/ phrases which are essential to an understanding of the whole, (e.g. overtake) and which may not be known.

From this point on record the lesson if possible, on cassette tape.

Go through the poem again, reading by stanzas, explaining as necessary, and asking the questions which you have developed. Maximum time twenty minutes. Close with one very general question:

What does this poem tell us about modern society?

Play back the tape and decide which answers to the experience/knowledge questions are more relevant to the final question. Which question was most successful in 'activating' the learners' experience? How was this experience then directly related to the poem itself?

As further exploitation, and with advanced learners, set the task of writing a report for a provincial newspaper, under the headline.

DRIVER KILLED ON A30 AFTER ARGUMENT WITH WIFE

Keep as close as possible to the information content of the poem.

Points for discussion

1 The authors state that 'any questions which the teacher asks about the context would probably be intended to check that the learner could relate the propositional content of the text to the wider world outside it'. This presupposes, of course, some knowledge of the 'wider world'. How important do you consider this in the study of literature? Suggest one text where knowledge of the world was very important, and one text where it was relatively unimportant.

2 Do you believe that drama *automatically* establishes a context, from the stage directions and dialogue in the text, or the set and stage props (plus of course the dialogue) when performed?

3 What knowledge of the world might be useful for either studying or watching the opening scene of *Macbeth*?

4 What general statements do you think can be made about dealing with vocabulary in teaching poetry to non-native speakers?
e.g. Learners should be trained to guess the meaning of unfamiliar words. Only words which are essential to the poem as a whole should be translated or explained.

5 'Context questions may be used less frequently than content of meaning questions.' To what extent do you think that content questions are used excessively in your own experience? Do you believe that a 'student-centred approach' (see 2.7 above) would be a better, if slower, way of achieving the same result?

6 Look again at the extract from *The Killers* (Hemingway) in this chapter. Why is it important to establish a context for this text?

7 Why might a work of literature become 'inaccessible' if we did not activate our experience?

8 Look again at the brief extract from *The Return of the Native* (p. 46). Do you think it is useful or important to have seen a real heath? What other factors are important in understanding Hardy's description?

9 In what ways do you think that a knowledge of 'mother-tongue literature' would help in the study and enjoyment of English literature?

10 Look back at the two poems 'Futility' and 'Neighbours' in Chapter 2. What 'knowledge of the world', if any, would you now say was necessary for an understanding of these poems?

3.4 Asking and sequencing questions: a summary

In this short section we attempt to summarise briefly the preceding discussion of question types, questioning strategies and the relationships between them. Perhaps the first point to stress is that, although many questions originate with teachers, questioning strategies should not be seen as automatically teacher-centred rather than student-centred in approach to a literary text. Above all, sensitive questioning is best seen as a form of *teacher intervention* which can be both positive and productive. Some teacher-centered activities can pre-empt a student's own discovery procedures and the heuristic process of a student's own response to a text; but subtle interventionist moves on the part of a teacher possessed of a range of questioning strategies can be a midwife to a learner's creative endeavour. It can be dangerous to see teacher-centred activity in too exclusive a way for there are many intermediate levels between teacher-centred and student-centred.

In a related way we should also recognise that terms such as:

open   v.   closed questions
high-order   v.   low-order questions

are not mutually exclusive and most questions can be arranged on a continuum, and that along such a continuum there can be questions which are not easily classifiable in such terms. We have tried to suggest that one does not exclude the other; in fact, they are often closely interdependent and interrelated.

We should also note that there is no fixed order to questions as the questions we choose to ask will above all be conditioned by the nature of the text and the students we are working with. While it is true that content questions normally precede questions which prompt understanding of a context of meaning, this is by no means an automatic procedure. Much depends on what will best encourage the student's own responses to a text – something which is very much a matter of a teacher's own judgement. And the teacher will always need to continue to seek the *generative* question (see p. 47) which will strike an imaginative resonance in the student.

We might conclude by suggesting, then, that the generative question is a mobile question type. It can prompt understanding by establishing a kind of bridgehead between content and context of meaning. Such questions can also suggest alternative routes and sequences. For example, in the case of some texts it can be appropriate to begin with relatively open, higher-order questions; subsequent questions might then concentrate on content and be relatively closed; but these can then be followed by a generative question which acts to stimulate students to see a context of meaning differently. This in turn can produce even higher-order questions which may, in fact, go beyond previous understanding of the text. At such points students may begin to produce questions of their own and the teacher will know that the previous questions and interventions have been particularly successful.

3.5
In another medium

Literature, and particularly the novel, is a much-used source for films and television series. The following are just a few of the works which have been watched by mass audiences in recent years:

3.5.1
Motivation of the learner

The Forsyte Saga – John Galsworthy
Tess of the D'Urbervilles – Thomas Hardy
A Passage to India – E.M. Forster
Brideshead Revisited – Evelyn Waugh

They are mentioned here because at least two of the above have been required reading for many thousands of examination candidates.

Before we become too concerned with the size of the television audience we should mention that there is nothing new about works of literature crossing media boundaries. Schubert's (1797–1828) famous *Lieder* (songs) are settings of lyric poems in German, many of them by famous poets, although their present-day appeal is almost certainly in the music, rather than the poetry, even for native speakers of German. Verdi's opera *Otello* follows Shakespeare's play closely, though in an Italian adaptation. Of the many films of Shakespeare plays, Lawrence Olivier's *Hamlet*, *Henry V* and *Richard III* were deservedly famous, retaining the atmosphere of a theatre production while still utilising the techniques of camera work, such as close-up. These films stayed very close to the original texts; others, such as Pinter's adaptation of John Fowles' novel *The French Lieutenant's Woman* were much changed, in spite of the period costume and setting. However good the film was, one could still read the novel and enjoy a quite different experience.

The question we need to address is 'How useful are interpretations of a literary text in another medium *for the teaching and study of literature*?'

There are, clearly, some benefits. Many people enjoy watching a film.

Even without subtitles it is relatively easy to understand the plot and to deduce from that the theme of a film, even where the text is complex. *Especially* if the text is complex, and the learner is likely to have difficulties, above all in getting interested in it, the film is a superb 'way-in'. Ideally the teacher might first give a short introductory talk, explaining the setting, the period and even outlining the plot of the whole. Excessive detail should be avoided. The learners then watch the film, without interruption. This is followed up immediately by a few general questions to find out if they enjoyed it, and what they particularly liked, followed by further 'What did he do next?' type questions, so that the main outline is established. All this is 'affective', in the sense of putting the learner in the right frame of mind to appreciate and enjoy the text. Teaching begins in the following lesson, which should not be more than a day or two after seeing the film.

In practice this is seldom possible. Few institutions are fortunate enough to have the film available at exactly the right time. The above 'programme' also rather assumes that the learner has little or no knowledge of either text or author, where, in fact, he may previously have had to study the same text, or another by the same author, in less favourable circumstances. In spite of the difficulties, any showing of the film, at whatever stage of study, should improve motivation.

3.5.2
Exchanges – visual appeal and textual richness

Beyond this point we should exercise care in the shifting of a text from the printed page to another medium. There is at least a danger that the new medium has a monopoly of appeal, and that the text is forgotten, or only half understood, as the audio, or audio-visual element takes over (note that this is not the same as reading aloud – usually of a poem – for which see 4.4 below). Broad outlines do become more clear through watching the film, and especially through watching it several times. But subtle textual detail is lost, and the effect of the choice of one word rather than another is never considered at all. In other words there is a point where it is necessary to return to the text, though this does not mean that learners must understand every word:

. . . . No, to be once in doubt,
Is once to be resolv'd: exchange me for a goat,
When I shall turn the business of my soul
To such exsufflicate and blown surmises,
Matching thy inference.
Shakespeare *Othello* III iii

The obvious question is 'What does *exsufflicate* mean?' which few native speakers could answer. But an equally interesting question is 'What does *blown* mean in the same line?' The listener to Verdi's opera would never be aware of the existence of the problem. The person who watched the film of *Othello* is unlikely to be troubled by the line in question, which is fine if you are not studying the play. If you *are* studying the play you may also consider it is not necessary to know, but, in a film, there will be many similar examples, leading to a point where several viewings have still given the non-native learner only a skeleton of the whole. This is inevitably true of an adaptation of a novel, where a lengthy text is compressed into about two hours, and where all such problems are excised.

In other words the film, or the picture, or the song (relatively rare in the teaching of literature) is an *aid*, as in language teaching. At no point can the teacher dispense with the text, though where a videotape is available, one section may be played through several times, to note a particular line or phrase, with the visual/auditory features supplementing the study of the printed version. Such study of the printed version will generally precede this 'detailed' viewing/listening. On the other hand, a viewing of the complete film/video – being fairly lengthy – could best be done at the beginning as mentioned above, and where practicable, again at the end.

3.5.3
Interaction and
production by
learners (1)

This leads to a further question: 'Is the potential for *interaction* with a cross-media production inevitably limited?' The answer is 'not necessarily'. It is possible to watch a movie and then set up a student-centred activity or debate (see 6.7). But, of course, it is as easy, or perhaps easier, to do so using the text.

Watching a video or listening to a recording of a literary work may certainly stimulate interest for some students, but for others it may be a passive process. Reading a literary work is certainly not passive, though it may be harder work than watching or listening. It should be remembered, however, that reading literature is a *learning process*, as well as, hopefully, a pleasure. The student is adding to his or her store of knowledge, which can be activated when reading further works of literature. The vast majority of these will not be available on film, of course. For example, we know of no film of Milton's *Paradise Lost*. Why then not make one? In other words to exchange merely watching for a more active, interactive, productive process.

In commercial terms of course the idea may present problems. Considerable modification of the text would be necessary to ensure a mass television audience for *Paradise Lost*. In complete form a video recording would defeat any but the most dedicated. But consider the following:

Treble confusion, wrath, and vengence poured.   220
   Forthwith upright he rears from off the pool
His mightly stature; on each hand the flames
Driven backward slope their pointing spires, and, rolled
In billows, leave i' th' midst a horrid vale.
Then with expanded wings he steers his flight   225
Aloft, incumbent on the dusky air,
That felt unusual weight; till on dry land
He lights, if it were land that ever burned
With solid, as the lake with liquid fire,
And such appeared in hue: as when the force   230
Of subterranean wind transports a hill
Torn from Pelorus, or the shattered side
Of thundering Etna, whose combustible
And fueled entrails, thence conceiving fire
Sublimed with mineral fury, aid the winds,   235
And leave a singed bottom all involved

With stench and smoke. Such resting found the sole
Of unblest feet. Him followed his next mate,
Both glorying to have 'scaped the Stygian flood
As gods, and by their own recovered strength,   240
Not by the sufferance of supernal power.
    "Is this the region, this the soil, the clime."
Said the the lost archangel. "this the seat
That we must change for Heaven? this mournful gloom
For that celestial light? Be it so, since he   245
Who now is sovereign can dispose and bid
What shall be right: farthest from him is best.
Whom reason hath equaled, force hath made supreme
Above his equals. Farewell happy fields
Where joy forever dwells! Hail, horrors! hail,   250
Infernal world! and thou, profoundest Hell,
Receive they new possessor, one who brings
A mind not to be changed by place or time.
The mind is its own place, and in itself
Can make a Heaven of Hell, a Hell of Heaven.   255
What matter where, if I be still the same,
And what I should be, all but less than he
Whom thunder hath made greater? Here at least
We shall be free; th' Almighty hath not built
Here for his envy, will not drive us hence: 260
Here we may reign secure: and, in my choice,
To reign is worth ambition, though in Hell:

Paradise Lost is a canonical text, and Book 1, from which the above extract is taken, is a required (i.e. examination) text in many literature courses. The inspired teacher of literature will have his or her own ways to make this text interesting, though it will never be easy to make direct links here between the subject matter and the learner's experience (see 3.3). In university courses the lecturer may give a lecture on Milton, or on *Paradise Lost*, and students are left to read through the text themselves. Alternatively, there is the teacher-centred approach, where the teacher works through the text more or less line by line, simplifying, summarising, noting the extended similes, glossing the many Latinate words (incumbent, sublimed, supernal) and asking questions to check comprehension. The inference here is that this is a difficult text *to teach*; there is a lack of either change of pace or relief in the text, and though the heavyweight lexical content no doubt fits Milton's purpose, it is just about as distant as one could get from the spoken language forms through which many non-native speakers will have learned a large part of their English. The change to another medium which we are considering may be a more satisfactory approach, allowing learners to work in groups, to interact, to use spoken language, and to work closely with the text itself without it being boring or solemn, in spite of Milton's serious subject.

    Students, then, are required to make a videotape of this extract. From this point on the exercise is make-believe, as there are normally no facilities in the classroom to make a videotape. They are making an **imaginary** videotape. *Students in other words are making an imaginative creation, similar to an intensive and successful reading of a literary text, but they do it in collaboration* *with fellow-learners, instead of individually.* The format we suggest is as follows:

1 A speaker, full-face to camera, gives a very brief talk on Milton.

2 A second speaker, also full-face, gives a brief summary of the poem up to the starting point.

3 Students make a video *of the text*, using any actors, location, sets, props, make-up, or, in this case special effects (as in the making of horror films, ghost films, etc.), which they require.

3.5.4
Interaction and production by learners (II) – some guidelines

Students may complain that they know nothing about the making of films or videotapes. Point out that they are not expected to, but that they are simply to enjoy themselves as if they had the chance. Hint repeatedly that they should look again at 'what it says in the text', or 'see if you can find any clues there', without making it appear that you are really asking them to work together in a group reading, which in fact is what the exercise is! Some very simple guidelines, which with minor variations could be used for any text, should be given. For (1) above:

a) The material must be researched. Suggest sources if the students are not experienced.

b) Decide in advance the exact length of the projected 'brief talk'. Two to three minutes is quite enough for this part, which must be scripted.

c) Decide the setting in which the talk is to be given. What will the speaker wear in the 'actual production'?

For (2) above:

a) Students should complete this as a group exercise, but it must be scripted.

b) Prompt suitable introductory remarks and conclusion, to link with preceding and following sections respectively. Each should be *very* short, comprising at most two or three sentences.

c) Decide the setting, if different from (1), and the speaker.

(3) is of course the important part, for which the text provides most of the necessary information:

a) Explain the 'voice-over' technique, by which one person reads the script but is not seen, and the visual commands attention. Decide on a reader.

b) Learners decide how to portray Satan; features of make-up; lighting and, particularly for this part, special effects –'chained on the burning lake'. (Use the learners' experience of horror films, etc.) Decide on how to convey size – 'extended long and large'.

c) Consider the setting for line 242.

d) Manner of speaking for Satan. Movement while speaking. Lighting.

The way in which the learners deal with these points, and any others which they or the teacher think should be considered, will give them an interesting and stimulating insight into literary text.

The 'production' method outlined above is relatively time-consuming, which suggests that it is for occasional rather than regular use, although if used frequently learners become familiar with what is required and correspondingly quicker, but also very much more productive and inventive. The big advantage is that it requires investigation of many different facets of a text. It is a way of encouraging and fostering a more open-ended response to a text. Instead of always responding to the teacher's questions, students may begin to ask questions about the text *for themselves*.

Note: Is there a setting and song in your country which would be appropriate, while still keeping the narration in English? Ask learners to consider *why* setting and/or song are appropriate.

In conclusion, consider any advantages or disadvantages of this treatment of the poem. What other ways are there of 'teaching' this extract? What is gained or lost by such ways of teaching?

Discussion

1 The authors state that 'it is probably fair to say' (i.e. the proposition is carefully qualified) that only a minority of students enjoy the texts they have to study for examinations. What are the qualities which you think make a text enjoyable *to students*? Conversely, what qualities will make the text disliked?

2 Suppose your learners are going to see a film of a 'set-book' which you are teaching. The authors suggest a short introductory talk beforehand, to prepare the learners. Make a draft version of such a talk for a text which is well-known to you, and for which a film and/or video exists. Discuss the amount of detail which you consider appropriate.

3 Summarise the advantages of a film or video (of a play or novel) as a teaching aid.

4 If you had to teach the extract from *Paradise Lost* Book 1, what techniques would you use to make it interesting? Do you agree that it is a difficult text to teach? Imagine the learner group to be non-native speakers, competent readers, but with limited vocabulary.

5 In what way is the making of an imaginary video similar to an intensive and successful reading of a literary text? It is, of course, much more time-consuming. For non-native students is this good or bad? Do you think the process might discourage repeated re-reading, from which much insight into text normally stems?

6 'The big advantage' (of this interaction/production process) 'is that it requires investigation of many different facets of a text'. What are these 'facets'? Rank the first five in order of importance.

3.6
Prediction: what happens next?

3.6.1 Prediction and the structure of literary texts

The title of this section, 'What happens next?' is virtually a set expression in English, that is, it is an invariable grouping of words which a fluent speaker uses in a certain situation, perhaps where somebody is telling a story in a slow or ponderous manner. The implication is 'Speed it up a bit. We are not interested in all this detail.' In a written text the author may intentionally withhold 'what happens', either to create a feeling of suspense, or to give the reader a deeper insight into the action. There is a parallel phrase, however, which deals not with the short or medium term prediction of 'next', but with the conclusion or resolution of the text: 'What happens in the end?' This too may be withheld, as in some of the short stories of Hemingway, so that we are forced to infer an end, and re-evaluate what we have read to do so. On the other hand certain literary genres rely to a greater or lesser extent on 'What happens in the end?' The reader knows this and his or her reading is the more acute on account of it. The reader is saying, in effect, not 'What happens in the end?' but 'I know your technique. Surprise me if you can.' The widely popular murder/mystery novel depends very heavily on this practice, with clues distributed throughout the text. At its most successful, the reader is constantly invited to predict, but is still surprised by the ending, saying perhaps 'Why didn't I think of that myself?' Although this type of text is seldom included in formal literature courses, it is scarcely unique in the way in which it exploits prediction, this 'longer-term' prediction being a feature of many short stories. In fact there is no reason for the short story, as a genre, to rely on prediction of ending, sometimes popularly or conversationally referred to as a 'twist at the end'. A number of writers, however, have done this to such effect that the reader becomes accustomed to it, and feels correspondingly 'let down' when there is no such 'twist' – when nothing particular happens at the end. The very widely-read stories of Somerset Maugham exploited this device to the full (see particularly *Rain*, *The Force of Circumstance* and *The Verger*) though we should be careful to see prediction as a backward-forwards type of reference, and not as a sort of bait: 'Read a Somerset Maugham story and you will get a prize at the end'. It is nevertheless difficult to separate this form of long-term prediction in a short story from the resolution of the story itself, which instead of unfolding gradually over a number of pages is reduced to a conciseness which can have the element of surprise.

3.6.2
Prediction and the
literature
classroom

Prediction, in this sense, is not specifically connected with literature, but is a normal reading strategy. We should also note that non-native speakers predict less well in a second language than they do in their mother tongue. This can be a serious impediment to the reading of literature. The reader does not want to pause or stumble at a key point in a text, whether that text is prose, poetry or drama, perhaps to look up a word in a dictionary. Additionally, non-literary text generally confirms prediction, especially in technical or 'special purpose' text, which has a higher factual truth value. Literature sometimes confirms and sometimes denies a prediction. The outcome of all these considerations is that learners need training and exercises in prediction, both as part of a pre-reading activity, and as a repeated but short exercise in the continuing literature classes.

Exercises in prediction are easy to construct and practice, and are generally enjoyable if they are not carried on for too long. At the word level, the preparation consists of nothing more than omitting a small number of words, but these are never random. The finding of suitable words to complete the text should be a corporate, discursive activity rather than a private dictionary/thesaurus-based one, always with the wider aim of getting the student of literature at least to consider 'Why this word rather than some other word?' and to consider what the 'correct' word contributes to the impact of the text as a whole.

3.6.3
Popular songs as
prediction
exercises

Do not confuse prediction with the common 'teacher talk' habit of leaving a sentence incomplete, inviting anyone in the class to provide an answer, or, by gesture, an individual student:

> Shakespeare was born in 1560 and died in . . . .
> A poem of fourteen lines, written to a prescribed rhyme scheme, is called a
> . . . .

Popular songs are a good starting point for exercises in prediction, and the teacher should not worry if the lines seem hackneyed or trite. The following is an example:

> 'You are my sunshine / my only sunshine / You make me happy / when
> . . . . '

If you are prepared to sing it, that is even better; *the teaching* of literature does not have to be earnest to the point of solemnity. Invite suitable phrases to fill this gap. If everyone knows it already of course, the exercise fails; it assumes that at least a majority of the class will have to invent. If one student provides the original ('when skies are grey') fairly quickly, do not immediately abandon the exercise. Encourage alternatives and accept all reasonable suggestions. Follow up with an example from a poem which has been studied in part, so that learners have some idea of the idiom of the poem.

3.6.4
A sample of
classroom
interaction,
inviting prediction

Remind students of Keats' 'Ode to Autumn', mentioned briefly in (2.8), and particularly the line 'Season of mists and mellow fruitfulness'. If the poem is not familiar, preface the following exercise with a 'word set', where learners shout out all words they can think of which are connected with autumn in a British or American context e.g. leaves, damp, fruit, apples . . . . The prediction here is based on another poem called 'Autumn' by the modern poet Vernon Scannell. In a somewhat teacher-centred version the lesson may run as follows:

> 'The first line of the poem is "It is the football season once more". The second line begins with "And . . . . " How do you think the poet expands that opening? /   /   Well, the actual version was "And the back pages of the Sunday papers". That limits your choice. If we link autumn with football, then what do you predict you'll find on the back pages of the Sunday newspapers? /   /   So, try and imagine that you are in England in autumn; think again of that word set which we made a few minutes ago. Now, the second stanza begins "In Maida Vale, Golders Green and Hampstead" – those are all inner suburbs of London – "Lamps . . . . .". Well, what do you think the poet is going to say about the lamps in London suburbs on an autumn evening? /   /   He mentions the pavements too: "The pavements of Kensington are . . . ." /   /   Yes, "damp" seems an obvious choice, but in fact it is not the word the poet used. Can you think of any other words which you might associate with the pavements in autumn? The next stanza, still in London, mentions a hotel. "The big hotel like . . . . ." What would the big hotel look like, perhaps in late afternoon or evening, as you were going home from work? /   /'
>
> (The above is essentially an introductory exercise, concerned primarily with prediction to complete meaning. If extended to consider the effect of

greasy v. damp – or any other word – or the impact of 'ripen' v. alternatives in the phrase 'Lamps ripen' – then it is probably a more intermediate level exercise. If the teacher tries to elicit *comparison* with Keats' poem, and to suggest likenesses, as in Keats' line

'And fill all fruit with ripeness to the core'

then that would be an advanced exercise.)
The first four stanzas of the Vernon Scannell poem are as follows:

Autumn

It is the football season once more
And the back pages of the Sunday papers
Again show the blurred anguish of goalkeepers.
In Maida Vale, Golders Green and Hampstead
Lamps ripen early in the surprising dusk;
They are furred like stale rinds with a fuzz of mist.

The pavements of Kensington are greasy;
The wind smells of burnt porridge in Bayswater,
And the leaves are mushed to silence in the gutter.

The big hotel like an anchored liner
Rides near the park; lit windows hammer the sky.
Like the slow swish of surf the tyres of taxis sigh.

3.6.5
Medium term prediction and invention

Prediction exercises with poems may be either 'controlled' or 'free'. For the 'controlled' lesson the teacher has the text, and invites learners to predict the meaning conveyed by the original. The teacher then has the option of evaluating different suggestions, or redirecting the learners if he or she considers a suggestion loses contact with the original poem. On the other hand it might be thought preferable to hand the whole process over to the learners, who then invent as much as predict. Any evaluation is done by an individual learner, in pairs, or in groups (with the usual warning that the latter might be time consuming, and tending to depart from the text rather than investigate it more closely). This can nevertheless be a rewarding exercise for, say, the completion of haiku, of which the first two lines only are given, or completing stanzas, as in the Vernon Scannell poem in 3.6.4, where the prediction of the second line of the stanza is controlled, but the learners are invited to invent the third line.

3.6.6
Long-term prediction

Long-term prediction, should be used only where *there is sufficient evidence to project into the future*. Prediction, therefore, needs to be distinguished from mere 'wanting to know'. At the opening of Thomas Hardy's novel *The Mayor of Casterbridge*, Henchard, having sold his wife while drunk, goes the next morning to an empty church, kneels before the altar, and says 'I, Michael Henchard, on this morning of the sixteenth of September, do take an oath before God in this solemn place that I will avoid all strong liquors for the space of twenty-one years to come . . . . . .'. We certainly want to know what will happen, during and/or after that time, but there is little point in asking students to predict, at that point. Prediction should never appear to be a mere filling-in of classroom time.

**3.6.7
Practical tasks**

1 Divide the class into *two* or *four* groups. Do not allow more than ten learners in one group. If practicable give instructions to Group A (or A1/A2 if there are four groups) and Group B (B1/B2) separately, so that the other group(s) do not hear.

These are the words of a popular song* by the pop group The Beatles. The words were written by Paul McCartney and John Lennon.

For Group A
Give the group the title and first FOUR lines of the song. Ask them to continue it for a further eight lines. The only instruction is that no line must contain more than six syllables.

For Group B
Give the group the following words as a single line:

'I give her all my love, that's all I do'

Do not give the title or reveal the source. The group must continue to 'predict' the next five lines of a six line stanza. Give no instructions as to use of rhyme, length of line, etc. But imply that learners are completing a 'poem'. Allow 15 minutes for completion.

Step 2
Groups exchange 'poems' and evaluate/discuss the work of the other group.

Step 3
Explain the slightly different tasks of the two groups, and put the original words of 'And I love her' on an overhead projector, if available.

Comment on obvious differences of the type and quality of production of the two groups.

> *And I love her*
> I give her all my love,
> that's all I do,
> and if you saw my love,
> you'd love her too.
> I love her.
> She gives me ev'rything,
> and tenderly,
> the kiss my lover brings,
> she brings to me,
> and I love her.
> A love like ours,
> could never die,
> as long as I,
> have you near me.
> Bright are the stars that shine,
> dark is the sky,
> I know this love of mine,
> will never die,
> and I love her.
> Bright are the stars that shine,
> dark is the sky,
> I know this love of mine,
> will never die,
> and I love her.

*This song and two others by the Beatles are used for prediction exercises for language learners in Davies, E and Whitney, N *Strategies for Reading* Heinemann

2 Here is an extract from a recent textbook, *Reading Literature* by Roger
  Gower and Margaret Pearson, 1986 Longman, in which a prediction activity
  is given. Answer all the questions. If you are doing the exercise in the
  classroom, the procedure is made easier by using an overhead projector.
  Write the poem on a transparency and mask all but the first two lines. Reveal
  the following lines as each set of questions has been attempted.

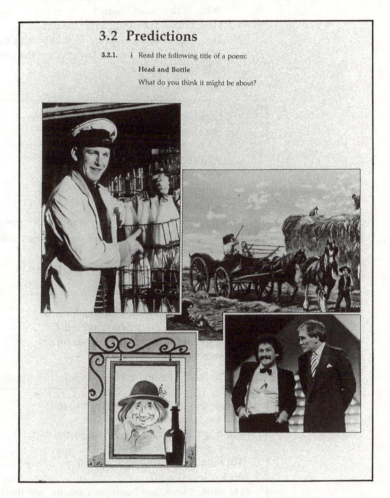

3.2 Predictions

3.2.1. i Read the following title of a poem:

Head and Bottle

What do you think it might be about?

ii   Read the first two lines:

GLOSSARY	The downs will lose the sun, white allysum
downs (1.I): treeless hilly land	lose the bees hum:
allysum (1.I): plant with yellow and white flowers	

Do you want to change your prediction about the subject matter?
What tense is used?
What time of year is being referred to?
What words are stressed more than the others?
Which words rhyme?

iii Read the next two lines:

> But head and bottle tilted back in the cart
> will never part

Do you want to change your prediction?
What do you think 'tilt' means?
What is the 'head' doing?
How long will he/she go on doing it?
Does the action take place in the town or the country?
Which words are stressed more than the others?
Which words rhyme?

iv Read:

> Till I am cold as midnight and all my hours
> Are beeless flowers

Why 'beeless'?
What is being suggested here?
Indicate stress and rhyme.

v Read:

> He neither sees, nor hears, nor smells, nor thinks,
> But only drinks.
> Quiet in the yard where tree trunks do not lie
> More quietly.

What sort of drink is he drinking?
What effect does it have on him?
Explain the metaphor in your own words.
Indicate stress and rhyme.

vi Read the poem again in its entirety without stopping.

> The downs will lose the sun, white allysum
> lose the bees hum:
> But head and bottle tilted back in the cart
> will never part
> Till I am cold as midnight and all my hours
> are beeless flowers
> He neither sees, nor hears, nor smells, nor thinks,
> But only drinks,
> Quiet in the yard where tree trunks do not lie
> More quietly.

Was it easy to understand when you had understood all the words?
Does the writer approve of the man?
Is he marvelling or impatient?
Is the title of the poem ennobling or belittling or merely descriptive?
How did your expectations change from the beginning to the end?
What do you think of the poem?

3.3.2
Notes   *The poem is by Edward Thomas (1878–1917). He tried to make his living as a writer but remained very poor. Much of his poetry and prose describes events that take place in the English countryside. He was killed in the First World War.*

What is the function of the photographs?

How effective are the questions?

Does the prediction exercise help with the reading of the whole poem?

Are the questions at the end of the section easier as a result of the prediction exercise? If so, why?

Discussion

1 To what extent do you agree that 'non-literary text generally confirms prediction'?

 Find one example from a literary text where prediction is denied.

 Present it in your discussion group and decide which is the most interesting example.

2 Does an exercise in prediction assist 'comprehension' of literary text, or do you see no obvious connection between the two?

3 What is the effect of withholding the resolution of a short story? Read the short story *Cat in the Rain* by Hemingway, and discuss to what extent prediction is confirmed and to what extent it is denied.

4 Retell to your colleagues *in summary form* any short story which you have read which has a 'twist at the end'. Stop at the appropriate point and ask them to predict the 'twist'. (Work in groups of four. Each member retells a short story.)

5 Why do the authors suggest that popular songs might be useful material for exercises in prediction? What are the possible advantages? What other 'non-literature' might be used in the same way?

6 In talking about prediction as a classroom activity the authors say that the teacher should 'accept all reasonable suggestions'. What is a 'reasonable suggestion?' Try it as a practical task in providing a fourth line for the stanza

> The curfew tolls the knell of parting day
> The lowing herd winds slowly o'er the lea,
> The plowman homeward plods his weary way
> And . . . .

7 Do you agree that prose text has more potential for student-centred prediction activity? Decide, with colleagues, on what would be a good text for such an activity.

8 What are the potential dangers of long-term prediction? Do you agree that it could be useful as a language learning exercise, but of little value for literature teaching?

**3.7
Character and
viewpoint: more
questions**

In the preceding section, various prediction exercises were discussed. The overall aim was to suggest ways of involving students with the developing process of a text. The most prominent of these processes is that of plot and, as we have seen, there are several possibilities which can be exploited to sensitise students to the meanings inherent in the twists and turns of a narrative. In this section we extend the discussion to the presentation of character, and suggest parallel ways in which involvement with character can be fostered. Crucial here is often the presentation of the character by the author and the resulting *point of view* from which a narrative is related. Our example is drawn from an opening paragraph which is often an important context for establishing character and viewpoint.

Examine the following worksheet with a text and questions. The strategy here is for students to complete the worksheet as a starting point for eliciting student responses to a) the characters of Tom Sponson and his wife Louie b) the presentation of character by the narrator of the story. Consider also how the passage might be exploited to *teach* about point of view. What further questions would you ask to draw attention to the above features? What particular points of language use would you wish students to notice?

Handout for students

Read the paragraph below and as you read decide who you think is going to be the main character in the story:

Tom ☐ Bob ☐ April ☐ Louie ☐

Tom Sponson, at fifty-three, was a thoroughly successful man. He had worked up a first-class business, married a charming wife, and built himself a good house in the London suburbs that was neither so modern as to be pretentious nor so coventional as to be dull. He had good taste. His son, Bob, nineteen, was doing well at Oxford; his daughter, April, aged sixteen, who was at a good school, had no wish to use make-up, to wear low frocks, or to flirt. She still regarded herself as too young for these trifling amusements. Yet she was gay, affectionate, and thoroughly enjoyed life. All the same for some time Tom had been aware that he was working very hard for very little. His wife, Louie, gave him a peck in the morning when he left for the office and, if she were not at a party, a peck in the evening when he came home. And it was obvious that her life was completely filled with the children, with her clothes, with keeping her figure slim, with keeping the house clean and smart, with her charities, her bridge, her tennis, her friends, and her parties.

(Joyce Cary: *The Breakout*)

A Tick one of the boxes, and give two reasons why you think so.

_____

_____

B Are there any *particular* words or phrases in the text that make you think this? If so, which?

_____

_____

C Do you like all four characters equally so far?

_____

Why (or why not?)

_____

_____

D You may not know some of the words in the paragraph. Try to guess what the following words mean by looking closely at the words and their context.

breakout _____

pretentious _____

frocks _____

trifling _____

3.7.1 Commentary	One first point to underline is that students need to develop the habit of continually asking themselves questions as they read, and that the reading process entails a constant activity of inferring, guessing and predicting. They should, however, always try to be prepared to give evidence for their predictions, and this is one of the reasons for the questions of the worksheet which ask for the supporting reference to 'particular words and phrases'. The class can then work through the worksheet examining their responses and giving reasons for them with reference to the language of the text. This is particularly relevant in the case of questions A and B, but question C also requires an answer which is likely to be conditioned by what we are told about the character and *how* we are told such things.

In this respect, the words 'all the same' in the middle of this opening paragraph are significant. 'All the same' indicates an opposite view is being developed, and represents a change from one point of view to another. It could be said that in the first part of the paragraph the reader is given the general view of Tom provided by the *society* in which he lives; in the second part there is a change in the direction to *Tom's own* point of view. Of course, the narrator of the story is addressing us all the time, but we do get a changing picture. From the outside Tom represents everything which is regarded as successful within and by the society he lives in; yet Tom himself is aware that 'he is working hard for very little'. It is at this point that students might be asked what they infer to be the main feature of Tom's character at this juncture of his life. They might also predict what the significance of the title is in the development of the story.

One conclusion which students may draw from reading the passage from *The Breakout*, following the worksheet and answering a range of questions, is that Tom Sponson, an *apparently* successful business man, apparently enjoying a happy family life, is *really* dissatisfied with his life and will 'break out' and away from this life. Such a conclusion or something close to it will have involved reading between the lines and paying close attention to language. The reading of a contrast between 'apparently' and 'really' is closely connected with the contrast signalled by 'all the same' and the change in point of view of the narrator.

It is also worth asking about Tom's view of his wife and how his view is presented. His view of her is that her life was completely filled with:

the children	the house	her tennis
her clothes	her charities	her friends
her figure	her bridge	her parties

This kind of diagrammatic presentation may also help to underscore the inference that all her activities appear to him to be of equal value. The lack of priorities and the suggestion that one thing is as important as another conveys an unflattering view of her, even though such a view is not *explicitly* stated.

3.8 Using grids and charts

Diagrammatic presentation, even of such a rudimentary kind as the above list, can assist in the perception of key components in the story. It can also help to store in our minds information about characters which may subsequently be

useful in making inferences or judgments about characters' actions and behaviour within a developing narrative.
For example:

1 Simple charts can be drawn up in which words are listed which are connected with a particular point of view or representation of a character. The first paragraph of *The Breakout* can be displayed in diagram form as follows:

Narrator

Point of view of society about Tom	Tom Sponson's point of view
successful	hard (work)
first class (business)	very little (reward?)
charming (wife)	gives him a peck (wife)
a good (house)	her life was completely
good (taste)	filled with . . . . . . (no priorities)
sensible (daughter)	

2 A chart can be made in which students list the *facts* that we know about the four main characters.

Tom	Louie	Bob	April

The list can be added to as more of the story is read. The main purpose here is to demonstrate the distinction between what we know and what we are left to infer and to interpret.

3 A related exercise is to list features of characters and of events in the story which can be marked as true or false.

		True T	False F	?
Tom Sponson	is pleased with his children			
	is happy with his wife			
	is successful			
	is proud of his success			
	is dissatisfied materially			
	is dissatisfied emotionally			
	. . . .			

The intermediate 'don't know' (?) category will again be used at those places where the narrator is forcing the reader to read between the lines or to make inferences and predictions. An interesting extension to this use of a chart or grid is to construct a series of statements about Louie. The exercise demonstrates how we know, at this stage at least, nothing about Louie except in so far as it is mediated to us through another's point of view. The point can be stressed further by an even more straightforward *re-writing* exercise in which Louie is presented to some extent *in the light of her own point of view.* In such cases a contrast in 'content' between the re-write and the original text can be additionally illuminating. For example:

> Louie hugged Tom warmly and kissed him when he left for the office and when he came back home. She often thought to herself how empty her life would be if it were not filled with her children, looking after their home and, most of all, her husband Tom.

We have to recognise the importance of viewpoint and the representation of character in fiction and how particular verbal signals can reveal much about what is being said. Some students require more time and reading practice to come to appreciate this and to learn to make constant inferences and predictions as they read. More extensive use of charts and grids can be a productive way forward.

It does, however, need careful monitoring, and, if the students do it without direct supervision, it is wise to make sure that a good and responsible student acts as producer/leader. More suggestions for different kinds of re-writing are made at 6.3 below.

3.8.1
Practical task

Work with a group of learners to make a complete 'production' of Wordworth's poem 'The Solitary Reaper'. (If another poem with a strong 'visual' component is already familiar to all learners, by all means use that poem.) Instead of the *two* introductory sections suggested for *Paradise Lost* above, use only *one*, combining a few sentences about Wordsworth with a brief introduction to the poem. This section should incorporate an explanation that the narrator/poet did not understand the language in which the girl was singing, hence line 17:

'Will no one tell me what she sings?'

Follow the procedure outlined in the section above but pay close attention to a) the setting b) the dress of the girl c) the song itself, which must be unaccompanied.

Consider the following as one approach to a 'production':

Stanza 1   – Visual – The 'Highland Lass'
              Sound – a) the girl's song
                      b) the poem – voice over
              How are these two combined, or kept separate?

Stanza 2 & 3 – What visual do you select?

Stanza 4   – Visual – the poet/narrator first motionless (wearing what? what age? etc.) then walking away into the distance, back to camera. Poem read, voice over, gradual fading out on the last two lines.

Note: This is a suggestion only and you should encourage all alternatives. Pay close attention to all details of appearance, position, dress, etc. and particularly of pauses in both the reading of the poem and the song. The above outline, however, is given primarily for teacher and group to discuss in detail the open question of *what visual to use for the second and third stanzas*.

**3.9
Conclusion**

This chapter has been almost exclusively devoted to strategies of questioning and to approaches to texts which result in productive questions. A main point made is that the more the students are involved with a text the more they will want to have their questions answered as well as to pose their own questions. It has been stressed that teachers can help to foster this kind of mental set if they give particular attention to the sequencing and type of questioning they ask. Underlying the whole chapter is the need for an imaginative response to be created. Approaches such as prediction and the re-creation of texts into visual media are designed to prompt imaginative and creative involvement.

4
Language-based approaches

4.0
Introduction

In the previous chapter we examined some classroom approaches to texts which were mainly directed towards eliciting responses to the themes and content of those texts by means of careful scrutiny of both the type and sequence of questions we ask. In this chapter the aim is to continue to elicit such responses. There is rather more emphasis on language, however, and on the ways in which attention to language can lead to a deeper understanding of a text. We title this chapter *language-based approaches*. In case this sounds forbidding we should stress that the procedures discussed here will certainly be familiar to teachers of English as a foreign language, and in many respects this chapter represents a continuation and extension of the previous chapter. We claim no originality in drawing on strategies such as jigsaw reading, cloze, re-writing, etc. But such procedures may be unfamiliar or not widely used in the teaching of literature. We aim to explore their relevance to the particular domain of literature teaching.

4.1
Jigsaw reading

4.1.1
Value as a
student-centred
activity

The term 'jigsaw reading' is borrowed from language teaching and is a parallel to the occasionally used 'jigsaw listening', whereby three or more groups listen to different tapes on the same subject, and thereafter pool their information to fill in a chart or table. Though the activity is widely practised, it generates relatively little language in the information-transfer stage. It is time-consuming to prepare, and it is difficult for groups to listen without interference from other groups. Jigsaw reading, on the other hand, is easy to prepare, and comprises the re-ordering of a text which has been scrambled. In the case of a poem this can be a difficult and challenging task, though the degree of difficulty depends, of course, on the poem which is selected for use. The phrase 'jigsaw reading' may suggest some sort of game. It is perfectly defensible, however, on the grounds that it is student-centred; it forces the individual to look closely at the language of the text and, more specifically, at the poetic discourse, and it stimulates learner–learner interaction in the solving of a puzzle.

4 1.2
Preparation and
procedure

It is important that before learners are asked to do an exercise of this type by themselves they should work through one example with the teacher. This, of course, applies to any exercise, but the purpose here is to indicate the type of question or prompt which will keep the interaction going. In this respect the term 'jigsaw' is appropriate as it indicates a series of small increments which, when added together, will 'complete the picture' i.e. reveal at least one complete level of meaning in the poem. The exercise is not simply a mechanical one, to get the poem into the right shape; nor does it resemble a crossword puzzle, where you try to find the solution, if necessary by guessing, as quickly as possible, and then move on to the next item.

For a sample exercise look at the well-known poem 'The Road Not Taken' by Robert Frost. As presented here the stanzas are not scrambled, but have been marked A B C and D for ease of reference:

The Road Not Taken

A   Two roads diverged in a yellow wood,
       And, sorry I could not travel both
       And be one traveller, long I stood
       And looked down one as far as I could
       To where it bent in the undergrowth.

B   Then took the other, as just as fair,
       And having perhaps the better claim
       Because it was grassy and wanted wear:
       But, as for that, the passing there
       Had worn them really about the same.

C   And both that morning equally lay
       In leaves no step had trodden black.
       Oh, I kept the first for another day,
       But, knowing how way leads on to way,
       I doubted that I should ever come back.

D   I shall be telling this with a sigh
       Somewhere ages and ages hence.
       Two roads diverged in a wood, and I,
       I took the one less travelled by,
       And that has made all the difference.

Robert Frost

The teacher should avoid beginning with the 'open' question: 'Which do you think is the first stanza?' Such a question invites 'hit or miss' answers but does not encourage investigation of the text. The following suggested questions do not form one half of a dialogue, because there is no attempt here to predict answers, but otherwise form an approximate sequence:
a) Who is the 'I' in stanzas A, C and D?
b) What does 'the other' refer to in stanza B?
c) What is the subject of 'took' in stanza B?
d) Why did he choose that road?
e) So why must stanzas B and C follow A, not precede it?
f) When did the incident described in stanza A take place?
g) What is the tense of the opening lines of stanza D?

h) Could D be the opening stanza?
i) If D were the opening stanza what information in A is redundant?
j) But is the sequence A D possible?
k) Why not?
l) Did the poet ever go back to the starting point?
m) How does the answer to (l) above determine the order of stanzas B and C?
n) Complete the sequence, using not more than five words for each item:
   1 The poet had an option
   2 He made his choice
   3 . . . .
   4 . . . .

Other questions are of course possible, and also follow-up questions to partial or tentative answers. Note that in general the lower-order questions (which, if understood by the learner, have a direct verifiable answer in the text) lead to higher-order questions (where in order to provide answers, it is necessary to make certain deductions, or evaluate alternative propositions). In some cases a low-order question leads directly to a higher-order question, as in g) – h). We suggest that anyone working through the above sequence to n) would have a fairly complete grasp of the poem's meaning, or be ready to make further inferences, from (here) *a guided process* of unscrambling.

**4.1.3
Preparing
questions for the
activity phase**

The following poem, also by Robert Frost, is here presented in scrambled form, and the reader is invited to consider what opening question(s) might be asked to set in motion the unscrambling of the poem *as a learner activity* (i.e. only the first two or three questions are required, but they should point the direction). In this poem attention should also be drawn to features of punctuation.

The Hill Wife

D
And work was little in the house,
She was free,
And followed where he furrowed field,
Or felled tree.

He never found her, though he looked
Everywhere,
And he asked at her mother's house
Was she there.

And once she went to break a bough
Of black alder.
She strayed so far she scarcely heard
When he called her –

She rested on a log and tossed
The fresh chips,
With a song only to herself
On her lips.

And didn't answer – didn't speak –
Or return.
She stood, and she ran and hid
In the fern.

It was too lonely for her there,
And too wild,
And since there were but the two of them,
And no child.

Sudden and swift and light as that
The ties gave,
And he learned of finalities
Beside the grave.

Robert Frost

73

(The practice of cutting and pasting the stanzas into an irregular pattern as above serves to isolate the stanzas and to focus attention on them one at a time as the learner tries to assemble the jigsaw.)

It is not, of course, essential to split up the stanzas of a poem, and a poem written in a continuous series of lines may also be used. In this case features of syntax and punctuation are certain to play a prominent part in the unscrambling process.

4.1.4
Jigsaw reading: 'Neighbours'

1 In this section we return to the poem 'Neighbours' introduced in Chapter 2. Here we have jumbled the stanzas of the poem. The task is to divide your class into small groups and to ask them to put the stanzas in what they think is an appropriate order. If they find the exercise difficult they can be told that the first and last stanzas are A and H respectively. When they have completed the exercise ask the groups to discuss with you the reasons for their choices. Did they see any parallels between stanzas B and E? Does that mean the stanzas go together? What is the time sequence relation between A and G? What is the sequence of the description of sizes? From large to small? From small to large?

2 Evaluate the task. Has the exercise been a meaningful one for the students? Do they seem more or less involved with the poem? Have they appreciated why the events occur in the order they do? Has the language-based activity taken your students into the subject of 'neighbours' and how we react to them?

A

I first noticed the neighbours were getting smaller
When driving away, he had to stand
To put his foot on the clutch.
She leant on tiptoe,
Getting the rubbish into the garbage bin.

E

Later we heard through the kitchen wall
Their quarrels like kittens mewing for milk.

D

And when it changed and I grew lower,
My chin on the basin, chest at the toilet top,
And my voice grew slower and weaker
And lesser as theirs grew louder
In sudden authority with their new-found height.

F

When I shaved
In the nude
In the morning,
The mirror reflected the wrong hair.
Soon I slept with my head up the chimney,
Feet out the window,
And outfaced the treetops, tip to tip.

H

I prayed they would do me no harm
As I had done them no harm,
Nor tread on a neighbour in or out of sight.

G

That evening, returning from work,
He set his shoulder to his briefcase.
Scraping it up the garden path
And reached to the heavens with his house-key.

C

Soon we'd be putting out birdseed for them:
But who was I to interfere?
For I was growing longer, day by night.

B

Later we heard through the bedroom wall
Their tiny cries of love like cries for help.

4.1.5
Discussion

1 This section lists at least three points which we believe make jigsaw reading a worthwhile teaching and learning technique with poems. Can you think of any other reasons for using it? What are the possible disadvantages?

2 Clarify what you understand by the term a 'mechanical exercise'. Why is jigsaw reading of poetry not a mechanical exercise?

3 Look at the poem 'The Hill Wife' on page 73. Why is this poem particularly suitable for scrambling and jigsaw reading?

4 Select a prose text from any literary work, preferably modern. It should consist of a series of short paragraphs. Scramble the text for jigsaw reassembly. Consider with your colleagues its value as an approach to literature. Do you think it merits the time spent on it by the *learner?* (i.e. not teacher preparation time)

5 Select a text which you know well and which you teach regularly, but which would *not* be appropriate for treatment as a jigsaw reading exercise. For example, we should consider lyric poems to be unsuitable because they rarely have a strong narrative line. Jigsaw activities are not well suited to non-narrative texts. Remember, too, that jigsaw reading can be time-consuming and that the length of the text is quite important. *Why* would your text be inappropriate? Now select one which you know well and teach regularly and which would be, by contrast, appropriate for jigsaw activities.

4.2
Matching

Matching exercises are related to jigsaw reading activities in so far as they involve a fitting together of different parts. Similarly, too, one aim of matching exercises is to enable students to use responses to the parts to build up sensitivity to the whole. One primary activity of matching is to collect examples of openings and closings to texts and invite students to match the relevant pairs. Doing so requires both recognition of stylistic similarities, continuities of character and thematic correspondences.

Beginnings and endings

Beginnings

1

THE Pottery House was a square, ugly, brick house girt in by the wall that enclosed the whole grounds of the pottery itself. To be sure, a privet hedge partly masked the house and its ground from the pottery-yard and works: but only partly. Through the hedge could be seen the desolate yard, and the many-windowed, factory-like pottery, over the hedge could be seen the chimneys and the out-houses. But inside the hedge, a pleasant garden and lawn sloped down to a willow pool, which had once supplied the works.

2

THEY were the idealists from New England. But that is some time ago: before the war. Several years before the war, they met and married; he a tall, keen-eyed young man from Connecticut, she a smallish, demure, Puritan-looking young woman from Massachusetts. They both had a little money. Not much, however. Even added together, it didn't make three thousand dollars a year. Still – they were free. Free!

3

MR LINDLEY was the first vicar of Aldecross. The cottages of this tiny hamlet had nestled in peace since their beginning, and the country folk had crossed the lanes and farm-land, two or three miles, to the parish church at Greymeed, on the bright Sunday mornings.

4

THERE was a man who loved islands. He was born on one, but it didn't suit him, as there were too many other people on it, besides himself. He wanted an island all of his own: not necessarily to be alone on it, but to make it a world of his own.

Endings

A

As he looked, the sky mysteriously darkened and chilled. From far off came the mutter of the unsatisfied thunder, and he knew it was the signal of the snow rolling over the sea. He turned, and felt its breath on him.

B

'We shan't see much of you then, as a son-in-law', said the mother, roughly but amicably.

'Not much,' he said.

Then he took his leave. Louisa went with him to the gate. She stood before him in distress.

'You won't mind them, will you?' she said humbly.

'I don't mind them, if they don't mind me!' he said. Then he stooped and kissed her.

'Let us be married soon,' she murmured, in tears.

'All right,' he said, 'I'll go tomorrow to Barford.'

C

'Europe's the mayonnaise all right, but America supplies the good old lobster – what?'

'Every time!' she said, with satisfaction.

And he peered at her. He was in the cage: but it was safe inside. And she, evidently, was her real self at last. She had got the goods. Yet round his nose was a queer, evil scholastic look of pure scepticism. But he liked lobster.

D

She stooped and kissed him. She had never kissed him before, not since she was a tiny child. But she was quiet, very still.

'Kiss him,' the dying man said.

Obediently, Matilda put forward her mouth and kissed the young husband.

'That's right! That's right!' murmured the dying man.

(We are indebted to Jane Spiro, Centre for English Language Education, University of Nottingham, for the ideas and suggestions given above.)

The exercise, which is also a heightened form of long-term prediction (see 3.6 above), may be useful as a pre-reading exercise for short stories or narrative poems. It is an exercise which can also be adapted to the requirements of different language levels and interpretive abilities; for example, the length of opening and ending can be extended or, if necessary, linking passages can be inserted with the link to different openings explicitly signalled. Other possibilities include: matching character descriptions from different stories; or matching three or more settings to a single story; or isolating the 'odd man out', that is, the description or setting or incident that does not belong to a particular story.

As far as drama is concerned the following matching activity has been suggested by Harold Fish[1]. It involves matching dramatis personae – as listed at the beginning of a play text – with a scene from the play. Here the dialogue alone provides the clue for students to match character and speech. The exercise is an especially productive one in the case of this play, *Golden Girls* by the contemporary dramatist Louise Page, which is thematically rich in confrontational issues such as racial tension, the position of women and sponsorship in sport. Once again the matching task can be adapted and simplified if necessary; for example, the number and/or gender of the characters speaking can be revealed. Here is the example:

Golden Girls was first presented by the Royal Shakespeare Company at The Other Place, Stratford-upon-Avon, on 20 June, 1984, with the following cast:

DORCAS ABLEMAN, *black athlete*	Josette Simon
MURIEL FARR, *black athlete*	Alphonsia Emmanuel
PAULINE PETERSON, *white athlete*	Katherine Rogers
SUE KINDER, *blonde white athlete*	Kate Buffery
JANET MORRIS, *black athlete*	Cathy Tyson
MIKE BASSETT, *white athlete*	Kenneth Branagh
LACES MACKENZIE, *coach*	Jimmy Yuill
VIVIEN BLACKWOOD, *doctor*	Jennifer Piercey
NOËL KINDER, *Sue Kinder's father*	George Raistrick
HILARY DAVENPORT, *sponsor*	Polly James
TOM BILLBOW, *journalist*	Derek Crewe
HOTEL PORTER, *white*	Norman Henry
THE GOLDEN GIRL, *everything the name suggests*	Jan Revere

1 In Carter, R A, Walker, R J and Brumfit, C J (eds) 1989 *Literature and the Learner: Methodological Approaches* Macmillan; MEP.

Directed by Barry Kyle
Designed by Kit Surrey
Music by Ilona Sekacz
Lighting by Wayne Dowdeswell

Acknowledgement
Special thanks to Ron Pickering for the sports commentary on page 61.

Can you do it?

Who can ever say?

Are you beginning to think of quitting?

Sometimes. (*Pause.*) I wanted a word.

With me?

Yes, I think so. (*Pause.*) It's a sort of question really. I hope you don't mind.

I'm flattered to be asked.

It's about Heidi Lynikova.

Yes.

There are stories in the camp –

Isn't gossip always rife amongst you?

Please.

I beg your pardon.

You know she was pregnant when she smashed the record in Oslo?

Fanny Blankers-Cohen in 1948 all over again.

Did you ever hear about the baby? (———— *thinks.*) It had everything wrong with it. They say it was a freak.

Really?

The American girls say it had something to do with some stuff she was taking. I wondered if you knew.

Why?

Pause.

     produces a capsule.

Oh!

It's legitimate. At least in the sense that nothing shows up.

A wonder drug?

We haven't had a bad season.

I thought it was the presence of Janet Morris amongst you. Youth snapping at your heels. Do you know what it is?

It's called hydro-something.

It's not cricket.

No. I don't want to stay in this game forever. Even if you want to your body starts to go and lets you down. I want to win here and then children. (*About the drug.*) We're running as fast as some of the men. (———— *takes it.*) It's not black market stuff. They come from the doctor.

Paid for by Ortolan?

I suppose so, in a manner of speaking. I thought you might have some way of finding out.

Hairy chests, anything like that?

It's not a steroid. It's made from rats.

It could be very messy.

Yes.

Drug analysis is expensive. The paper's money. They'll expect to be able to make a story.

Yes.

You'll be pilloried in every paper, every sports club –

Find out what it does. Please. Isn't it what they call a scoop.

Yes.

Matching is an activity with infinite possibilities for extension within the class. We have explored some basic principles; here are some further ideas for matching activities:

Match:

quotations or sayings with characters

pictures, photographs with characters or places

descriptions, profiles with characters

plot abstracts or summaries with beginnings or endings of texts

texts with genres[1]

stories or poems with titles (see also 5.1.4 below)

prose or poetry or drama dialogue with epoch or period

texts or settings or even characters with particular pieces of music

sentences jumbled together from two different works to form two separate stories[2]

Two-in-one story

The Stork/The Company Chairman

1   The cook stole a leg from a beautiful roast stork just before it was served to the king.
2   'But, your Majesty, you didn't clap last night.'
3   He glowered at them. 'Gentlemen, I have something I must say: half of you are idiots.'
4   The king asked him angrily why the bird had only one leg.
5   One day a company chairman got very angry with his board of directors.
6   The king clapped his hands and the birds flew off. 'There,' he said, 'You see, they all have two legs the moment I clap.'
7   'Very well', the chairman said, 'I withdraw it – half of you are not idiots.'

1 A further extension here is to write out three texts in prose (one is a poem) and students are asked to identify the poetic text and to give reasons for their choice and why they have identified the remaining passages as prose.

2 This final suggestion illustrates that activities such as matching can never be totally discrete. This two-in-one jumbled story, for example, involves both activities of matching and of text reconstruction or reassembly. This idea and the following example are taken from Berer, M, Frank, C and Rinvolucri, M 1987 *Challenge to Think* OUP p. 28. For further discussion of jumbling exercises see 4.1.4 p.74.

8   Next morning the cook and the king went down to the river and saw the storks all standing on one leg.

9   One of the directors stood up and banged on the table. 'I demand that you withdraw that last observation, Mr Chairman.'

10 The cook replied, 'Storks only ever have one leg – come to the river with me tomorrow and I will show you, Your Majesty.'

4.3
Gap-filling

Another way of drawing the students' attention to the language and form of a text and of exploring their relation to the text's meanings is by means of a targeted cloze procedure. Rather more informally, we term this well-known strategy 'gap-filling'.

Cloze is an established procedure in tests of language competence, and one of its dangers is that students may associate it with language examinations. However, it is increasingly employed for purposes of language development where the aim is to draw attention to the use of particular linguistic features such as connecting words between sentences or signalling words across paragraphs. In this sense the cloze becomes targeted, for the gaps are not made at random (or even systematically every nth word) but are removed because they have a particular function. In the case of cloze with literary texts it is important that by removing words the students' attention is drawn to items which are performing an important literary job.

As with most gap-filling exercises, the teacher can decide whether to ask students to retrieve a word or words without guidance or with reference to a group of words listed beneath the text. In our example here, based on D.H. Lawrence's poem 'Piano', we have chosen to supply a list and would only *not* supply such choices in the case of very advanced students. Five words have been removed and the lists of choices are in the order in which the gaps occur.

Softly, in the dusk, a woman is singing to me;
Taking me back down the _____ of years, till I see
A child sitting under the piano, in the boom of the tingling strings
And pressing the small, poised feet of a mother who smiles as she sings.

In spite of myself, the insidious mastery of song
_____ me back, till the heart of me weeps to belong
To the old Sunday evenings at home, with winter outside
And _____ in the cosy parlour, the _____ piano our guide.

So now it is vain for the singer to burst into clamour
With the great black piano appasionato. The glamour
of childish days is upon me, my manhood is cast
Down in the flood of remembrance, I _____ like a child for the past.

1 vista	2 calls	3 hymns	4 singing	5 cry
tide	betrays	songs	black	sing
	wins	fires	passionate	call
	forces		tinkling	weep

4.3.1
Advantages

1 The strategy of gap-filling in the literature class is well suited to pair and group work. It can be a student-centred activity.

2 It leads to *involvement* with the text. This involvement works on two levels: first, there is a natural interest in the success or otherwise of one's lexical predictions (even though it should be stressed that filling the gap with the 'right' word is not the point of the exercise); second, the making of any kind of choice depends on reading the *whole* text carefully and on checking how one word fits with other words.

3 The exercise raises a number of useful points of language use, even though the main point is to promote sensitivity to the use of words for *literary* purposes.

4 It is a task-based, activity-centred strategy which makes the teacher's role a supporting and supportive one. The teacher should, however, encourage students to justify their choices at all stages and be prepared to account for their choices to others in the group.

5 Gap-filling activities emphasise that a student's engagement with a text needs to be both linguistic and experiential.

6 It is a productive way of increasing the students' awareness of the *patterns* of words in a literary text. Choices of words in the above exercise depend on sound patterns as much as on meanings.

4.3.2
Conclusion

For further examples and further discussion of the uses of gap-filling in the literature class see Carter, R A and Long, M N 1987 *The Web of Words* CUP, especially Unit 8 which contains an exercise on the poem 'Futility' by Wilfred Owen discussed in Chapter 2 above. See also the article by Carter (especially pp. 112–113) in Brumfit, C J and Carter, R A (eds) 1986 *Literature and Language Teaching* OUP.

4.4
Reading aloud

In this section we explore the advantages and disadvantages of reading aloud in the classroom on the part of both teacher and students. Reading is normally a silent activity but we have to ask whether classroom understanding can be improved by giving a literary text an oral treatment or enactment.

4.4.1
To read or not to read: the teacher

In the teaching of a foreign language the teacher can quite often begin a lesson by reading out an opening sentence, or paragraph, or dialogue. This practice still seems to be quite common, even if what follows is 'communicative', inventive, and employs many of the tactics of current 'methodology'. In defence of the practice the teacher may be said to be 'modelling' the text.

In the teaching of literature an identical procedure is common, almost to the point of being a tradition. This time, however, it has little to do with modelling, and if pressed, many teachers would justify it by saying that story telling, and poetry, are part of an oral culture stretching back at least as far as any literary texts which we have, and probably a great deal longer; and that drama, by definition, is a refined and formalised oral mode. So the teacher reads and the students listen.

There are, of course, problems that will be encountered by the teacher and by the student when the teacher reads a text aloud to the class. First, few teachers are trained in reading aloud and not all may have the necessary skills in managing changes in pitch and tempo and in the effective use of pauses. Normally, reading a text in a monotone will do nothing to bring a text alive. Second, in itself the activity of a teacher reading aloud will not necessarily aid comprehension; in fact, hearing a difficult text may cause some students to become confused by the text and to switch off – particularly if it is a long text. Thirdly, choice of texts is vital. Some texts do not gain from being read aloud and may be better read silently.

On the other hand consider the following:

> I was not a clever child, academically speaking. I was alert, bright, chatty and energetic but by the age of seven I could barely read. Thompson was by then attending the Royal High School, where my father hoped eventually to send me. However, it soon became clear that my difficulties in reading and writing were going to make entry into that strict establishment uncertain. Thompson had been taught to read, had been read to nightly, by my mother. Oonagh, as I have said, was illiterate. I spent my days with her as an infant and it was she who put me to bed at night. Without fail, I would ask for a story and she would tell me one. She spoke to me in Gaelic – old folk tales, I like to think – but I was completely entranced. The room dark, one lamp glowing, Oonagh's haunch warming my side, and her soft lilting accent with its sonorous, soft gutterals. Oonagh's square face crudely mimicking the effects of shock, surprise, horror, fabulous joy . . . It was more than enough. I am sure, too, that here lies the key to my development as an artist, that this was why my personality took the maverick course it did. In those crucial, early days my imagination was not formed by any orthodox literary or pedagogical tradition. Oonagh's entrancing, meaningless tales and her big expressive face were sufficient fuel. I am convinced that it is this factor that separates me from my fellow artists, and it is this that makes my vision unique. Inchoate sound and dramatic expression were the foundations of my creative being. Sense, logic, cohesion played no part. Oonagh's mysterious voice and the bold analogues of her grimaces set my mind working independently.

(from *The New Confessions* by William Boyd 1987 Hamish Hamilton)

An effective oral rendering of a text can bring a text alive for students, even if not every single word is understood at first reading, and a class can be put in touch with a whole text in a unique and memorable way. An effective reading aloud by the teacher can also serve to clarify difficulties: difficult words can be 'enacted' and unclear or complex syntax can be unravelled in the process of an oral dramatisation.

Much depends, of course, on how well it is done, and it is impossible here to discuss in detail how it can or should be done. However, the following example may illustrate some relevant considerations. It is a single sentence from a novel by Charles Dickens.

> I thought it had the most dismal trees in it, and the most dismal sparrows, and the most dismal cats, and the most dismal houses (in number half a dozen or so) that I had ever seen.

(from *Great Expectations*)

If read aloud the repetition of the word 'dismal' becomes even more marked than in the printed version, and possibly also has an onomatopoeic effect, emphasising the drabness of the setting. Moreover, it accentuates a technique familiar to the cinema, moving from the trees, to the sparrows, to the cats, and finally to the most dismal feature of all, namely the houses, and allows the reader to add the phrase 'that I had ever seen' almost as an afterthought, so as not to divert attention from the universal dismalness. This of course is a fairly detailed analysis of a single sentence, and there is no need to rationalise in this way to learners. Select the sentence or unit of text which you consider will make a greater impact for being heard. Isolate it, i.e. make a marked pause before it and after it, and do not allow it to merge with the general flow of 'teacher talk'. Read it with as much expression as you can give it, imagining yourself for the moment on a stage, or before a television camera. Have learners look at you during the reading, though not, of course, by saying 'Look at me. I am going to read aloud'. Usually a lengthening of the initial pause will be sufficient.

The considerations here can gradually be extended to longer texts. In general, teachers should be concerned to improve their own reading, and much can also be learned by students from a discussion of how a particular reading reflects a particular interpretation of a text. If a teacher feels uncertain about his or her own reading then a practised reading could be put on tape, or commercial tapes or records used; alternatively, most commercial literature course books are accompanied by a tape. In general, our view is that generally more is gained than lost if the teacher develops the habit of reading aloud to his or her class.

4.4.2
To read or not to read: the student

In this section we explore some advantages and disadvantages to *students* reading aloud in the literature class. And we begin with an observation that there are few classes in both native and non-native speaker contexts where students do not *enjoy* the process of reading a text aloud.

There are, of course, a number of questions relevant to the practice of students reading aloud. Some of the main ones are:

1 What kinds of texts are best suited for reading aloud?
2 In the course of reading a text in class *when* should it be read aloud by the student? Should it be done first by teacher or by student?
3 How should it be done? Are there any guidelines which might help improve reading aloud by students?
4 Is reading best done by an individual student reading aloud to a class? Is choral reading effective? Can reading aloud be done in groups?

Clearly some texts lend themselves better than others to reading aloud. In general, a text which has a clear narrative line is better than one which is more descriptive, which presents a lyrical evocation of things or which presents ideas in a cerebral manner. Also important are *contrasts*. There might be contrasts between characters, contrasts in action or contrasts in mood. Reading the text aloud allows contrasts to be heightened by changes in pace or pitch. It is important to select texts which allow marked patterns, preferably of action in the early stages, to be clearly and energetically signalled. This will lead to a greater sense of involvement on the parts of both the students reading and those being read to.

In a class which is to be devoted to students reading aloud it is generally preferable if the students read the text *first;* otherwise they may be influenced by the teacher's style or by the particular interpretation which the teacher's reading supports. There are no hard and fast rules, of course, and a demonstration performance by the teacher even of the first sections of the text may be necessary as a way of modelling the texts for the students. It should be a matter for the teacher to decide, however, whether to conclude a study of the text with his or her own reading. It is important that students do not feel inferior; on the other hand it may provide an opportunity for the teacher to indicate some ways in which improvements to reading aloud can be made.

The teacher must also judge *when* reading aloud is most effective for the class's understanding and appreciation of a text. It may sometimes be helpful to discuss the text in advance of a reading; on the other hand, reading aloud first can supply pointers towards discussion. A general rule is that it is beneficial to read a text more than once at different stages in the exploration of that text. Remember that reading aloud can be a relief, it can heighten the impact of a line or phrase, it can effectively dramatise key points in the action and it can reveal humour which may not otherwise be noted in the printed word.

The question of how reading aloud is best done is difficult since the provision of guidelines may suggest that there is a correct way in which it is to be done. Texts cannot be subjected to a grid which is followed to produce a good reading. Different texts require different readings. However, a good starting point is to introduce potential readers to the idea of contrasting variables. Students can be offered an initial choice of reading the text:

loud or soft?
fast or slow?

with the choices related to the content of the text and the reader's interpretation of that content. After discussion of these main variables, further choices (e.g. high pitch v. low pitch) can be added and the text(s) re-read with reference to them. Students will also note that it is unlikely that variables would remain constant; a reading can change from slow to fast and from loud to soft and back to loud again during the course of the reading. For further exemplification see 4.4.4.

The following poem, from the First World War, is an extreme case of 'requiring to be read aloud'. Though each teacher/reader might have his or her own interpretation, *we* suggest that it should be read in the manner of a music-hall compere, or of a radio show host presenting pop records; that in this way the effect of the two lines

That in the fighting for this patch of wood (spoken very quickly, almost level pitch)
Were killed somewhere above (short pause) *eight* (sharp rise in pitch at the beginning of the word) *thousand* (slightly lower pitch) *men* (sharp fall in pitch)

achieves a greater poignancy than if read in a sombre or restrained manner, which is anyway not suggested by the opening:

Ladies and gentlemen (very loud, almost a shout, to attract attention; much lengthened second vowel in 'Ladies'; fall in pitch on 'gentlemen', though still very loud)

High Wood

Ladies and gentlemen, this is High Wood,
Called by the French, Bois des Fourneaux,
The famous spot which in Nineteen-Sixteen,
July, August and September was the scene
Of long and bitterly contested strife,
By reason of its High commanding site.
Observe the effect of shell-fire in the trees
Standing and fallen; here is wire; this trench
For months inhabited, twelve times changed hands;
(They soon fall in), used later as a grave.
It has been said on good authority
That in the fighting for this patch of wood
Were killed somewhere above eight thousand men,
Of whom the greater part were buried here,
This mound on which you stand being . . .

Madame, please,
You are requested kindly not to touch
Or take away the Company's property
As souvenirs; you'll find we have on sale
A large variety, all guaranteed.
As I was saying, all is as it was,
This is an unknown British officer,
The tunic having lately rotted off.
Please follow me – this way . . .

the *path*, sir, *please*,
The ground which was secured at great expense
The Company keeps absolutely untouched,
And in that dug-out (genuine) we provide
Refreshment at a reasonable rate.
You are requested not to leave about
Paper, or ginger-beer bottles, or orange-peel,
There are waste-paper baskets at the gate.

Philip Johnstone (1918)

Such preparation of the text for reading aloud can be done both individually and in groups. Our preference is for group work where students work together to rehearse a reading on which they can all agree and then appoint a reader to perform the agreed version. The different groups in the class can then vote to decide which rendering of the text they judge to be the best.

A variant of this would be for a short piece of text to be read aloud by one student and then read again by another student – leading to the question of why might one reading appear to be more appropriate than another. We would prefer such procedures to the practice of choral reading in a group or whole class. Choral reading – where everyone in a class reads the text together at the same time – has the advantage of helping the less confident students to participate; but it has the disadvantage of blurring individual or small group interpretations, of allowing some students to participate without actually doing or learning very much and of distracting attention from the decisions required as to how a particular text is to be read to its full effect.

In conclusion to this section we would stress once again the importance and value of encouraging students to read aloud. If students make errors, then opportunities can be found for learning from such errors. If we want students to explore literary texts and to explore their own experience in relation to such texts, then we have to trust them, to *encourage* them to try reading aloud. In this way they can come to gain insights into what a text means.

4.4.3
Practical task

This poem requires some background information in that it imitates the rhythms and uses some of the phrases of a quite well-known English hymn, the original being a thanksgiving for harvest. The poem is, of course, basically satirical. With a suitably advanced group decide 1 What is the underlying feeling of the poem? Is it, for example a) conviction b) humour c) indignation d) regret e) some other emotion? 2 We consider that this is a poem which *should* be read aloud. Do you agree? Why? 3 Decide *how* you would read it (see 4.4.2 above). 4 What is the potential of this poem for exploitation, quite separately from reading aloud?

Harvest Hymn

We spray the fields and scatter
  The poison on the ground
So that no wicked wild flowers
  Upon our farm be found.
We like whatever helps us
  To line our purse with pence;
The twenty-four hour broiler-house
  And neat electric fence.

All concrete sheds around us
  And Jaguars in the yard,
The telly lounge and deep-freeze
  Are ours from working hard.

We fire the fields for harvest,
  The hedges swell the flame,
The oak trees and the cottages
  From which our fathers came.
We give no compensation,
  The earth is ours today,
And if we lose on arable,
  Then bungalows will pay.

All concrete sheds . . . etc.

John Betjeman

4.4.4
Further
exploration

The following is a further extract from a course book for EFL students of literature. One of the units in the book is particularly devoted to reading aloud. We have extracted a section from the beginning of the unit – an orientation –

which introduces a specific framework and some suggested categories for reading a text in performance. This is then extended to a reading of 'The General' by Siegfried Sassoon.

Attempt the exercise yourself and with a class and consider a) the extent to which the suggested categories are useful b) how far your rendering of the poem represents an interpretation of it c) whether 'The General' is a poem better suited for reading aloud than the other war poem 'High Wood' discussed at 4.4.2 above.

Introduction for the student

This unit is designed to help you explore some of the factors involved in reading a literary text aloud. Just as writers exploit grammar and vocabulary for literary effect, so they pattern sounds for expressive purposes. This is a feature which can best be brought out by reading aloud, and many literary texts gain from this element of 'performance'.
You will find the cassette particularly useful for this unit.

Orientation

There are many different ways of reading a text. Factors such as speed, pitch and emotion all help to convey the reader's interpretation of the piece. Below is a set of eight such 'variables' (you may think of more) which the reader can select from and combine to give added meaning to the words on the page.

i)   loud   – soft
ii)   fast   – slow
iii) high pitch – low pitch
iv)   tense   – relaxed
v)   smiling   – grim
vi)   'chin up'   – 'chin down'
vii) emotive   – non-emotive
viii) 'breathy'

The first five pairs above are probably self-explanatory. The following brief notes are added for the remainder:

vi)   Consider the exchange:
      A: My father died last night.
      B: I'm sorry to hear that.

Utterance B here is likely to be spoken with 'chin down'. It is also likely to be soft rather than loud. For 'chin-up' consider:
      'I am proud to announce that your company has again achieved . . .'

vii) If I say, 'Take the second turning to the left' that is likely to be non-emotive, and as such 'neutral'. 'Emotive' would include any utterance which involved the expression of emotions such as excitement, anger, disappointment etc.

viii) 'Breathy' refers to the mode of speaking frequently associated with television advertising and intended to be persuasive and, in some cases, sexy. There is no obvious 'opposite' to 'breathy' to form a pair.

Reading aloud 1

1 Listen to this reading of 'The General' by Siegfried Sassoon. We shall look at this poem again in Unit 6 where we examine associations of particular words. Here we concentrate on how to express the meaning orally.
    Now look at the poem and read it through chorally.

The General

'Good-morning; good-morning!' the General said
When we met him last week on our way to the line.
Now the soldiers he smiled at are most of 'em dead,
And we're cursing his staff for incompetent swine.
'He's a cheery old card,' grunted Harry to Jack   5
As they slogged up to Arras with rifle and pack.

                    *

But he did for them both by his plan of attack.

Siegfried Sassoon

2 Consider the following features and practise them in groups. Make comments on each other's performance.

Line 1 Greeting high pitch. 'The General said' low pitch.
         Greeting also 'chin up'. Try and speak as a superior speaking to inferiors or subordinates.

Line 2 Continue low pitch, quick rather than slow. No variation of pitch. Consider also loud versus soft, tense versus slack.

Line 3 Grim. Stress on 'dead'. Very tense; relaxed speaking loses the meaning entirely.

Line 4 Grimmer than 3. Definitely emotive (anger? contempt?). Consider especially the articulation * of the word 'swine' (and also its associations – see Unit 6, Section A, *Orientation*).

Line 5 Complete change from 4. First part of line smiling – 'chin up' – in spite of the verb 'grunted'. Remainder of line low pitch.

Line 6 Less marked than any other line, but consider loud versus soft, quick versus slow.
         For effect, follow by a pause of full three seconds, and time this.

Line 7 Tense, but lacking the bitterness of 4. Soft – appropriate to the presence of death.

**4.5
Alternative
versions: the
uses of
paraphrase**

One of the advantages of gap-filling (4.2) as a language-based strategy is that students come to compare alternative versions of texts. They explore different lexical choices, evaluating the different effects of one word over another by considering the grammatical, semantic and, in the case of poetry, sound patterns into which they fit; they may even prefer some of their choices to the ones eventually revealed to be the poet's choices.

An extension to this activity can lead to an exploration of the possibilities of paraphrase. The technique is a relatively simple one of juxtaposing two or more versions from texts which are being read or are to be read – one the original and the other(s) a re-written alternative version. Clearly, paraphrasing texts can work most successfully if the texts are short or are opening lines or stanzas. As with texts which are compared for thematic correspondences, the basic principle is that the essential qualities of something are most effectively and memorably highlighted by means of simple contrast. The process of comparing alternative versions leads, too, to an active involvement with a text and to a sense of the text as something dynamic and fluid, open to creative exploitation, rather than as a static fixed order of words on a page served as if to a passive consumer.

Paraphrase holds out numerous possibilities. For example, key lines in a poem can be extracted and paraphrased in order to help students to isolate particular stylistic or tonal qualities. In the poem 'Futility', for example (see 2.4.2) a paraphrase of lines 10–11 such as:

> Are dear-achieved limbs and still warm
> full-nerved sides too hard to stir?

– which involves a teacher in little more than transposing adjectives – can be compared with the original:

> Are limbs, so dear-achieved, are sides
> Full-nerved – still warm – too hard to stir?

The paraphrase is deliberately not staccato, broken by syntactic embeddings or uneven in movement. The original serves to express the broken grief and emotional hesitancy of the persona of the poem. Its tone is appropriate.

Paraphrase can involve alternative versions in which words or phrases are put in a different order or it can adopt a more extreme but rather more playful strategy of *mimetic paraphrase* in which comic versions of well-known (and serious) texts are produced. For example, here are two versions of William Blake's poem 'The Tyger':

> Tyger Tyger burning bright,
> In the forests of the night;
> What immortal hand or eye,
> Could frame thy fearful symmetry?
>
> Rabbit Rabbit, freezing dull,
> In the plains of the day;
> What mortal foot or ear
> Could copy thy timid disproportion?

In this case several words are simply translated into their opposites but the effect can be to focus attention on the original from a different perspective.

Here are some examples of paraphrase exercises. In each case opening lines or short poems are taken and key words or phrases re-written. The paraphrasing takes the following forms:

1a) 1b) 1b) is the original version and 1a) involves changes to key verbs, rhymes and to a central adjective – diurnal/daily.

2a) 2b) Here 2a) is a re-write of the original, 2b), only in so far as the layout on the page is concerned. The aim is to focus on the purpose of the particular lineation adopted by the poet.

3a) – f) 3d) is the original version. Changes are made to vocabulary, syntactic structure and to deixis (i.e. *the*, *a*, *these*, etc.)

1   'A slumber' (Wordsworth)

a)   A slumber did my spirit feel;
     I shed no human tears:
     She seemed a girl who could not heal
     The touch of earthly years.

     No movement has she now, no force;
     She neither feels nor sees,
     Rolled round in earth's daily course
     With rocks, and stones, and trees.

b)   A slumber did my spirit seal;
     I had no human fears:
     She seemed a thing that could not feel
     The touch of earthly years.

     No motion has she now, no force;
     She neither hears nor sees,
     Rolled round in earth's diurnal course,
     With rocks, and stones, and trees.

2   'The Red Wheelbarrow' (William Carlos Williams)

a)   So much depends upon
     A red wheelbarrow
     Glazed with rain water
     Beside the white chickens

b)   So much depends
     upon
     a red wheel
     barrow
     glazed with rain
     water
     beside the white
     chickens

3   In a Station of the Metro' (Ezra Pound)

a)   An apparition of these faces in the crowd.
     Like petals on a wet black bough.

b)   The appearance of these faces in the crowd.
     Petals on a wet black bough.

   c)   The apparition of these faces in a crowd.
        Petals on a wet black bough.

   d)   The apparition of these faces in the crowd;
        Petals on a wet, black bough.

   e)   The apparition of these faces in a crowd;
        Petals on a wet brown bough.

   f)   The apparition of these faces in a crowd.
        Was like petals on a wet black bough.

Paraphrase is a language-based approach which, with only a small measure of re-writing by the teacher, can put a text and its organisation in focus and which can aid appreciation of how form and meaning are interrelated.

For further discussion of paraphrase and re-writing see essays by Widdowson and Nash in Brumfit, C J and Carter, R A (eds.) 1986 *Literature and Language Teaching* OUP. The general issues raised here are examined further in sections on re-writing in the next chapter.

4.6
Writing creatively in a foreign language

Some teachers resist the idea that students of English as a second or foreign language should write creatively in English. It is felt that they have enough difficulty manipulating the language in correct structures and that managing the kinds of deviant 'creative' structures of a language can produce problems without any clearly mitigating advantages. However, such a view discounts the benefits in confidence and in appreciation of language use which can be derived from simple language-based exercises, designed to promote sensitivity and to develop interpretive skills by exploiting awareness of patterns of language 'from the inside'.

These ideas can be clarified by examination of some basic exercises. The exercises involve writing in English according to particular patterns. The exploitation of patterns is designed to enhance awareness of the interrelationship between form and meaning. They try to achieve a balance between a particular topic or theme and the form selected to represent it. Encouraging a student to respond to a theme or to content is important but, for purposes of developing literary appreciation, it may be dangerous to focus on what is said in isolation from *how* it is said. Listed below is a sample of possible exercises for writing according to clearly specified language-based patterns:

1 *Focusing first line*
Students are given a key line, e.g.

    It was so boring

    I was frightened and alone

and invited to complete the poem by a series of observations. For example:

    I was frightened and alone
    The trees were waving dark and lonely
    I was frightened and alone
    The owl hooted
    I was . . . . .

2 *Thin poems*

A 'thin' poem consists of just two words per line. Less basic versions can be written in stanzas of two lines and can involve alliterative patterns. For example:

> Soft sand
> Bright shells
> Kids shout
> Sun shines
> Salty smell
> etc.

3 *Cinquain*

This is a five line poem with two syllables in the first line, four syllables in the second line, six in the third, eight in the fourth and two syllables again in the final and fifth line. For example:

> Cold room
> Ice at windows
> Arctic whistling outside
> The fire at last burns more brightly
> Warmth glows.

4 *Sound poems*

Here students are given combinations of initial syllables and have to make patterns of related words:

a) in a *shape* which has some relation to the sound produced, e.g.

> splASH!
> spl u r g e
> sp͜ᶻ

or b) contrasts have to be produced using words with the same initial letters:

> fridge
> freeze
> frost
> freedom
> frank

5 *Noun phrase poem*

This poem is based on sequences of noun phrases without a main verb which have to be arranged in an appropriate 'picture' on the page. For example:

The Teacher's Desk		
The steady job	The daily work	The cup of tea
The bulky desk	The constant loss	The sinking feeling
The same ideas		The safety cage
The familiar prison		The occasional dream
The private life		The same faces
The sticky seat		The comfortable chair

This example was written by a German student of education training to be a teacher.

6 *The Magic Box*

This is a more open-ended and less formally restrictive exercise which is widely used in schools in England and which can carry over into EFL classes. Here students are read a sample version and given the main structural frame to the poem. They are then invited to say what they would put in the 'box' and what they would then do with it. The frame for the poem is as follows:

- It has a refrain: 'I will put in the box', which can be followed by a range of objects as unusual as the student's imaginative and linguistic resources will allow.
- It should contain a stanza which describes the box.
- It should contain a stanza in which the writer says what he/she would do with the box.

Here is a 'Magic Box' poem written to this formula by an Italian secondary school student.

The Magic Box

I will put in the box
flowers of gold held together
by silver chains,
diamond stars and moons.

I will put in the box
the little man from the blue moon,
a marvellous day with mum and dad
the schoolbag of a violet octopus

My box is made out of sea
shells and
lightning, rainbows and
golden rays of sunshine.

I shall go with my box
to a desert island and play alone
with the gold and silver and touch
the rainbows where no-one will see me.

4.6.1
Creative writing in the classroom

In this section only some very preliminary possibilities[1] have been explored and the potential for developing this work into pair, group and class poems should not be overlooked. The aim throughout is to foster an awareness *from the inside* of what is involved in the creative shaping of a text and to increase understanding of the mutual reinforcement of form and meaning. Frequently, such appreciation is fostered from the outside by analysis and discussion of a finished product; exercises in creative writing, however rudimentary, put students in touch with the processes of a text and with processes of language and form which are their own. This can lead to greater confidence and

---

[1] For further examples see Carter, R A and Long, M N 1987 *The Web of Words* CUP especially Unit 5 'Patterns of Language'. Many more extensive examples can be found in Maley, A and Moulding, S 1985 *Poem into Poem* CUP.

enjoyment and perhaps to a realisation that writing creatively is a property available not exclusively to 'great' canonical writers, or even to native speakers only, but to all users of a language. Even small steps in this direction can lead to larger strides in literary competence.

4.7
Conclusion

In this chapter some preliminary language-based aproaches to literary study have been reviewed and illustrated. These approaches are preliminary in that they are well-known and widely used in the language class, and are also preliminary in that they are designed to produce a creative involvement with a text which lays a firm basis for subsequent more detailed analysis, discussion and evaluation. The approaches are also related to one another as strategies for generating greater awareness of the properties of language use in literary texts. The chapter ended with an invitation to teachers and students to work progressively through a number of basic exercises leading to their writing creatively and for themselves in a foreign language. A final task for readers to undertake at this point might be a) try out *two* of the patterns at 4.5 in their own classrooms b) add to the list of basic patterns by at least two more suggestions which stimulate controlled creative writing.

5

Hearts and Hands: a case study

**5.0
Introduction**

In this short chapter a preliminary teaching plan is proposed for a complete short story. The story is *Hearts and Hands* by the American writer O'Henry. The story is printed in full on pages 30–32. In the first section of the chapter we present a list of teaching suggestions more or less in the order in which they might be presented to a class. The points begin with questions to elicit a basic understanding of some themes in the story and then proceed to more language-based approaches. The next sections provide a commentary on the teaching plan with particular attention given to sequencing of questions and to integration of approaches. A main aim of the chapter is to explore ways of bringing together, in relation to one text, language-based approaches covered in Chapter 4 with the more general approaches covered in Chapter 3.

**5.1
Teaching points**

**5.1.1
Pre-reading
activities**

One possibility here may be a pyramid discussion which focuses on attitudes to money and personal wealth. The theme of money recurs in a number of places in the story, both directly and indirectly, and there are even two statements concerning money which might number among the various citations we could list. (Money isn't everything; Money has a way of taking wings.) As in 2.3 above, students are invited here to work in groups to decide which of the statements they agree with most at each point, and should be able, of course, to say why they are eliminating particular statements.

> Money can't buy you love

> Money isn't everything

> Money talks

> A fool and his money are soon parted

Money doesn't grow on trees

The love of money is the root of all evil

Money has a way of taking wings

Money makes the world go round

Everyone has their price

Other possibilities for related pre-reading activities in theme-sensitisation include a ranking activity in which the statements have to be ranked in order of truth to experience either for a group or for individuals working on their own; or a true/false exercise can be devised, again for a group, pair or individual in which starker choices are presented. For example,

	True	False
Money makes the world go round:		
The love of money is the root of all evil:		

insert ✔

The true/false activity is deliberately designed to enforce decisions, though it will probably emerge that some statements are true or false depending on the context. It is also important to guard against pre-empting readers' responses to the text and *necessary* to suggest that 'money' is not *necessarily* the main or only theme of this story.

**5.1.2
Prediction**

The story has a relatively strong narrative line and lends itself well to prediction exercises. Listed below are some points at which a group reading of the story might pause to consider predictions of what is to follow:

l.6 'The two were handcuffed together'.

What is the story going to be about?
What happens to the 'pretty young woman'?
Who is the prisoner? The younger man or the large, 'roughly dressed' man?

l.25 ' . . . with his sharp searching eyes'

What is the relationship between the young man and Miss Fairchild?
What does the sad-faced man say next?

l.55 'The bound travellers rose to their feet'

Is there a reconciliation between Miss Fairchild and the young man?
Is the young man really the marshal or is he the prisoner?
How does the story end?

5.1.3
Read aloud

The story can then be read aloud by the teacher with particular emphasis given to the statements about money.

5.1.4
Questions

The next point in the lesson is to elicit responses through questions. A range of questions related mainly to theme and character are offered, beginning with more closed questions and moving to questions which are more open and which require the student to make greater inferences.

1 Which country do you think this story is set in?

2 Which period of history do you think the action takes place in?

3 How many characters are there in the story and which are the three main ones?

4 Which two of them are old friends and where did they know each other formerly?

5 Which character could these words best refer to:
    rich,   confident,   fashionable?

6 Which character could these words best refer to:
    solemn,   alert,   compassionate?

7 Make a list of adjectives to describe the third main character.

8 Why do you think the writer has called the young lady 'Miss Fairchild'?

9 This story is full of opposites (e.g. right v. left; east v. west;). Make a list of words, phrases or images that are opposites of each other.

10 What do you think is the significance in the story of these oppositions?

11 Which words are most repeated in this story?

12 What is the significance of the repetitions?

13 What is the significance in the plot structure of these lines:
    'You'll excuse me for speaking, miss. But I see you know the marshal here. If you'll ask him to speak a word for me when we get to the pen, he'll do it.'?

14 From whose point of view is the story told?

15 Give one example of irony in this story.

16 What is the 'shining bracelet' referred to in the story?

17 What is the surprise in the last three lines of the story?

18 What is the counterfeiter's name?

19 Is there a clue in the story about why he may have needed to commit this crime? If so, where?

20 Which of these titles do you think is most suitable for this story and why?
    a) East and West
    b) The Counterfeiter
    c) Hearts and Hands
    d) Handcuffs
    e) Money isn't Everything
    f) Everyone has their Price

(Note that initially the teacher would need to present the story without its title.)

5.1.5
Post-reading
activities

There are a number of possibilities for follow-up questions and activities which can serve to reinforce preceding work and to promote further interpretation of the story. Here are two such possibilities.

1 *Letters: Diary*
Students can be asked to write a letter from Miss Fairchild to a close friend in which she recounts the meeting with Mr Easton, or a letter from the marshal to a friend explaining his actions in allowing Miss Fairchild to assume he was the prisoner, or an entry for that day in Mr Easton's diary. The point of a letter to a close friend or a diary is that it is an appropriate context for revealing inner feelings and provides an opportunity for hypothesising about and exploring the relative points of view of the three main characters. The results will be in contrast to the story itself which is understated and implicit in such areas. The contrast can help with appreciation of *how* the story is written. Further re-writing exercises involving switches in point of view are suggested in the next chapter (6.3).

2 *Scenario: In another medium*
Here groups can work on the production of a video or short film of *Hearts and Hands*. The following list of points can be given for consideration/decision-making by the groups. Several of the points depend on how the story is interpreted and what its principal meanings are taken to be.

1 Is the film in colour or black and white? Part colour and part black and white?

2 Is there a soundtrack?
If so, what form does it take?

3 Are there any flashbacks?

4 At what points in the narrative will there be close-ups on the different characters?

5 How will the handcuffs be filmed?

6 How can the significance of left hand/right hand be brought out visually?

7 Is it possible to represent the east/west distinction (the freedom and opportunity – ironically so in the case of Easton – of the west, compared with the primary concern with money, 'style and manner' in the east?) If so, how?

8 Describe or find photographs of an actress to play Miss Fairchild. What are the reasons for your choice?

9 How important is the setting? (i.e. the meeting on a *train*?) What will be emphasised in the filming?

10 Hands can be filmed but how can hearts be represented visually?

5.2
**Sequencing and
integrating
approaches**

In this chapter we have combined a number of strategies and approaches. The strategies have been outlined in the preceding two chapters but a number of them are applied here to a single text to form an integrated approach to the teaching of *Hearts and Hands*. The strategies are presented, too, in a particular sequence. In this section we try to draw some general conclusions concerning the sequencing and integrating of approaches.

In the case of *Hearts and Hands* the order of strategies is listed here, together with an indication of a rationale for the putting of each activity in its particular place in the sequence:

1 The pyramid discussion is the first approach and is designed to encourage a response to a *theme* (here, 'money') and a prior personal involvement with a topic which is represented in the story. Personal experience is also invoked from the beginning.

2 The prediction exercise is designed to develop sensitivity to plot and character formation. The completed exercise builds towards a sense of the whole story and an initial awareness of the relationship of the theme of money to the way the plot develops and the way the characters are presented.

3 Reading aloud reinforces a sense of the whole.

4 A series of questions prompts further involvement and responses. The questions are, in turn, sequenced. They begin with information-based questions, the answers to which can be relatively easily retrieved from the text itself. The questions then involve transposition of single words to particular characters. There is then a question which touches on more symbolic associations. This question is then followed by more linguistic questions involving more detailed textual analysis. These then lead to a consideration of point of view and the presentation of the structure of events – which require attention both to language and to the formalistic mediation through language of character, character interrelationships and the developing themes of the story. The questions develop from this exploration of form and language towards questions which require fuller inference and interpretation. The questions conclude with open responses where they had begun with rather more focus on closed and factual answers.

5 The general sequence for this story may be set out as follows:

Questions 1–4   Content, information-based
Questions 5–7   Initial attention to language
Question 8   Prompt to interpretation
Questions 9–12   Linguistically-orientated questions; further prompts to interpretation
Questions 13–17   Relationship between form and meaning; attention to the structure of the story and its significance
Questions 18–20   Further prompts to interpretation and exploration of the meanings of the story

6 Post-reading activities are designed to *integrate*:
    a) language-based approaches: students are using language for expressive and purposive activities
with b) further exploration of theme and character and a developing interpretation of the text
with c) further creative involvement with the text through a process of formal comparison and contrast
with d) methodologies which are learner-centred, activity-based and productive of language and which draw on students' own experiences.

**5.3
Conclusions**

It is, of course, dangerous to attempt to establish any principles when the conclusions are necessarily general and provisional and are drawn from an example of only one short story. The points we have made here are intended to do no more than prompt discussion. Each story will require different approaches and not all strategies work equally appropriately on all texts; similarly, different sequences and different degrees of integration will be applicable with other stories and with the different genres of poetry and drama. There are also issues to do with:

sequencing of language
sequencing of content
sequencing of activities
sequencing of objectives

which will be relative to a particular course, culture, language-situation, range of students' experience, etc. We do hope, however, to have drawn some attention to the importance of such issues (some of which will be discussed in greater detail in Chapter 7) and established an initial framework within which such issues can be examined in a systematic way. The case study of this specific example also serves as a bridge between the discussion of teaching approaches in Chapters 3 and 4 and further exploration of them in the chapter which now follows and which is devoted to activities and approaches for the more advanced student of literature.

A Theoretical Postscript

> Striving to construct a coherent sense from the text, the reader will select and organize its elements into consistent wholes, excluding some and foregrounding others, 'concretizing' certain items in certain ways; he or she will try to hold different perspectives within the work together, or shift from perspective to perspective in order to build up an integrated 'illusion'. What we have learnt on page one will fade and become 'foreshortened' in memory, perhaps to be radically qualified by what we learn later. Reading is not a straightforward linear movement, a merely cumulative affair; our initial speculations generate a frame of reference within which to interpret what comes next, but what comes next may retrospectively transform our original understanding, high-lighting some features of it and backgrounding others. As we read on we shed assumptions, revise beliefs, make more and more complex inferences and anticipations; each sentence opens up a horizon which is confirmed, challenged or undermined by the next. We read backwards and forwards simulataneously, predicting and recollecting, perhaps aware of other possible realizations of the text which our reading has negated. Moreover, all of this complicated activity is carried out on many levels at once, for the text has 'backgrounds' and 'foregrounds', different narrative viewpoints, alternative layers of meaning between which we are constantly moving.
>
> Eagleton, T 1983 *Literary Theory: An Introduction* Blackwell p.77,
> describing work by Wolfgang Iser and Roman Ingarden.

This quotation, referring to the work of the leading theorists of reader-response criticism (also known as Rezeptionsästhetik or reception theory), illustrates the relative closeness between process-based strategies drawn from the language teaching classroom and accounts of the reading process given by literary critics and theorists. Thus, prediction, be it at the level of a paragraph,

99

sentence, clause, phrase or word, as a teaching strategy is argued to be close to natural processes of reading in which a reader is active in filling gaps, resolving indeterminacies and ambiguities, constructing and revising interpretive hypotheses and reading beyond the text in all kinds of ways. We draw attention to this coincidence here in order to underline the importance of pedagogies which are doubly sensitive to and integrate linguistic and literary procedures.

Clearly, texts such as *Hearts and Hands* which require a high degree of *inference*, can help to promote this kind of reading activity. This is particularly true if teachers continue to devise questions and related activities along the lines outlined in 5.2 above.

6

Activities for the advanced class

6.0
Introduction

This chapter describes a number of activities for upper-intermediate to advanced students of English. The aim here is to offer procedures which fully *integrate* literature and language study, suggesting, we hope, as much for the language development of the student as for the development of capacities for literary understanding and appreciation.

6.1
Language and literariness: using a cline

Is there anything special about the *language* of literature to which we can direct the learner's attention? Indeed, there would seem to be a great deal. Everybody knows what literature is, namely that which was written by one of the authors mentioned in a history of literature, or in a survey course. But we persist with our question. Is there anything special about the *language*? Well, of course. Literature has rhythm, and quite often rhyme and …… . Yes, some of it does, but by no means all of it. Is there anything special about the language of prose, for instance?

This sort of dialogue may be continued for some time, and as it develops it would become increasingly evident that while the language of literature has 'something' (though it may be difficult to categorise it because it is a combination of many features) a vast selection of other texts also have some of those features, though the texts may not otherwise be classified as literature. But why not? There are no rules to decide what can be accepted as literature and what can not. Why not devise a scale or cline of literariness, personal and individual for each reader, and thus available for constant reassessment, which allows the reader to place a text higher (or, of course, lower) on the scale at a second or later reading, when the language was found to be richer or more subtle, or more moving, than at first thought? As the cline is personal, it does not need rigid external criteria, which are obviously difficult to establish in saying what sort of language is 'rich' or 'subtle' or 'moving'. Put slightly differently,

'The answer (to what is specifically literary about certain texts) may be a primarily sociological one and lie with the disposition adopted by the reader towards the text. In terms of actual words employed, there can certainly be no quantitative distinction between literary and non-literary texts. However, differences in the way language is used are discernible, though it has been argued that such distinctions may be less a case of yes/no decisions than one of a gradient or cline of literariness. In the language and literature classroom it is necessary to approach such issues with an open mind ....'

from an article 'Linguistic models, language, and literariness' by R.A. Carter
in Brumfit, C J and Carter R A (eds.) 1986 *Literature and Language Teaching* OUP

The idea is the more appealing in that it avoids other value judgements on what constitutes 'great literature', by which anything by 'a famous author' has to be rated highly, although at certain points it may be quite awful (or, in your assessment, always awful), while other texts, plucked from a wide general reading, quite separate from a *study* of literature, may be superb, deserving of a high rating on the cline, and exactly what you, as teacher, need as exemplifications.

6.1.1
Setting a standard with well-known lines of poetry

The cline cannot begin to work until you set a standard. But it must be remembered that, in the last resort, it is *your* standard and nobody else's. You are therefore under no obligation to accept other people's judgements.

Remember, secondly, that you are not making value judgements. You are, in fact, trying to do the impossible, namely to make a scientific evaluation of a piece of language, to make the same sort of statement as 'iron has a higher molecular weight than aluminium', or 'a chimpanzee is a more highly developed creature than a kangaroo'. The criteria of course are not verifiable in the same way, but this does not matter.

Suppose we begin with:

The plowman homeward plods his weary way   (see p.38 above)

We know that it is poetry, which predisposes us to a high rating rather than a low; but, as we saw on p.38, it has also a number of readily identifiable literary features, although rhyme is not one of them unless we take a larger unit. However we will assign it as follows, where 'low' and 'high' refer to relative literariness:

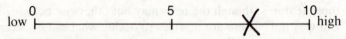

Now consider the two lines:

Behold her, single in the field
Yon solitary Highland lass

As no criteria other than overt and recognisable literariness are involved, we might place this higher, on the grounds that 'Behold her', as an opening, 'single in the field' to express the idea that she was alone, 'Yon' as a conscious archaism even when the poem was written (though that is using our knowledge of literary history), and the use of the word 'lass', mean that virtually everything in the ten words is in some way 'marked'. However we look at it, it is very distant from something like 'Look at that girl over there in the field. She looks a bit lonely' as a proposed spoken version of the same proposition. We therefore rate it as follows:

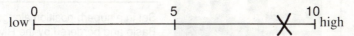

Thirdly, the opening of the poem 'Snake' by D.H. Lawrence:

> A snake came to my water-trough
> On a hot, hot day, and I in pyjamas for the heat,
> To drink there.

There seems here a closer correspondence with spoken language, or for that matter written language, though it is difficult to place it exactly, especially with the phrase 'I in pyjamas' (a personal letter? a diary?). But remember that nothing requires us to do so. We relate it only to one or more of the other texts. Thus:

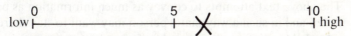

The next line of the same poem, however, is:

> In the deep, strange-scented shade of the great dark carob tree

Note that no new proposition is here involved; it is only an adverbial phrase. Does your assessment of the 'literariness' of the text change? We leave this question unanswered. It is for you to decide.

6.1.2
Evaluating prose types

Note that the above is a sensitisation process only. Nothing is to be gained by making large numbers of ratings of small segments of many poems, all of which tend to ignore the discourse structure of the poem as a whole, and the impact of a particular word or phrase, or line, in a longer extract, or indeed of the whole, which may otherwise be very high, or relatively low, on our rating. Without abandoning the previous section let us start from a completely different angle. Look at the text at the top of page 104:

The Bath Hotel

Widcombe Basin, Bath.
Tel: (0225) 338855

Set in a superb position alongside Widcombe Basin and bordered by the River Avon, Bath's newest hotel provides excellent 3 star Accommodation and facilities just a few minutes away from Bath's historic centre. Our 96 well appointed bedrooms all with private bathrooms offer every modern convenience. Both our Carvery Restaurant and Thimble Mill Restaurant offer a cuisine that will satisfy all tastes.

BHRA £ ⓘ ♿ ☒ ⊟
⬚ P V ⬚ ⬚ ⬚ ☎ P 18 9 H/C

The above text attempts to convey as much information as possible about a hotel, and in such a way that a person may want to stay there. The picture is intended to reinforce the varied features of attractiveness, contained in such phrases as 'superb position', 'newest hotel', 'every modern convenience', etc. We would give it a very low rating on a literary scale, but it would be possible to find texts with a lower rating (e.g. a page from an advanced mathematics textbook using largely symbols and formulae and scarcely any language at all). Rating:

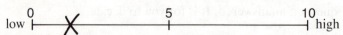

0 ———X————————— 5 ————————————— 10
low | | | high

The process, and its potential usefulness, should become clear when we move to the following example:

The first of its magnitude to open in Phuket, this five-star resort–convention hotel combines gracious Thai hospitality with French flair in offering the ultimate in hotel accommodation and facilities. With just the right setting for that perfect getaway holiday by the sea, Le Meridien stands amidst forty acres of lush tropical greenery in secluded Relax Bay on the west coast of the island.

These are but a few of the delights awaiting guests at Le Meridien Phuket. The hotel's impressive structure, depicted in its contemporary Thai architecture, combines the best of both East and West in a rare ambience that is carried right through the intricate interior details.

A distinctive flower, the lotus, has been selected as the design motif. And to complete this total look of sophistication, the theme is reflected on the murals, floors, furniture, and even staff uniforms as well as in the serenity of the hotel's 470 guest rooms.

An international mangement team provides the finishing touches to Phuket's latest hotel – Le Meridien – which continually grooms its staff so that the deluxe facilities are fully complemented by the very best service. All these, and much more, make Le Meridien Phuket a truly tropical island hideaway.

Compared to the previous example, this text considerably lowers the information content and greatly accentuates the promotional element. That there may be a good reason for this does not concern us here. The corresponding effect is undoubtedly higher on the cline, though the repeated use of noun phrases which attempt to appeal to the reader (the ultimate in hotel accommodation/that perfect getaway holiday by the sea) are not of course 'literature' – except for the subcategory of 'promotional literature' – and may even defeat their own purpose. Yet it nevertheless does what literature does, namely create an effect through words. How we *rate* such a text is highly subjective and depends on how 'open minded' (see Carter above) we are when we read it. If we are sitting at home in England on a cold winter evening, and contemplating a holiday on a tropical island, having just won a large sum of money in a lottery, we may well give it a considerably higher rating than if it is presented to us without comment after a fascinating study of an English novel with our favourite teacher. Better then to specify a *range* on the cline:

```
        0              5                10
low  ├──── XXXX ───────┼──────────────┤ high
```

The third text in this section is, immediately and obviously, very different:

> The Hotel du Lac (Famille Huber) was a stolid and dignified building, a house of repute, a traditional establishment, used to welcoming the prudent, the well-to-do, the retired, the self-effacing, the respected patrons of an earlier era of tourism. It had made little effort to smarten itself up for the passing trade which it had always despised. Its furnishings, although austere, were of excellent quality, its linen spotless, its service impeccable. Its reputation among knowledgeable professionals attracted apprentices of good character who had a serious interest in the hotel trade, but this was the only concession it made to a recognition of its own resources. As far as guests were concerned, it took a perverse pride in its very absence of attractions, so that any visitor mildly looking for a room would be puzzled and deflected by the sparseness of the terrace, the muted hush of the lobby, the absense of piped music, public telephones, advertisements for scenic guided tours, or notice boards directing one to the amenities of the town. There was no sauna, no hairdresser, and certainly no glass cases displaying items of jewellery; the bar was small and dark, and its austerity did not encourage people to linger. It was implied that prolonged drinking, whether for purposes of business or as a personal indulgence, was not *comme il faut*, and if thought absolutely necessary should be conducted either in the privacy of one's suite or in the more popular establishments where such leanings were not unknown. Chambermaids were rarely encountered after ten o'clock in the morning, by which time all household noises had to be silenced; no vacuuming was heard, no carts of dirty linen were glimpsed, after that time. A discreet rustle announced the reappearance of the maids to turn down the beds and tidy the rooms once the guests had finished changing to go down to dinner. The only publicity from which the hotel could not distance itself was the word of mouth recommendations of patrons of long standing.
>
> (from *Hotel du Lac* by Anita Brookner
> 1984 Jonathan Cape)

This, clearly, is very different from the two previous examples. It is neither a record of what the hotel offers, nor a promise of 'the ultimate'. It is immediately noticeable that it does not give unreserved praise ('Its furnishings, although austere, were of excellent quality ....'), although this does not of itself constitute literariness. But what does it set out to do, other than to describe? This question is more difficult to answer, and indeed the lack of overt or obvious purpose may itself be one of the qualities which make it 'literary', in contrast to the other examples dealing with hotels. Again we leave 'open' the rating on the cline which you may wish to give it.

6.1.3
Literariness
outside established
literary texts

We hope that the principle of using a cline is helpful, above all else in detecting 'differences in the way language is used' and thereafter in recognising more and more works of literature which make a unique appeal to you, and having a better grasp of why they do so. We must nevertheless be careful. It would be quite wrong to suggest that it is only literature which earns a high rating on the cline; that literature is the preserve of the good and the beautiful; that literature requires a particular heightened sensibility, granted only to a talented few, to appreciate it.

In fact we are proposing the opposite of this, namely that there is a great deal of writing which is literary, and which rates highly on the cline, although it is not normally regarded as literature at all. The following examples are intended to illustrate this. The first, which is well known, is Sir William Napier's account of the Battle of Albuera, 16 May 1811:

Such a gallant line, issuing from the midst of the smoke and rapidly separating itself from the confused and broken multitude, startled the enemy's masses, then augmenting and pressing forward as to an assured victory; they wavered, hesitated and, vomiting forth a storm of fire, hastily endeavoured to enlarge their front, while a fearful discharge of grape from all their artillery whistled through the British ranks. Myers was killed, Cole, the three colonels, Ellis, Blakeney and Hawkshawe, fell wounded, and the fusilier battalions, struck by the iron tempest, reeled and staggered like sinking ships: but suddenly and sternly recovering, they closed on their terrible enemies, and then was seen with what strength and majesty the British soldier fights. In vain did Soult with voice and gesture animate the Frenchmen; in vain did the hardiest veterans, breaking from the crowded columns, sacrifice their lives to gain time for the mass to open out on such a far field; in vain did the mass itself bear up, and fiercely striving fire indiscriminately upon friends and foes, while the horsemen hovering on the flank threatened to charge the advancing line. Nothing could stop that astonishing infantry. No sudden burst of undisciplined valour, no nervous enthusiasm weakened the stability of their order, their flashing eyes were bent on the dark columns in their front, their measured tread shook the ground, their dreadful volleys swept away the head of every formation, their deafening shouts overpowered the dissonant cries that broke from all parts of the tumultuous crowd, as slowly and with a horrid carnage it was pushed by the incessant vigour of the attack to the farthest edge of the height. There the French reserve, mixing with the struggling multitude, endeavoured to restore the fight but only augmented the irremediable disorder, and the mighty mass, giving way like a loosened cliff, went headlong down the steep: the rain flowed after in streams discoloured with blood, and eighteen hundred unwounded men, the remnant of six thousand unconquerable British soliders, stood triumphant on the fatal hill.

(Quoted in *The Face of Battle* by John Keegan 1978 Penguin)

Keegan says:

'Now, as Romantic prose passages go, this is clearly a very remarkable achievement, rich in imagery, thunderous in rhythm and immensely powerful in emotional effect; it almost vibrates on the page ....'

We do not have to agree with him, of course, although we are more likely to do so when we consider that *The Face of Battle* has no connection with literary studies at all, and is in fact a study of how soliders react to the stresses of battle. As a record of the actual battle, Napier's report may be inaccurate; we may think that it is too self-consciously literary. But it would be difficult to give it a *low* rating on a cline of literariness.

The following extract is very different, but serves to show that literariness is not dependent on a wide selection of adjectives (iron tempest; dreadful volleys; tumultuous crowd), which the previous passage may suggest. This is from *The Fatal Impact* by Alan Moorehead, and is an account of exploration and travel in the South Pacific in the eighteenth century. The setting of this passage is Australia; there is a strong narrative line, and the suspense is heightened by the lack of unnecessary detail:

April 29 was a hot sultry day. In the afternoon a hurricane blew up with heavy clouds, but there was no rain. However, they chose a place to camp where there were flat rocks which would catch water if rain fell in the night. They made their customary breakwinds of bushes, and Eyre took the first watch while the others slept. Their remaining arms and provisions were piled together under an oilskin, but Baxter kept his own gun beside him. The night was cold, with the wind blowing clouds hard across the moon, and after a time Eyre went off to gather in the horses which had grazed away through the scrub. He was returning with them around half past ten when he saw a sudden flash in the darkness and heard the report of a gun in the camp, about a quarter of a mile away. Thinking that Baxter must have awoken and fired so as to guide him back to the camp Eyre called out to him. There was no answer. In some alarm Eyre abandoned the horses and hurried on. Wylie came running out to meet him, calling for him to come quickly, and on entering the camp Eyre saw Baxter lying covered with blood on the ground. He had been shot through the left breast and the two boys had vanished. The cache of arms under the oilskin lay scattered about on the rocks, and both Eyre's and Baxter's double-barrelled guns were missing. Baxter was beyond help; he collapsed and died without a word. Wylie could explain nothing; he had been woken by the report, he said, and had found that the overseer had been shot.

The wind was now howling through the camp, and Eyre wrote later in his diary: 'Suffering and distress had well-nigh overwhelmed me, and life seemed hardly worth the effort to prolong it. Ages can never efface the horrors of this single night, nor would the wealth of the world ever tempt me to go through similar ones again.'

His chief concern was that he was now entirely in the power of the two boys, since they had taken away the only serviceable firearms; all that he was left with was a brace of pistols for which he had no cartridges.

(from *The Fatal Impact* by Alan Moorehead 1968 Penguin)

This too seems to merit a high rating on the cline, and maybe one not lower than the more sonorous Napier text.

6.1.4
Exceptions and exclusions – a warning

The principle we are here proposing is, of course, well-established, in that the Bible is studied, in university courses in English literature, as a literary artefact, for which it qualifies because the language earns a very high rating on the (possibly unacknowledged) cline of generations of academics. But the same principle requires a warning, namely that it is quite easy to find *literary* works that are very distant from the 'thunderous in rhythm' style of writing of the Napier passage quoted above. An example would be the extract from *Victoria Station* (see 6.5) by Pinter, or the same author's short play *Last to Go*, where an elderly newspaper seller and a coffee stall attendant carry on an apparently inconsequential conversation. This, however, does not invalidate the principle. These texts are low in *some* aspects of literariness, and we may give them a correspondingly low rating, certainly at a first reading. Later we may give them a higher rating *for other qualities*, as there is a tendency at first to equate literariness with sonorousness, which is perhaps just what Pinter is trying to avoid; alternatively we may say that the very realism of the text, imitating 'the actions of men', makes the language intrinsically literary, and therefore deserving of a high rating on the cline. It depends, then, on the 'disposition adopted by the reader', as it does when we read an historical record, a personal letter, or an advertisement, all of which may rate highly, but not, usually, a service manual or a legal document, which have explicit functions for which literariness is not suited.

6.1.5
Practical task

1 Write up the advertisement on page 109 on a transparency for OHP. Do *not* put 'Advice to the unwary . . .' or the title at the top.
2 Reveal only the first paragraph on the screen. Keep the remainder covered. Ask each individual to give a rating from 1 (low) to 10 (high) on a cline (or scale), of literariness.
3 Repeat the process with paragraphs two and three, after only a single showing of the transparency and sufficient time to read it once only. Then ask learners to make a further rating, but this time for the whole, that is paragraphs one to three. They may increase or reduce their original rating, but should have some reason for doing so.
4 Allow a few minutes for general discussion of ratings. Remind learners they do not have to agree – if one person gives a rating of 2 and another 8 it does not mean that one is 'wrong'. Display the transparency again if there is considerable disagreement.
5 Explain that 'the City' is the financial/banking district of London.
6 Display the final two paragraphs of the text. Ask learners to make a separate rating for this. Ask them if they wish to revise their rating of paragraphs one to three now that they have read the final paragraph.
Go through the text. Ask learners to consider the literariness of individual phrases, but do not give a rating to them. Note for example:

Advice to the unwary abroad in the City, or

HOW A YOUNG UPWARDLY MOBILE BEE FELL FOUL OF A DASTARDLY VEGETABLE PLOT.

IT had been the very essence of an English summer's day. Buckets of rain, a skittering of sleet, massed ranks of cloud. But now the rain had stopped. A segment of sun peeped through. The lawn sparkled like a jeweller's window.

A swarm of pinstriped bees was sweeping across the garden. They had turned the hive into a profitable business. "Money from honey" was their slogan. But one wily worker bee knew better than the rest.

Perched on a branch high above the flower beds, he mocked their giant hollyhocks, scorned their cornflowers, chuckled at their honeysuckle. For, lurking by the cold frame at the head of the garden were the biggest flowers he'd ever seen. Great white globes, eight or nine inches across. Like an actor in a bee movie, he tugged up his collar and glanced around shiftily. Good: the coast was clear.

On whirring wings, he divebombed the first enormous flower head. He sniffed the air: there was no bouquet. He rummaged for the nectar, delved deep for the pollen. But the cauliflower, in spite of its name, had none.

The City, too, has its quota of people with harebrained schemes for extracting uranium from Arctic sleet or honey from cauliflowers. Naturally, they all come with promises of positively gargantuan returns. But our shrewd investor will always opt for a scheme that is much more soundly based. With their wealth of experience and the resources of Mercury Warburg Investment Management, Mercury can supply you with all the help and advice you need.

For details of our ten unit trusts, please write to: The Client Services Director, Mercury Fund Managers Ltd, FREEPOST, London EC4B 4DQ, (01-280 2800) or contact your usual financial adviser.

a) A segment of sun peeped through (acceptably literary)
b) The lawn sparkled like . . . (does the comparison work?)
c) A swarm of pinstriped bees . . . (pseudo-literary; comic; reveals that the whole is a joke)

Get learners to discuss *how* and *why* paragraph four is lower on the cline, and paragraph five very low indeed.

Discussion

1 The authors state that 'there are no rules to decide what can be accepted as literature and what cannot'. But what judgements or criteria are usually applied? Make a list – this could be quite extensive.

2 Why does poetry predispose us to a high rating (on a cline of literariness)? You may disagree with the proposition if you wish.

3 Look at the advertisement for The Bath Hotel (p.104). How many features can you list which mark it as 'non-literary'? – i.e. that are likely to give it a low rating on a cline of literariness.
Begin: a) there is a picture
(Count the row of symbols as one feature only)
Compare with one other person and try to decide why each feature is unlikely in more literary texts.

4 Read again the extract from *The Fatal Impact.* Are there any *words* which are noticeably literary?
'The night was cold, with the wind blowing clouds hard across the moon . . .'
Do you think the writer is using diary entries here or inventing?
Does the extract sound more like history, or a novel? Why?
What other reasons would you give for giving it a high rating on a cline of literariness?

5 Do you agree that we often equate literariness with 'sonorousness' (high-sounding language)? Select *two* extracts (one poetry, one prose) to which you personally give the very highest rating on the cline. Present them to a group of four or five colleagues and ask them to say if they are 'sonorous'. If not, ask them to find features which merit your high rating.

6.2 Analysing metaphor

The 'traditional' approach to figures of speech and literary tropes

15. Point out the figures of speech involved in the following extracts:
(i.) A father that whipped his son for swearing and swore himself while he whipped him, did more harm by his example than good by his correction.—FULLER, *Holy State.*
(ii.) It could not perhaps have been avoided, and it cannot now be healed or even concealed.—*Lord Rosebery's Speech*, July 17, 1901.
(iii.) Rend with tremendous sound your ears asunder
With gun, drum, trumpet, blunderbuss, and thunder.

POPE.

(iv.) Such methods will land us ere long in the vortex of the maelstrom, in the current of which we are now drifting.—*Nineteenth Century* p. 726, May 1990.

(v.) China is a country where you often get different accounts of the same thing.—*Lord Salisbury's Speech.*

(vi.) His honour rooted in dishonour stood,
and faith unfaithful kept him falsely true.—TENNYSON.

16. What figures of speech do you find in the following, and what is your opinion of their respective merits?—

(i.) A treacherous calm. A sullen sky. A frowning rock. Pitiless cold. Cruel heat. A virgin soil.

(ii.) We believe that the embers of municipal patriotism have never ceased to burn and glow in these smaller communities into which London by historical and physical necessity, has been divided. We will do nothing to quench these embers. Rather we will tend them and fan them, until over the whole of these communities they have shed an equal and a vivifying light and warmth.—*Duke of Devonshire's Speech*, Feb. 15, 1898.

(iii.) The repose of repletion may not be a very heroic attitude to a great nation like the English; but even a lion sleeps after a full meal.—*Review of Reviews*, p. 8, Jan 1898.

(iv.) Savoy and Nice, the Keys of Italy and the citadel in her hands to bridle Switzerland, are in that consolidation of the French power.—BURKE.

(v.) The sky shrunk upward with unusual dread,
And trembling Tiber dived beneath her bed.—DRYDEN.

The above exercises are taken from Nesfield's *Matriculation English Course*, first published by Macmillan & Co. London in 1914, and reprinted as late as 1956. This book identifies, defines and exemplifies no fewer than twenty-eight different figures of speech, and follows this with several pages of exercises of the above type. To call this a 'traditional' approach may be unfair, but it is certain that large numbers of learners have been required to perform such tasks. This process is not recommended, either for teaching or testing. It is, first and foremost, a labelling task, and is largely mechanical. The figures of speech to be labelled are taken out of context, and, where learners are required to give an opinion on 'their respective merits', the figures tend to be either odd or laboured, inviting an adverse opinion. In context they may have been effective. In any event the process makes the figure more important than the text in which it originally occurred. The exercises quoted would appear to be extreme, and are more likely to occur as tests than as teaching material. But with less grandiose and rhetorical extracts the process has survived; who has not been asked to 'give an example of personification from stanza 3'?

6.2.1
Enter the trope and the lost lamb with a shopping basket

We must nevertheless recognise that literature frequently has a high concentration of metaphor or figurative language – but so do many other texts that are not normally classified as literature. Our problem is not the existence of metaphor or figurative language, but what to do about it, firstly in teaching (that is, in a teacher-centred classroom situation) and secondly to establish learner-centred strategies for dealing with language used in other than its normal literal sense. As a first step we recommend the use of the word 'trope'. This is a low-frequency word, and the teacher should indicate that it has no value outside the classroom (it does not occur in the Collins COBUILD

English Language Dictionary, 1987). Its use is to avoid unnecessary nomenclature, and concern about unusual figures of speech, to be presented (and possibly even tested) more for their own sake than for any significance they may have in a text. The teacher says, in effect 'There's a trope here. In what way is the word/phrase .... special?'. This of course is only a focusing device. It does not of itself explain anything.

A good starting point is to analyse a non-literary text. In this case you need not feel that you are dealing with a sacred and revered object, or that there is a certain sublime quality about a figure of speech, which the Nesfield examples above suggest. For the purpose of creating awareness of how *language* is used, 'She walks around like a tramp' is every bit as much a trope as Byron's 'She walks in beauty like the night' (except that the latter is incomplete, you have to read on to the next line of the poem).

Collect a number of such texts, from any sources. For example:

> The current financial year is going to be one of consolidation and seed planting in formulating our firm plan of growth for the future. A major stepping stone for Amstrad and one which, I predict, in years to come will be recognised as one of the major strategic milestones in the Company's history. There is a temptation to follow the experience of other companies which have risen, like Amstrad, to great heights. The phenomenon of meteoric growth followed by the question "What do we do for an encore?"
> The answer is often that the company wanders like a lost lamb with a shopping basket, surveying the shelves of the company lists in desperation, buying profits at a high cost to cloud the on-going issue.
>
> (from the Annual Report 1986/87 of the Amstrad Computer Company)

Instead of Nesfield's evaluative 'What is your opinion of their respective merits?' ('their' referring to the figures of speech) ask, simply and informally, 'How did the *seed planting* get into this text?' 'How did the *milestones* get in?' 'How did the *lost lamb with a shopping basket* get in?'. When learners are ready to evaluate any trope allow them to do so with such questions as 'What is a "strategic milestone"?' and 'Have you ever seen a lost lamb with a shopping basket?'

Although the above example, incorporating such a large number of heterogeneous items, each in a 'non-literal' sense, is exceptional, such language is common. Tropes are by no means the preserve of literature. Consider:

> It is unfortunate Great Britain should hit full stride just when the rest of the world decides to take a rest, but the economy cannot walk alone. The stockmarket doesn't want to try walking alone.
>
> (from a financial advice sheet published in Hong Kong)

> 'Cuckney could be downright rude, but I soon realized that he was just tired of knocking into shape young MI5 recruits of generally poor caliber. He was altogether different from the average MI5 officer. He refused to submit to the monotony of the dark pinstripe, preferring bolder styles. Cuckney was his own man and had broad horizons beyond the office.'
>
> (from *Spycatcher* by Peter Wright Heinemann Australia 1989)

6.2.2
Tropes in literary texts

It is a relatively short step (itself a trope) from the foregoing to:

> That time of year thou mayst in me behold
> When yellow leaves, or none, or few, do hang
> Upon those boughs which shake against the cold,
> Bare ruined choirs, where late the sweet birds sang.

and it does the Shakespearean sonnet no disrespect to ask 'How did the leaves get in there?' 'How did the choirs get in there?' and then 'Where might you see a ruined choir?' etc. The difference from the earlier texts is largely in a) appropriateness and b) originality, and as learners develop literary familiarity they might be asked to discuss these features. Incidentally the above sonnet (No. 73) depends entirely on extended tropes, and develops two quite different ones after the 'trees/choir' sample. An advanced exercise would be to discuss their respective merits, or, in the learner-centred activity, to say which you like best, and why. Such exercises should be short, and fairly frequent, until learners are fully familiar with a wide range of tropes. It is preferable to discuss each one as it is met in a text, rather than presenting learners with a block or set as in the Nesfield English Course at the beginning of this section. Learners should discuss in groups, which is best arranged if they are *permanently* in groups in the literature class, whether the activity is teacher-centred or learner-centred. (This gets round the objection that a teacher is not going to arrange group work just to discuss one trope.) Again it could be useful to use a cline (see 6.7) and to compare the rating given to any trope with that given by a neighbour group.

6.2.3
Rating a trope on a cline

We must make quite clear once more that in an activity of this type there are no single correct answers.

In addition to appropriateness and originality learners should also consider the *centrality* of a trope to the text in which it occurs. That is, is the trope essential, or merely an addition or afterthought? In spoken language if I say 'you are as white as a sheet' (red as a beetroot, hungry as a wolf) 'as a sheet', though perhaps part of a set phrase, is by no means essential. An interesting point for discussion here would be the sentence from the Conrad text quoted on p.165:

> 'A magnificent <u>death</u> had come <u>like a grace</u>, <u>like a gift</u>, <u>like a reward</u> to that old ship at the end of her laborious days.'

As a literary trope *death* is central to the text; are the other phrases underlined also central? It is necessary to look at, at least, the paragraph in which it occurs before deciding any answer.

Let us now return to the lines from the Shakespeare sonnet above. For centrality the trope must be rated right at the top, as the whole proposition is dependant upon it.
Thus:

Not central ├──────────────────────────✕┤ Central

Appropriateness must also have a high rating, as there is a similarity, though not necessarily of course a correlation, between autumn ('that time of year') and advancing age. In fact we take this similarity rather for granted; on inspection there are features which are also dissimilar. But compare this for a moment with the idea of a company 'wandering like a lost lamb with a shopping basket'!

Rate as follows:

Inappropriate ├─────────────────────────────X─┤ Appropriate

In saying (above) that we take the similarity between advancing age and autumn 'rather for granted' we are in fact commenting on its originality. Even in Shakespeare's time it is likely that 'in the autumn of his life' was a worn-out image. We might consider however that Shakespeare brings freshness to it by avoiding the word 'autumn', but giving it an indeterminate quality with 'yellow leaves, or none, or few', and by extending it to the starkly visual 'bare ruined choirs'.

Thus:

'Worn/threadbare' ├──────────X──────────────┤ Original

Overall rating: ├────────────X────────────┤

As a process learners should be instructed not to take this too seriously. The theme of the poem is serious, but this does not mean that discussion of the language need be funereal. Literature teaching is still perhaps some way behind language teaching in introducing an element of fun into the classroom.

6.2.4
Dealing with the unexpected

The rating of a trope, as exemplified above, is an occasional activity which can generate a good deal of discussion and can assist the learner in peeling off some of the multiple meanings of a literary text. In terms of literary competence it is nevertheless less important than being able to deal with the unexpected. The 'labelling' approach mentioned at the beginning of this section would seem to be of very little help in training a learner, whether native speaker or not, to decode an unexpected word or phrase and to consider possible reasons why the author used it. The best way of approaching this would be a variation of the learner-centred discussion mentioned in (2.7) and approved by the inspectors. Instead of trying to formulate a generalised proposition for a poem or text, learners should be given quite explicit instructions. For example:

> *Now pick out all the tropes in this poem and discuss the meaning. The poem itself is easy enough. The poet says that an owl is his favourite bird, and then goes on to tell us some of the characteristics of owls. But look at 'a nothing' in line 2. Why does he say 'flies like a nothing? And what is the effect of 'flies like a nothing through the night'? There are several other words which are rather unusual, or unexpected, and I*

want you to talk about each of them. The difficult one is the 'gold rings'. How did they get in there?'

Owl

is my favourite. Who flies
like a nothing through the night,
who – whoing. Is a feather
duster in leafy corners ring-a-rosy-ing
boles of mice. Twice

you hear him call. Who
is he looking for? You hear
him hoovering over the floor
of the wood. O would you be gold
rings in the driving skull

if you could? Hooded and
vulnerable by the winter suns
owl looks. Is the grain of bark
in the dark. Round beaks are at
work in the pelletey nest,

resting. Owl is an eye
in the barn. For a hole
in the trunk owl's blood
is to blame. Black talons in the
petrified fur! Cold walnut hands

on the case of the brain! In the reign
of the chicken owl comes like
a god. Is a goad in
the rain to the pink eyes,
dripping. For a meal in the day

flew, killed, on the moor. Six
mouths are the seed of his
arc in the season. Torn meat
from the sky. Owl lives
by the claws of his brain. On the
branch

in the sever of the hand's
twigs owl is a backward look.
Flown wind in the skin. Fine
rain in the bones. Owl breaks
like the day. Am an owl, am an owl.

George Macbeth

At least one or two group leaders should be asked to report back, and the class thereafter invited to comment on any word/phrase/trope which has not previously been mentioned. A first stage in literary competence is achieved when lexis and syntax cause the reader to pause only on very rare occasions. A trope, however, can always be opaque, and cause the reader to pause, no matter how much literature he or she has already read. It is not, of course, necessary to 'work it out' on every occasion, but the really original trope may always startle the reader. He or she may in some cases wish to return to it. He or she may ask, simply, 'how did that word get in'? Using Nesfield's broad categories, the learner may ask if there is some resemblance, association, imaginative use, or sound quality (to use four of Nesfield's six categories) which accounts for the trope. Neither the learner nor the experienced reader will ever exhaust the range of new usages and new tropes which he or she will meet. Some, like the lost lamb with the shopping basket, are just ridiculous. The teaching of literature is in part a training in evaluating all such usages.

6.3
Guided rewriting

6.3.1
Shifting the angle

Imagine that you are a photographer. You have an opportunity to photograph one of the world's most magnificent buildings – say the Taj Mahal. You do not take one picture of course. You take many. You take them from different positions and different angles. You shift the angle because you know that this can give a totally different impression of the whole – or indeed of one part.

This comparison must not be carried too far. When the photographer takes a picture from a different angle the building remains unchanged. When we rewrite a text, to see the same incident, or situation, or proposition, from a different angle, the new piece of writing may bear little relation to the original.

If a text is rewritten it is the *reader* who gets a totally different impression, as in photography it is the viewer. But in this case we are asking learners to be *writers*, or to take a more productive role than that of viewer or reader, however interesting the new and varied angles may be. By becoming a writer, however, the learner is being asked to look more closely at the *original* angle, and the special impression produced by that particular (literary) angle. By rewriting, he or she will appreciate the singularity, possibly even the strangeness, of the literary angle.

6.3.2
Practical examples

Look again at the extract from *Hotel du Lac* (p.105) above. Suppose that we ask learners to rewrite it as an entry for a guide book. The opening line of the quotation is: 'The Hotel du Lac (Famille Huber) was a stolid and dignified building, a house of repute, a traditional establishment . . .'

Although this gives it a positive (i.e. 'good') image, we can scarcely use the same words in the rewriting exercise. 'Stolid' is only marginally positive; 'dignified building' is not the sort of information we expect in a quick survey; 'a house of repute' – we would hardly expect less for the price – is not the language of guide books. In other words, the author has taken a very special angle, emphasising the slight dullness of the hotel, which is offset by its worthiness and reliability. The learner/reader will appreciate this angle more thoroughly and also how it is achieved if he or she has to rewrite it as follows:

Hotel du Lac

A highly reputable hotel providing high class accommodation with a long tradition of respect for the privacy of its guests. The hotel occupies comfortable premises and provides a high standard of service unequalled by most modern hotels. The policy for some years has been to avoid tourist groups, with the result that most of the public rooms recall the quiet but luxurious calm of a former era. Staff are highly trained and attentive to detail, though for the most part unnoticed. This hotel will appeal particularly to the well-to-do traveller who dislikes piped music, and objects to the distractions of video tape and television as a constant presence.

A detailed analysis of the two texts is of course possible to see what has been retained of the original ('well-to-do') and what has been omitted; and secondly, to assess if the much shorter rewrite retains the essential information of the original, and, if so, what the literary text gained by its greater length. This, however, would take us more into the area of stylistics. Our concern here is only that the *principle* of rewriting focuses attention very effectively on a literary text. At the same time it is also excellent advanced language training, though it cannot be attempted successfully unless learners already have some idea of language appropriateness in English.

While there is virtually no limit to the *range* of rewriting exercises learners may be asked to write, it will usually be from the literary text into some other, non-literary, form. The reverse process is both too difficult (highly-educated native speakers cannot necessarily write a text with genuine literary qualities) and, of course, loses the purpose of close reader attention to the language of the literary text. There can still be a wide imaginative leap between the original and the product, and remember that this is one of the few tasks in this book which does require a *product*, most others being concerned with the *process* of study. Consider this as a possibility:

Rewrite the following nursery rhyme as a newspaper report:

> Litle Bo-peep has lost her sheep,
>   And can't tell where to find them:
> Let them alone, and they'll come home,
>   And bring their tails behind them.
>
> Little Bo-peep fell fast asleep.
>   And dreamt she heard them bleating:
> But when she awoke, she found it a joke,
>   For they still were all fleeting.
>
> Then up she took her little crook.
>   Determin'd for to find them;
> She found them indeed, but it made her heart bleed,
>   For they'd left all their tails behind 'em.
>
> It happen'd one day, as Bo-peep did stray,
>   Unto a meadow hard by:
> There she espy'd their tails side by side,
>   All hung on a tree to dry.
>
> She heav'd a sigh, and wip'd her eye,
>   And over the hillocks went stump-o;
> And tried what she could, as a shepherdess should,
>   To tack again each to its rump-o.

Newspaper item:

SHEEP MAIMED BY MYSTERY ATTACKER

A mystery attacker has mutilated a flock of sheep in the Barfordshire village of Woollyton. Twenty-four sheep had their tails cut off, though they are otherwise unharmed.

Audrey Bopeep, 17, a shepherdess, was looking after the sheep but fell asleep under a tree. When she awoke the sheep were missing, though a gap in the hedge revealed that they had only gone as far as a nearby meadow. During the short time that the sheep had been outside her care, all their tails had been cut off. The tails were found hanging on the branch of a nearby tree, apparently hanging out to dry, though the purpose of the attack is not clear.

Miss Bopeep, who was reportedly much distressed by the incident, says that she thought she had heard the sheep bleating while she was asleep. She was so alarmed at finding the tails that she at first tried to attach a tail to each animal, before realising that this was impossible.

Though the sheep seem none the worse for their ordeal, the police have been informed and a close watch is being kept on the area.

Both versions contain a narrative, however bizarre this may seem. There is nevertheless a marked change, in this case from the fantasy world of the nursery rhyme to the apparent earnestness and objectivity of the newspaper report. More important is how the *language* is used in each case. In the newspaper report we are told that Miss Bopeep 'was much distressed by the incident', for the 'it made her heart bleed' of the original. This is just one example in which the language used in the rewriting cannot be transferred to the 'literary' text (and there is little doubt that nursery rhymes have some literary features), and vice versa. By rewriting we gain an insight into the unique quality of the literary text, sometimes to the point where the changing of a single word changes the whole quality of the original.

Other rewriting exercises with the above text are of course possible. For example Bopeep could be asked to record the whole incident as a monologue for inclusion in a radio programme 'Special Events of My Life'; another possibility would be a court report in which somebody was accused of the tail-cutting. In terms of *literary competence* these exercises are essentially 'intermediate', but a high level of language proficiency is required to do them well.

6.3.3
Narratives and letter writing

For the teacher, rewriting exercises are easy to set up, and thereafter they are essentially learner-centred, in that each learner and/or group is forced to investigate a literary text for a message/proposition/narrative, while the rewriting will isolate and reveal at least some of the special qualities of the original. One or two such activities should be completed in the classroom, in detail, and thereafter set as an out-of-class/homework activity.

One useful exercise is to ask learners to rewrite the narrative component of any literary text as if it had happened to them, and to include it in a personal letter. After all, every student of literature will have had some experience of writing personal letters. You may even permit learners to write it in their own language at first.

As a classroom example take Wordsworth's poem 'The Solitary Reaper'. Suggest a starting point which has the features of a personal letter. Thus:

> There are all sorts of things I want to tell you about the holiday, but most of them will have to wait until I see you. There were many beautiful moments, like the day I was walking in the hills and I saw a girl working in the fields by herself. She was singing to herself and the sound echoed around the hills. I called to her but she didn't notice . . .

As a narrative, of course, this is fairly unremarkable. What it does do, however, is to draw attention to the lines in which Wordsworth describes, by way of comparison, the beauty of the song:

> No Nightingale did ever chaunt
> More welcome notes to weary bands
> Of travellers in some shady haunt,
> Among Arabian sands:
> A voice so thrilling ne'er was heard
> In spring-time from the Cuckoo-bird,
> Breaking the silence of the seas
> Among the farthest Hebrides.

Learners may have to be warned that they are not asked to *paraphrase* the literary text: it is a 'rewriting', or a complete shift of angle. The purpose is for them to see that while they may use any words they like here to describe the beauty of the song, they will not recapture, in the words of a personal letter, the unique quality of the literary artefact. In other words, if the exercise is successful, they will have understood better the literary quality of the original. (While this 'narrative to personal letter' approach has very wide possibilities of application, another text which is recommended, in addition to 'The Solitary Reaper' is the poem 'Snake' by D.H. Lawrence.)

6.3.4
Rewriting
viewpoints

Shifting the angle of perception involves seeing things through new eyes. Further extensions to the ideas outlined in this section are provided in Chapters 3 (3.7 and 3.8) and 5 (5.1.5) above. There the emphasis was less on rewriting linguistic choices and more on seeing events and characters from the viewpoint of another character, usually one different from that selected by the author as the focal point for the narrative.

The following list of suggestions for rewritings is itself only preliminary, and teachers will be able to produce alternatives and elaborations for themselves:
a) as suggested, rewriting a text from a different viewpoint e.g. rewriting 'Futility' (p.21) as a story told by a character who finds the body of the dead soldier.
b) rewriting a text in such a way as to incorporate a reordering of events e.g. rewriting the opening to *Hotel du Lac* (p.105) during a bomb scare.
c) rewriting a text to include an additional character e.g. rewriting 'The Solitary Reaper' in conversation with a girlfriend.

6.3.6
Practical task

The practical task in this section is entirely for *teachers*. Read the following extract, which is the opening of *The Mimic Men*, by V.S. Naipaul.

Suggest as many 'guided rewriting' exercises as you can, based on these three paragraphs. One example might be an advertisement, offering accommodation at three guineas a week. What other possiblities are there?

> When I first came to London, shortly after the end of the war, I found myself after a few days in a boarding-house, called a private hotel, in the Kensington High Street area. The boarding-house was owned by Mr Shylock. He didn't live there, but the attic was reserved for him; and Lieni, the Maltese housekeeper, told me he occasionally spent a night there with a young girl. 'These English girls!' Lieni said. She herself lived in the basement with her illegitimate child. An early postwar adventure. Between attic and basement, pleasure and its penalty, we boarders lived, narrowly.
>
> I paid Mr Shylock three guineas a week for a tall, multi-mirrored, book-shaped room with a coffin-like wardrobe. And for Mr Shylock, the recipient each week of fifteen times three guineas, the possessor of a mistress and of suits made of cloth so fine I felt I could eat it, I had nothing but admiration. I was not used to the social modes of London or to the physiognomy and complexions of the North, and I thought Mr Shylock looked distinguished, like a laywer or businessman or politician. He had the habit of stroking the lobe of his ear and inclining his head to listen. I though the gesture was attractive; I copied it. I knew of recent events in Europe; they tormented me; and although I was trying to live on seven pounds a week I offered Mr Shylock my fullest, silent compassion.
>
> In the winter Mr Shylock died. I knew nothing until I heard of his cremation from Lieni, who was herself affronted, and a little fearful for the future, that she had not been told by Mrs Shylock of the event of the death.
>
> (from *The Mimic Men* by V.S. Naipaul 1969 Penguin)

If you wish to try out the exercise, divide the class into groups and assign one rewriting task to each group. On completion, get the leader of each group to read out the completed task. Applaud any imaginative use of information/content of the original text. What is the effect, if any, of knowing that V.S. Naipaul is Indian?

Discussion

1 What do you understand by the term 'the strangeness (of a literary text)'? In what sense are literary texts strange?

2 Consider again the quotation:
'The Hotel du Lac (Famille Huber) was a stolid and dignified building, a house of repute, a traditional establishment . . . '
Can you think of any context for these 19 words, in spoken or written English, *except* literature? (You may make minor modifications e.g. 'is' for 'was'.)
If you think it could occur only in literature, what are the 'literary' qualities which mark it?

3 Rewriting requires some knowledge of language appropriateness. That is, the learner/writer needs to know how guide books, advertisements of various

kinds, formal reports, etc. employ syntax, and particularly lexis, in English. Do you think literature also depends on language appropriateness, or is an author free to make his own rules of what is or is not appropriate to his or her subject?

4 Look at the extract from *Lord of the Flies* on page 137.
What possibilities does this text suggest for guided rewriting?

5 Example: a) *Iago*:
        O, beware, my lord, of jealousy;
        It is the green-eyed monster, which doth mock
        That meat it feeds on:

                              (*Othello* III iii)

        b) *Psychiatrist talking to patient*:
        Well, Mr Othello, we really must get you to shake off this
        jealousy. Terrible thing, when you let it get a hold of you.

Take this as an extreme case of where *the language of the literary text* cannot be transferred to the rewriting.
Find other examples where transfer of exact words from literary text to rewriting is impossible.

6 Do you agree that rewriting 'does not trivialise the original'?
Do you see any potential dangers in guided rewriting exercises?

7 Two recently published books contain a number of ideas for rewriting from different character viewpoints: *Openings* by Brian Tomlinson 1987 Lingual House p.xv; *Class Readers* by Jean Greenwood 1988 OUP especially Section D pp. 127–143 and sections on 'assessment of character through altered perspective' pp. 101–105.

6.4
Stylistics: further
possibilities

Each section of this chapter has involved progressively more conscious attention to language and to its uses for literary purposes. *Stylistics* is an approach to the study of texts which involves analysis of language use in literary texts. A main aim is to employ analysis of the forms of language to try to account for particular effects in a text. Another aim is to use the analysis to promote understanding of the literary purposes and functions to which particular uses of language are put. One outcome of stylistic analysis is to be able to explore the relationship between what is said and how it is said. It is clearly an approach which is suited to both the *study* of literature and advanced students. There have been, however, previous examples of 'preliminary' stylistic analysis in the book where analysis was shown to be useful in providing a basis for explaining how advertisements, jokes, etc. exploit 'literary' uses of language (see 2.8).

    There is space here to do no more than illustrate two examples. The first is drawn from the opening stanza of a poem by e e cummings:

    yes is a pleasant country:
    if's wintry
    (my lovely)
    let's open the year

The lines here are 'ungrammatical' in that they deviate from standard English grammar in the following ways:

1 *Yes* is not normally followed by a verb and does not normally occupy what is here the position of a noun:
   France is a pleasant country   (✔)
   Yes is a pleasant country   (✗)

2 *If* follows a parallel pattern:
   Sweden is wintry (✔)
   If is wintry   (✗)

3 'My lovely' appears to be detached from the communication and is not anchored to a verb. It is possible, however, to interpret it as a kind of interjection:
   'I wish, my dear, that we could speak more often.'
   'England is cold, Ann, so let's go abroad.'

4 The verb *open* and the noun *year* do not normally collocate. Semantically, too, we normally 'open' physical objects such as doors and windows. To 'open a year' is anomalous and as with the above deviations forces the reader to seek a satisfactory interpretation of meaning.

A possible interpretation of these lines is as follows:

> The poem is a love poem and is a discourse between lovers. The speaker is trying to persuade another to be positive and affirmative, to live in a world (country) where saying 'yes' is normal not deviant. To answer by using the word 'if' would be a cold response because the word 'if' imposes conditions. The couple should, therefore, start a new year (metaphorically) by moving from a wintry country to a warmer more pleasant one.

There are, of course, other possible interpretations, but some conscious attention to grammar and to the forms and meanings of words can serve to increase understanding of the effects of the poem and lay a basis for fuller interpretation. We would argue that it is difficult to get to grips with the poem *without* some stylistic analysis; indeed, we feel that analysis can demonstrate that the poem is not as difficult as it may at first appear. The process can also give students confidence in reading poetry, which, as a genre, regularly contains unusual or deviant uses of language.

 Our second example is taken from the famous opening to Charles Dickens' novel *Bleak House*.

> LONDON. Michaelmas Term lately over, and the Lord Chancellor sitting in Lincoln's Inn Hall. Implacable November weather. As much mud in the streets, as if the waters had but newly retired from the face of the earth, and it would not be wonderful to meet a Megalosaurus, forty feet long or so, waddling like an elephantine lizard up Holborn Hill. Smoke lowering down from chimney-pots, making a soft black drizzle, with flakes of soot in it as big as full-grown snowflakes—gone into mourning, one might imagine, for the death of the sun. Dogs, undistinguishable in the mire. Horses, scarcely better; splashed to their very blinkers. Foot passengers, jostling one another's umbrellas, in a general infection of ill-temper, and losing their foot-hold at street-corners, where tens of thousands of other foot passengers have been slipping and sliding since the day broke (if this day ever broke), adding new

deposits to the crust upon crust of mud, sticking at those points tenaciously to the pavement, and accumulating at compound interest.

Fog everywhere. Fog up the river, where it flows among green aits and meadows; fog down the river, where it rolls defiled among the tiers of shipping, and the waterside pollutions of a great (and dirty) city. Fog on the Essex Marshes, fog on the Kentish heights. Fog creeping into the cabooses of collier-brigs; fog lying out on the yards, and hovering in the rigging of great ships; fog drooping on the gunwales of barges and small boats. Fog in the eyes and throats of ancient Greenwich pensioners, wheezing by the firesides of their wards; fog in the stem and bowl of the afternoon pipe of the wrathful skipper, down in his close cabin; fog cruelly pinching the toes and fingers of his shivering little 'prentice boy on deck. Chance people on the bridges peeping over the parapets into a nether sky of fog, with fog all round them, as if they were up in a balloon, and hanging in the misty clouds.

One marked feature of the language use in this opening is the omission of a main finite verb from each sentence. For example:

Dogs, undistinguishable in the mire.
(Dogs are undistinguishable in the mire.)
Implacable November weather.
(There was implacable November weather.)

One effect of this 'ungrammatical' style is to create a sense of confusion and disorientation. Without verbs the reader is not sure how one statement relates to another or whether a phrase is the subject or object of a sentence; without verbs there is also no tense and the reader does not know the time order in which events are being narrated.

Analysis of such a stylistic feature again helps to raise awareness of the patterning of language. With this awareness it is important that students are prompted to account for or interpret the effects. One interpretive equation here is between verbless sentences, a consequent sense of disorientation and Dickens' creation of a London shrouded in fog and in which disorder and confusion are prevalent. This is, of course, not the only possible interpretation, but it is a reasonable one.

We believe that stylistic analysis can assist awareness of language use, can heighten sensitivity to literary styles and purposes and foster confidence in reading and interpreting texts. If students are regularly encouraged to explore equations between linguistic forms and meanings, then they are becoming more effective and accurate readers. As we have argued in our opening chapter (1.3), it is important to maintain a balance between accurate and fluent reading in the teaching of literature in a foreign language. Stylistics is an approach especially suited to the development of close, accurate readings of all texts in which language is deployed for creative purposes.

6.5
Reader's theatre: drama in the literature class

Where drama is included for study in a literature course it generally receives 'equal treatment' with other types of text; that is, it is broken into sections for study in each lesson, and thereafter the text is 'used' for comment or question by the teacher. The dimension of performance is seldom considered an essential part of literature teaching.

123

6.5.1
The problem of performance

Most teachers would be happy to resolve this problem by showing a film of the play being studied, where such is available, or getting the learners to see a local production. But, as has already been mentioned in 3.5.3, to see a play performed, once only, will give a very incomplete knowledge of the *text* of the play, even supposing a good performance and a high level of language skill in the viewer. For a class, or group, to produce the play being studied may be desirable, but is for the most part impracticable; among non-native speakers the learning of a large 'part' may be a task which is too difficult, and may take up a disproportionate amount of time if the literature course is to be more than a single play. There are many other potential difficulties, among them entirely different conventions of acting and play production in the native culture. Yet performance makes drama accessible in a way which does not exist with any other literary genre. The teacher must look for compromise methods.

6.5.2
'Remember your lines'

It never does any harm to remind ourselves that drama 'imitates the actions of men'. Such an imitation involves 'action' and, usually, speech. The speech is the easiest to reproduce in the classroom. Audio recordings, by professional actors, should, where available, be played for short sequences after a 'light' teaching, that is, without trying to extract all possible meanings from the text. Frequent replays will reinforce the impact of the words. The focus may be the sharper for the lack of the visual element, and the teacher should always draw attention to 'manner of speaking' i.e. the multiple prosodic features which characterise the way in which a line, or speech, is spoken. Learners, even at intermediate levels, should be encouraged to repeat single lines imitating – in a slightly different sense – the model of the tape as closely as possible. Take as a paradigm the line from *Macbeth* 'Is this a dagger I see before me?' and refer back to it every time you want learners to recall how to rehearse a line. Practise *frequent* choral and individual recital, but of single lines or very short sections only. Do not worry if learners parody the line outside the classroom; it is only likely to stimulate greater interest in drama as a spoken art.

6.5.3
The problem of play-reading

Play-reading may, at first glance, seem an activity which is suited to group work, giving a fairly large number of speakers a participatory role. In fact, with non-native speakers, it can be one of the least successful applications of all for group work. Though in this book we encourage virtually all innovations, we do warn particularly against group play-reading. With all but the most advanced students, misreading of lines is a frequent occurrence. Speakers will typically look at their script and will concentrate on 'correctness' (of pronunciation) rather than the 'feeling' of the line or the fact that they are speaking *to* somebody. Colleagues in the group are probably listening with less than total attention, eyes down on the script for their own entry. It is almost impossible for the teacher to monitor closely, at least if there are several groups. If you do choose to use this activity, appoint a good student as 'director' in each group, and allow him/her to stop the activity to demand re-readings, and to say how she/he thinks lines should be spoken. In other words, simulate 'rehearsal', rather than 'production'. It may be helpful at this stage to read aloud the sections devoted above to 'reading aloud' (4.4) which give guidance and advice in the promotion of this kind of classroom activity.

6.5.4
Reader's theatre

'Reader's theatre', on the other hand, which is used as the title of this section, is an ideal group exercise, involving *discussion* rather than *performance*, and multiple features of drama rather than just manner of speaking. Students are here invited to involve themselves in the complexities of drama production but with only the text as their source material, and through interaction with peers. This almost ensures a particularly close engagement with the text – the exercise is essentially intermediate, but can be used in just the same way with the most advanced students, and also at more elementary levels with more teacher guidance and control. For all levels guidance will be necessary in the first few attempts.

Select a part of the play being studied which is markedly 'dramatic', that is, which would be 'taught' by any other means as being a significant part of the plot. Put clear limits on the starting and finishing point – if possible about thirty to forty lines. Make sure that any lexical items which are essential to the whole are known by all. Get learners to work in groups of five or six and appoint a group leader. In the first such exercise give a list of questions generally applicable to the production of a play, but do not try to cover all possibilities. For example:

a) Where is each person standing?
b) What movements or gestures accompany each line, word, utterance, etc.?
c) How is the line spoken (e.g. loud, soft, quick, tense, etc.)?
d) Could any adverb be applied to the way in which a line is spoken (e.g. resignedly, happily, furiously, etc.)?
   Other features where not indicated by the author:
e) What furniture or stage props. are needed?
f) What lighting would be appropriate?
g) What is each person wearing?

Invite learners to extend this list. Point out that answers can only come from the text itself. Where there is no clear answer, the group must consider what hints can be used to provide an answer. The following example is a good one for practice. In addition to the information contained in the text – which is extensive on close examination – tell the students only that Ronnie, aged 14, has been sent home from Naval College accused of theft, although he claims he is completely innocent. The family are upper class and Arthur is a commanding father figure. The year is 1912. In this extract the adverbs (see question d) above) are well supplied by the author, but all other answers must be worked out. When a similar exercise is done in connection with a play being *studied*, learners will know a great deal more about the *context* than is revealed from this extract:

> ARTHUR (to CATHERINE): Did *you* know Ronnie was back?
> CATHERINE: Yes.
> ARTHUR: And you, Dickie?
> DICKIE: Yes, Father.

ARTHUR: Grace? 5

GRACE (*helplessly*): We thought it best you shouldn't know—for the time being. Only for the time being, Arthur.

ARTHUR (*slowly*): Is the boy ill?

(*No one answers.* ARTHUR *looks from one face to another in bewilderment.*) 10

Answer me, someone! Is the boy very ill? Why must I be kept in the dark like this? Surely I have the right to know. If he's ill I must be with him—

CATHERINE (*steadily*): No, Father. He's not ill.

(ARTHUR *suddenly realizes the truth from the tone of her voice.*) 15

ARTHUR: Will someone tell me what has happened, please?

(GRACE *looks at* CATHERINE *with helpless enquiry.* CATHERINE *nods.* GRACE *takes the letter from her dress.*)

GRACE (*timidly*): He brought this letter for you—Arthur.

ARTHUR: Read it to me, please— 20

GRACE: Arthur not in front of—

ARTHUR: Read it to me, please.

(GRACE *again looks at* CATHERINE *for advice, and again receives a nod.* ARTHUR *is sitting with his head bowed.* GRACE *begins to read.*)

GRACE: "Confidential. I am commanded by My Lords Commissioners of the Admiralty to inform you that they have received a communication from 25 the Commanding Officer of the Royal Naval College at Osborne, reporting the theft of a five shilling postal order at the College on the 7th instant, which was afterwards cashed at the post office. Investigation of the circumstances of the case leaves no other conclusion possible than that the postal order was taken by your son, Cadet Ronald Arthur Winslow. My 30 Lords deeply regret that they must therefore request you to withdraw your son from the College." It's signed by someone—I can't quite read his name—

(from *The Winslow Boy* by Terence Rattigan 1946 Hamish Hamilton)

6.5.5
'Reader's theatre'
with non-dramatic
text

The next step is to exploit the dramatic potential of novels, and occasionally poems, in the same way as drama (6.5.4 above), for reader's theatre need not be limited to plays. The first two chapters of Hardy's novel *The Mayor of Casterbridge* have great potential for this type of exercise. First a dialogue must be constructed, as the novel provides only a limited amount of direct speech. The construction of the dialogue is an effective and useful exercise in combined language learning and literature: students are forced to investigate the text closely before deciding what was said, and then deciding on the most appropriate form in which to say it. This should be very much a group exercise.

6.5.6
Simulated play
production

The extension of the above is to ask the students to imagine that they are making a film or videotape of the literary text. They work in groups. The group has the collective responsibility of the producer. They can, in imagination, have whatever resources they require, whether of actors, actresses, costume, lighting and make-up. The final 'take' can be done where they choose, either on location – anywhere in the world – or in the studio or theatre. That, broadly, is the 'brief'. There are several considerations to be taken into account:

a) Students generally object at first that they have no experience of such production. The answer to this is that the production is imaginary, but the *process* is the all-important factor, and this depends entirely on a careful reading of the text. It is, nevertheless, essential to take learners through an example, indicating basic production methods, and 'voice over' techniques. The make-believe element is entertaining, and students usually enter quickly into the spirit of the exercise. There is also a *product*, in the form of a script, with marks for pauses, movements, lighting, etc., and details of fade-in or fade-out of picture, and students here will need to be acquainted with a metalanguage of production such as *close-up; fade-in/out; pan; slow-motion*, etc. The nature of the exercise is intermediate, shading to advanced for intelligent and interesting productions, which can of course be *actually* produced on videotape, where the facilities exist. For an example worked out in detail see Carter, R A and Long M N 1987 *The Web of Words* CUP Unit 2. See also 3.5 on 'In another medium'.

b) Most productions require some sort of lead-in, introduction, brief background, etc., for example, the opening may be marked by a commentary on the relevance of the author's life to the piece being produced. This requires special experience and usually some minimal research. Teacher assistance would be necessary, but the exercise is still an advanced one. Lack of such a lead-in, however, does not invalidate the exercise, and where the linguistic and literary competence of the learners is at a lower level it may be omitted.

c) Care needs to be taken with the selection of texts. Lyric poems are generally unsuitable, as is the satirical poetry of Pope and Dryden. Shakespeare however, can be unexpectedly successful; students are diverted from details of lexis or complexity of phrasing and focus on the obvious action potential, even in soliloquies.

| 6.5.7 Shakespeare | 'Drama in the literature class' cannot avoid Shakespeare, although there is clearly no single formula which applies to Shakespeare but not to other drama. The name, however, often creates a certain consternation among students, and this in turn is sometimes transformed into difficulties which are created by scholarship, footnotes, critical evaluation, etc. It is important to remind students that there is an excellent play to be enjoyed, and that this should not be spoiled because it has also to be studied in the classroom. |

1 Make sure that *all* learners know 'what is going on' i.e. the plot. Explain in small sections and review frequently with low-order questions. The comedies often have complex plots.

2 Use 'reader's theatre' techniques at least once for each act of the play. Allow sufficient time to work out the 'video production' thoroughly. Encourage acting out small stretches, even if students have little aptitude. But do not allow students to be embarrassed.

3 Make students learn, and repeat regularly, very short sections, even single lines, with full attention to 'manner of speaking', and a professional (taped) model where possible.

4 Do not try and exhaust every possible detail of meaning from the play. You will not succeed, and are more likely to make the play formidable and unentertaining.

5 Set context questions (see 3.1.3) *in advance* of the study of each scene, and allow time for these to be followed up as a group activity after the formal teaching.

6 Use whatever audio-visual aids are available, but if 'audio', break into small stretches, with comprehension questions in the breaks.

6.5.8 Practical task

1 Set the following as a reading task, in advance of the lesson. It is the opening of a short play by Harold Pinter, called *Victoria Station*.

Lights up on office. CONTROLLER *sitting at microphone.*

CONTROLLER: 274? Where are you?

Lights up on DRIVER *in car.*

CONTROLLER: 274? Where are you?

Pause

DRIVER: Hullo?

CONTROLLER: 274?

DRIVER: Hullo?

CONTROLLER: Is that 274?

DRIVER: That's me.

CONTROLLER: Where are you?

DRIVER: What?

Pause

CONTROLLER: I'm talking to 274? Right?

DRIVER: Yes. That's me. I'm 274. Who are you?

Pause

CONTROLLER: Who am I?

DRIVER: Yes.

CONTROLLER: Who do you think I am? I'm your office.

DRIVER: Oh yes.

CONTROLLER: Where are you?

DRIVER: I'm cruising.

CONTROLLER: What do you mean?

Pause

128

Listen son. I've got a job for you. If you're in the area I think you're in. Where are you?

DRIVER: I'm just cruising about.

CONTROLLER: Don't cruise. Stop cruising. Nobody's asking you to cruise about. What the fuck are you cruising about for?

Pause

274?

DRIVER: Hullo. Yes. That's me.

CONTROLLER: I want you to go to Victoria Station. I want you to pick up a customer coming from Boulogne. That is what I want you to do. Do you follow me? Now the question I want to ask you is this. Where are you? And don't say you're just cruising about. Just tell me if you're anywhere near Victoria Station.

DRIVER: Victoria what?

Pause

CONTROLLER: Station.

Pause

Can you help me on this?

2 Discuss briefly with learners how they might produce this play. Where would you place *Controller* and *Driver* on a stage? How would you separate them? What lighting would you use for each?

3 Then construct discussion points which investigate the thematic content of the interaction. One suggestion is
   'Pinter's characters seem to suffer from a serious problem of communication.' This may be because
   a) The driver is deliberately uncooperative;
   b) The controller is bullying and rude;
   c) The two men dislike each other intensely;
   d) The driver does not understand the messages passed to him.
   Extend this list by at least two more propositions.
   Note: You are free to devise a completely different set of discussion points, but they should be related to the theme of the play.

4 Allow students to discuss in groups, and ask each group to select the proposition which they feel is at the 'core' of the play. Each group may select any proposition, but should be prepared to defend their choice by reference to the text.

6.5.9
Discussion points

1 The authors say that 'to see a play performed, once only, will give you a very incomplete knowledge of the *text* of the play'. What, on the other hand, will seeing a play performed give to the learner that the classroom cannot give?

2 How important do you consider 'manner of speaking' in repeating/ memorising 'key' lines of a play? What lines can you think of, from any play in English, which have come to be associated with a certain interpretation, or manner of delivery?

3 In dealing with drama, especially in literature teaching, how do you equate discussion v. performance? To which do you give more time, and for what reasons? If you consider performance to be valuable and important what are the potential drawbacks?

4 Discuss a non-dramatic text, (not necessarily in English) known to all people in the discussion group, which would lend itself to the 'reader's theatre' teaching approach. What reasons support your choice?

5 If you teach/have taught any play by Shakespeare, what were the relative 'weightings' given to
   a) enjoyment/entertainment?
   b) performance?
   c) text study, including translation into mother tongue or translation/ paraphrase into modern English?
   d) critical evaluation; readings about the Shakespeare 'canon'?
What do you think are the correct weightings, for your own teaching situation? Do you agree that the 'reader's theatre' approach is, or could be, 'unexpectedly successful' for the teaching of Shakespeare?

6.6 Developing background research

6.6.1 Introduction

In section 2.1 above we approached the question of whether literature represents experiences which are true, or not. While we were unable to give a clear 'yes/no' answer we were nevertheless able to find examples, such as *War and Peace*, and *In Cold Blood*, which contain a great deal of verifiable fact. The authors of those works, however, were not merely presenting a record for the archives. The importance of the historical data to the work as a whole ensured that in each case we as readers would not be puzzled by who people were, or the significance of any events. But there is a great deal of literature in which some event in the author's life is embellished or expanded to become the core of an imaginative work. The author does not refer to 'what' or 'when', but indirectly asks the reader to assess the work quite independently of the event which stirred his or her imagination. To know it may be important, or it may not. 'I wandered lonely as a cloud' will not be greatly improved if we learn where and when Wordsworth saw daffodils on the edge of a lake, though a great deal has been written about that. Indeed the challenge of finding out the origin of any work of literature is an important reason for the vast amount of material of a biographical/investigatory nature about authors. The question for the teacher of literature however is quite different. It is 'When does the learner need to know more?' and 'How do we train him/her to find out?'

6.6.2
A needs analysis
for literary
background

Look again at the list of quotations in section 2.3. All except one are propositions. We may agree or disagree with them. We may give to them an additional measure of authority or wisdom because they are attributed to well-known literary figures. But no 'background' is needed, either to understand them, or to select two for a particular purpose, as you are asked to do on p.17. We may smile at the quotation 'No man, but a blockhead, ever wrote for money' because we *already have* some background about Dr Johnson, and we form a jolly picture in our minds of the great man, much overweight, delivering his opinions to an appreciative audience in a London coffee house. But such background is not *needed*. It does not matter if the reader has never heard of Dr Johnson.

There is one exception in the list in 2.3, however. That is the quotation 'And forgive us our trespasses as we forgive them that trespass against us' which is then attributed, 'The Lord's Prayer'. The first, and most obvious question, is why does it occur among a set which are all taken from well-known 'writers'. Is it a prayer *by* the Lord, or *to* the Lord? It contains an injunction, not a proposition. To whom? What 'trespasses' do 'we' ask forgiveness for? What does 'trespass' mean anyway, though if we could imagine a native speaker of English who had never seen this before, he/she may recognise that it is an archaism. If you are an English-speaking Christian there is no problem; you would recognise it immediately as an integral part of your religion. If, however, you know nothing about Christianity you need more information. You need *background*, in this case an outline knowledge of the Christian religion.

'We forgive them that trespass against us' as a context question might be concerned with 'we' and in what circumstances we forgive. Background is concerned not simply with relationships but with a historical, religious, political, philosophical or psychological framework. It is within such a framework that the *literary* text has particular resonances and the reader, therefore, needs to know at least an outline of that 'framework'. Thus in the quotation from *Paradise Lost* in 3.5.3 it is by no means necessary to know all the references. But there is a firm 'need', as in the quotation from the Lord's Prayer, for some knowledge of the Christian religion.

Note that in the above example *background* is a vastly wider concept than *context* – see 3.1.3. If the quotation were merely:

'Thus Satan, talking to his nearest mate'.

then this represents a 'need'. You need to know who Satan is, and by implication the background.
Lines 200–1, however,

'or that sea beast
Leviathon, which God of all his works . . .

does not represent such a need. Leviathon is introduced for purposes of comparison. If we know nothing about it/him we can still read the text.

6.6.3
Recognising the need for background

Look at the following poem:

In Flanders Fields

In Flanders fields the poppies blow
Between the crosses, row on row
  That mark our place; and in the sky
  The larks, still bravely singing, fly
Scarce heard amid the guns below

We are the Dead. Short days ago
We lived, felt dawn, saw sunset glow,
  Loved and were loved, and now we lie
    In Flanders fields.

Take up our quarrel with the foe:
To you from failing hands we throw
  The torch; be yours to hold it high.
  If ye break faith with us who die
We shall not sleep, though poppies grow
    In Flanders fields.

John McRae
(*died in Base Hospital, 1918*)

The first warning signal in this poem is the proper noun 'Flanders', which occurs both in the title and in the first line. It is not, however, a difficulty in itself, though in line 2 we might wonder why there should be crosses 'row on row' in Flanders. 'Guns' in line 5 gives us the clue for war, and we then wonder about 'the foe'. The message of the poem is otherwise clear and uncomplicated, though the additional words beneath the name of the poet, 'died in Base Hospital, 1918', tell us that the poem is not just a generalised statement about death in war and battle, but a reference to a particular war, an historical reality. When we recognise this we need to know what or where Flanders is, as it is mentioned no fewer than four times in all. The death of the poet *in 1918* is sufficient. As soon as any curiosity at all about this war is aroused then we realise that the poem is a small and poignant artifact from a vast and massively recorded 'background'. It is one step from there to placing the poem against a particular literary and historical background, namely, the poetry of the First World War.

A similar series of steps, sometimes prompted, sometimes the result of the habit of extended reading or rereading, is likely to occur in recognition of the need for background in any text.

6.6.4
Access to background: the teacher as resource

Background is a learner need. The best way to satisfy that need is by teacher input, preferably by a short and economical lecture.

This may appear to be a reversal of much that we have said in this book, where we have repeatedly suggested methods by which learners at fairly low levels of language competence may evaluate a text from their own resources, and hopefully thereafter appreciate it and see reasons why it was selected for study. This process may gain from a learner-centred approach, which encourages direct engagement of the learner with the text.

But background is not text, and to acquire the requisite information can be a time-consuming business, and unless adequate library facilities are available, a near impossible task. Consider again the poem 'In Flanders Fields'. *The Oxford Companion to English Literature* (Fourth Edition 1978) has no entry for McRae, the poet, or Flanders, or the First World War, or war poems. The learner who remembered having studied 'Futility' and looked up Wilfred Owen would find the following:

> OWEN, WILFRED (1893–1918), poet of the First World War, killed just before the Armistice and before he was able to complete the book of poetry he had planned, of which he said in the preface 'My subject is War, and the pity of War'. His *Collected Poems* were published in 1920 by his friend Siegfried Sassoon, a new edition appeared in 1931 by Edmund Blunden, and a third in 1963 by C. Day Lewis, with a memoir by Blunden.

In other words, virtually nothing about the war which produced a very rich outpouring of poems, and a tendency towards literary history rather than background. (Incidentally the *Oxford Companion to English Literature* has no entry for the Lord's Prayer. It would be equally difficult to establish a religious background from this reference book.) What is required is a framework, within which the literary text can be studied with as much knowledge as is needed to avoid mystification about the propositions, events or characters described. Unfortunately it is difficult to find a collection of background articles of the right length, partly of course because the range of disciplines, and within those disciplines the periods and the topics, are so varied. It is for this reason that the teacher is by far the best resource. The 'input' should be economical, that is, it should not contain a large mass of superfluous detail, and the broad outlines of the framework should be clear. For this, a lecture seems to be an appropriate way of transferring information. While no firm rules can be laid down, it is suggested that a five to ten minute input should be sufficient. If this begs the question of where the teacher gets his or her information this is because the teacher

a) has access to a wider range of resource materials;
b) has built up a store of facts about the background, perhaps acquired as small increments from various sources;
c) knows where learner needs will occur, and selects the text for study either because of or in spite of these needs.

In other words, the teacher has an informal involvement with 'research', before presenting any text.

For further discussion of examination/test questions in relation to different curricular philosophies, including those which stress the relevance and importance of background surveys, see section 7.5.

6.6.5
In-depth studies of background

The 'art' of background is to relate to needs but to avoid irrelevance. 'Irrelevance' here means that the background information contributes nothing to an understanding of a literary text. Biographical data, or 'author

133

background' is a potential danger area, and though perhaps not normally a problem with the teaching of English literature to non-native speakers, it is worth mentioning that Virginia Woolf and James Joyce, for example, have in recent years been more read about (i.e. background) than read. The extent to which such author background is a real 'need' is by no means clear. Shakespeare is studied with very little of such background, largely because the detail is notoriously sketchy. It is a matter of dispute whether studies of Shakespeare suffer unduly as a result.

On the other hand there is a significant number of literature teachers who would argue that a text can only be fully appreciated with some knowledge of the social, economic and political conditions under which it was written, or even which *caused* it to be written. This is rather different. If the study is of a full length novel, or several novels by the same author, then some framework undoubtedly helps. This would be specially true for novelists like Dickens, Bennett, Lawrence, and Priestley, where the writer tries to create the reality of the society in which he lived. It certainly helps to know more about the forces which influenced that society, and though these may be portrayed in the works themselves, it will be by hints, references and increments, rather than as a concise description. To get that description may, in the first place, again be the responsibility of the teacher, but thereafter the learner/reader should make a check list of all major references, and should only, therefore, be directed to books of author background and, where appropriate, social history, or other related areas.

The latter implies adequate library facilities and a fairly advanced and/or mature learner. As 'background' can be a problem additional to any posed by the text itself, it should as far as possible be avoided with younger learners or those whose language proficiency is relatively low, unless, as with nursery rhymes (which abound in curious references and invite 'research') and young children, the background is ignored. This cannot be done with an author study and a related 'term-paper', though even here as much as possible of the material should be gleaned from the text itself, supplemented where possible by teacher input, and only at genuinely advanced levels by the reading of biographical/critical studies of the author. Even here care is needed, so that background, with its many parts and almost limitless 'research' potential, does not become more important than the literary text. If and when that happens we are in an area which is no longer the concern of this book.

Practical task	'Research' the novel *Schindler's Ark* by Thomas Keneally 1982 Penguin. This work provides sufficient information to avoid puzzlement and therefore does not require background as 'a learner need'. But in what way is it literature? How does it deal with 'verifiable truth'?

Do you consider it appropriate that the book should have won a prize *as fiction*?

(Note: Where this book is readily available and the class comprises fairly fluent readers allow perhaps one month for everyone to read it. Then undertake this practical task, which will raise many issues connected with 'background' and 'research'.)

Discussion

1 What work of English literature do you know which contains a 'great deal of verifiable fact'? Do you consider the 'fact' to be self-explanatory from reading the text, or is additional background necessary?

2 Consider again the work discussed in 1 above. In what way does the literariness of the work differ from a purely factual account, or 'record for the archives'? Do you think the literary work
a) improves on a factual record?
b) distorts a factual record?
If so, in what way?

3 Do you agree that the quotation 'And forgive us our trespasses as we forgive them that trespass against us' requires some background of the Christian religion? How might it be interpreted by someone who was a fluent English speaker but who knew little or nothing of the Christian religion?

4 To what extent do you think it is a good idea for the teacher to provide 'needed' background? Do you think the learners should be encouraged to do their own 'research', as they would have to do if they were simply reading the text and not studying it? By providing information is the teacher encouraging laziness?

5 What work of literature (any literature, as long as the group is familiar with it) do you know which might be studied *because of* the background – that is, because it opens up a potentially interesting study of a period, religion, political movement, etc.?
Do you consider any of the following to be in this category?
a) *Gullivers Travels* by Jonathan Swift
b) *Animal Farm* by George Orwell
c) *The Empire of the Sun* by J.G. Ballard
d) *The Raj Quartet* by Paul Scott

6 Do not attempt this point unless you have read the poems *Absalom and Achitophel* (1681) and *Mac Flecknoe* (1682) by John Dryden.
Do you consider these poems can be read and enjoyed as a skilful and spirited attack on rogues and fools, or that background is essential to understand them? If you think the background is needed, do you think it too complex for the non-native learner? In other words, do you think these poems should be avoided?

**6.7
Forum: the uses
of debate**

6.7.1
Debate with a
small 'd'

In a great variety of different cultures throughout the world it is quite common for any group of people who meet regularly to start the day by talking about the previous evening's television programmes. The discussion could equally well be about a film, or a book, but with a somewhat lesser chance that each person has recently seen or read it. People who read books like to talk with others who have read the same books, or other books by the same author. In short they like to share their experience. It is easy to list conversational openings, on the pattern of 'Did you enjoy . . . ?'/'Yes, I thought it was . . . ', through to disagreement and contention, at the opposite extreme. This is debate, of a kind, though without any formal structure. It is debate with a small 'd'.

6.7.2
Debate and literary text: source material from within

Topic is still seen by most teachers as the central focus of classroom discussions. To my mind, it is certainly important, but not central: the crux is not *what* to talk about, but *why* you need to talk about it.

The above quotation is from *Discussions that Work* (a *language* teaching book) by Penny Ur 1981 CUP. It is equally true of literary texts. Topic is not of itself a sufficient reason for holding a discussion.

In fact there are two principal reasons why we should want to hold a debate about a literary work – as opposed to just talking about it conversationally, as in 6.7.1 above. These are

a) because there is some uncertainty or ambiguity in the text that we wish to resolve,

or b) we think that the author in some way distorts life ('. . . people aren't really like this . . . '), and we wish to correct the record.

In both cases, to argue it convincingly the reader must examine the words which are written. Of course to make a debate at all, two opposing points of view are required, and it requires the teacher to formulate those points of view, and for the students, after suitable preparation, to talk about them.

The subsequent debate may not reveal what the learners themselves believe, and certainly does not necessarily require them to express opinions concerning the success or otherwise of the text; but it will force them to examine the text closely.

6.7.3
Taking issue with the author

In b) above we suggested that debate could be a learning device when we 'think that the author in some way distorts life'. We must, of course, recognise that the creative role of the author allows him or her to portray the world exactly as he or she likes, but we frequently feel that we accept it only with reservations. In other words, we attempt a form of criticism of the author's world view. To do this, however, someone else must be prepared to debate a view which, roughly speaking, is more sympathetic to the author's outlook. In both cases you 'need to talk about it' because the text is intrinsically interesting, not because you want to win an argument, and certainly not because the learners should be able to differentiate 'great' writing from that which is flawed. The latter is not a concern of any of the three main levels to which these exercises are directed.

Consider the following as a fairly complete 'worked example'. Read this extract, which is from William Golding's *Lord of the Flies*, first published in 1954.

The boys chattered and danced. The twins continued to grin.

"There was lashings of blood," said Jack, laughing and shuddering, "you should have seen it!"

'We'll go hunting every day—'

Ralph spoke again, hoarsely. He had not moved.

"You let the fire out."

This repetition made Jack uneasy. He looked at the twins and then back at Ralph.

"We had to have them in the hunt," he said, "or there wouldn't have been enough for a ring."

He flushed, conscious of a fault.

"The fire's only been out an hour or two. We can light it up again—"

He noticed Ralph's scarred nakedness, and the sombre silence of all four of them. He sought, charitable in his happiness, to include them in the thing that had happened. His mind was crowded with memories; memories of the knowledge that had come to them when they closed in on the struggling pig, knowledge that they had outwitted a living thing, imposed their will upon it, taken away its life like a long satisfying drink.

He spread his arms wide.

"You should have seen the blood!"

The hunters were more silent now, but at this they buzzed again. Ralph flung back his hair. One arm pointed at the empty horizon. His voice was loud and savage, and struck them into silence.

"There was a ship."

Jack, faced at once with too many awful implications, ducked away from them. He laid a hand on the pig and drew his knife. Ralph brought his arm down, fist clenched, and his voice shook.

"There was a ship. Out there. You said you'd keep the fire going and you let it out!" He took a step towards Jack who turned and faced him.

"They might have seen us. We might have gone home—"

This was too bitter for Piggy, who forgot his timidity in the agony of his loss. He began to cry out, shrilly:

"You and your blood, Jack Merridew! You and your hunting! We might have gone home—"

Ralph pushed Piggy on one side.

"I was chief; and you were going to do what I said. You talk. But you can't even build huts – then you go off hunting and let out the fire—"

He turned away, silent for a moment. Then his voice came again on a peak of feeling.

"There was a ship—"

One of the smaller hunters began to wail. The dismal truth was filtering through to everybody. Jack went very red as he hacked and pulled at the pig.

"The job was too much. We needed everyone."

Ralph turned.

"You could have had everyone when the shelters were finished. But you had to hunt—"

"We needed meat."

Jack stood up as he said this, the bloodied knife in his hand. The two boys faced each other. There was the brilliant world of hunting, tactics, fierce exhilaration, skill; and there was the world of longing and baffled common-sense. Jack transferred the knife to his left hand and smudged blood over his forehead as he pushed down the plastered hair.

Piggy began again.

"You didn't ought to have let that fire out. You said you'd keep the smoke going—"

This from Piggy, and the walls of agreement from some of the hunters drove Jack to violence. The bolting look came into his blue eyes. He took a step, and able at least to hit someone, stuck his fist into Piggy's stomach. Piggy sat down with a grunt. Jack stood over him. His voice was vicious with humiliation.

The story is about a group of schoolboys who are trying to survive on an island after a plane crash. They have to appoint their leaders, and make all their rules, without anyone to guide them, and things go very wrong. (To be extended according to specific learner requirements.) You are going to debate two differing views of this situation, but you should build your argument as much as possible on what you have actually read here. What you are really arguing is whether the author has made the boys seem worse than they are (View A) or as they are (View B):

A Boys are not really like this; these boys are victims of a situation that is too complex for them.

B The boys show the true nature of human beings, who respect only the powerful and the persuasive.

6.7.4
Developing a battery of topics on a single text

The preceding exercise (*Lord of the Flies*) is pitched at an intermediate level. It is quite possible to develop more than one forum on a single text, where 'forum', the title of this section, refers simply to developing *two* contrasting or opposed views on that text. Consider this poem by Thomas Hardy: (we resisted the inclination to call this an *unusual* poem!)

Her Second Husband Hears Her Story

'STILL, Dear, it is incredible to me
        That here, alone,
You should have sewed him up until he died,
And in this very bed, I do not see
How you could do it, seeing what might betide.

'Well, he came home one midnight, liquored deep –
        Worse than I'd known –
And lay down heavily, and soundly slept:
Then, desperate driven, I thought of it, to keep
Him from me when he woke. Being an adept

'With needle and thimble, as he snored, click-click –
        An hour I'd sewn,
Till, had he roused, he couldn't have moved from bed,
So tightly laced in sheet and quilt and tick
He lay. And in the morning he was dead.

'Ere people came I drew the stitches out,
        And thus 'twas shown
To be a stroke.' – 'It's a strange tale!' said he.
'And this same bed?' – 'Yes, here it came about.'
'Well, it sounds strange – told here and now to me.

'Did you intend his death by your tight lacing?'
        'O, that I cannot own.
I could not think of else that would avail
When he should wake up, and attempt embracing.' –
'Well, it's a cool queer tale!'

We return to the point made by Penny Ur: 'The crux is not *what* to talk about, but *why* you need to talk about it'. In this poem the *topic* is the *story*, but the reason for talking about it may be any one of an extensive list:
a) The story lacks all credibility.
b) Stranger things are reported every day in the newspapers.
c) It is difficult to imagine in what circumstances the story would be told.
d) The husband seems to know the story anyway.
e) Coincidence overrides misfortune.
f) The story is really about the death of an evil man.

g) What preceded the story? To what is the opening line an answer?

h) What follows the last line? What do you predict as the 'ending'? etc.

There is virtually no limit to *why* one should talk about a poem, while the apparent oddity of the theme in this poem only serves to make the list more extensive. There is, perhaps, a degree of uncertainty as to the wife's intention ('Did you intend his death by your tight lacing?') but we have only her answer, and there is no substance for a 'forum' there. What we need to do is to develop topics which incorporate the greater part of the poem, and for which some evidence can be established in the poem itself. Thus:

A This poem could only be a confession. The wife pours out a story which has been troubling her for a long time.

This needs to be balanced with a view which is in some way 'opposite', or invites a different interpretation. We suggest (perhaps tentatively):

B This is really a love poem. The wife shows her love for her new husband by telling something of the horror of her previous marriage.

Though to argue either A or B requires close attention to the text, the level of the exercise remains essentially intermediate. It is quite possible to lift this to an advanced level by widening the topics to include other works by the poet:

A.1 The poem is one of many by Hardy where he enters the mind of someone who has suffered deeply.

B.1 The poem typifies Hardy's love of strange little folk tales, often with a comic or ironic twist.

To hold a forum to A.1 – B.1 requires knowledge which cannot be extracted from this one poem. But though distinctly advanced, the topic is still related to the poet's 'world view', and requires a close reading of the poem itself.

6.7.5

Practical task

Divide the class into groups of six or eight. Select a text where there is some element of ambiguity, for example 'Neighbours' (see p. 20 above). Write up two statements which are possible interpretations. Try to make them wide-ranging, and inclusive of the whole. Avoid a 'debate' on what one line or stanza 'means'. This is better resolved by direct questioning. For 'Neighbours' the following are examples:

A This poem is about social status; people always look down on those they think are inferior.

B This poem is about personal fantasies; people are afraid of everybody and everything when they are in a neurotic frame of mind.

Within each group one person is selected to speak for each 'side'. Allow up to ten minutes for preparation, with equal numbers on each side helping the speaker. The preparation can be conducted in first language (where relevant) to explore close differences in meaning in the poem which may be too difficult to attempt in English, but the final presentation should be in English. Set a realistic time length for this presentation. This could be three, four or five minutes per speaker, at the discretion of the teacher, and depending on both the literary competence and the language proficiency of the learners. Allow a shorter time if there are a large number of groups. Take the presentations in an A–B / A–B sequence after appointing two students as secretaries, to note the main arguments on each side. Point out that members of the class may interrupt or ask questions, but the speaker has the right to ignore both if he or she wishes. The point here is that we wish to make the debate as lively as possible, and the teacher should try to avoid the situation where each speaker has a three minute task to complete, but otherwise no one has much interest in the points being made. It is vitally important that everyone should listen to the arguments. After all arguments are completed, get the secretaries to make a summary of the points made, one secretary representing all 'A' arguments and one all 'B' arguments. Allow a vote on which side has made the more convincing argument.

Note: where different conventions for debate are already familiar, the teacher should follow those conventions, but without allowing the exercise to become too formal. Do not try to resolve the debate, but applaud any points which seem to indicate a perceptive and intelligent response to the text.

6.7.6
Discussion

1 Can you suggest *several* reasons why 'people who read books like to talk with others who have read the same books'? To what extent do you think such talk promotes an interest in literature?

2 Consider any text that is well known to you, and which at some time you have 'talked about' i.e. discussed informally with a colleague or peer. Try to establish *why* you needed to talk about it.

3 The authors gave a) ambiguity and b) distortion of the real world as reasons for 'talking about' a text. Why do you think they did not also include 'liking it very much'? Should they have done so?

4 Do you think it is still possible to enjoy reading a text (especially a novel or short story) even if you think the author is distorting the real world?

5 Look again at the quotation from *Lord of the Flies* (p.137). In your own view does it support argument A or B given beneath it? Do you agree that it is a text/extract that you would want to talk about? If so, why?

SECTION III
GENERAL ISSUES

7

The literature curriculum

7.0
Introduction

In this chapter we return to some of the more general issues which affect the teaching of literature in a foreign language. The issues will, of course, vary from one country to another and will crucially depend on what the objectives are for the teaching of a literary text. However, questions of which texts to select, establishing criteria of difficulty and deciding on how to evaluate students' performance are fundamental. These are the main issues explored in this chapter.

7.1
Some criteria for text selection

In any subject in the curriculum there is a large number of students who achieve only very modest success, and who leave the subject at the first convenient stopping point. In one's 'first literature' there is always a chance that you come back to the subject, perhaps informally and without tuition, at a much later date, perhaps through the stimulus of a movie or television production, or simply through recommendations in conversation; somebody tells you that a certain work/book/poem/play is 'great – you should read it'. For non-native speakers this 'second chance' is less likely. It is, therefore, particularly important that those who part company with the subject at an early date should not do so through having been forced to study unsuitable texts.

Other issues which are important for text selection also need to be considered. These are:

1 General availability of the printed text.

In many countries where English literature is taught, only a limited range of books in English is available. For a short poem, if the teacher has a copy, this is not a problem, but for a full length prose work it is. The teacher may like to select a text written in English by a local writer (see 5 below) but this may not be readily available at the start of a course. Also, if a book which the teacher would like to select is too expensive for all students to have a copy, it may have to be omitted.

2 The texts provide a representative selection, however small, of the literature as a whole.

With a literature as extensive as that in English, and including British, American, Australian and 'other' (without any implication that items from the latter group are less worthy of consideration), to make a 'representative selection' is difficult. But for the non-native learner it would not be a good idea if all selected texts were, say, nineteenth-century British novels, simply because such a choice is insufficiently representative of the literature as a whole. A selection that is too narrowly based has a greater risk of not appealing and thereby discouraging the learner from reading further.

3 Familiar/established/'canonical' text v. unfamiliar/not widely-known text.

This is possibly the most emotive of all topics in the teaching of literature. It cannot be resolved here, but is referred to again in the 'Discussion' section at the end of this section, where readers are themselves invited to make points 'for' and 'against'. A related point is, of course, to consider how 'survey' (see 6.6) is handled. The student of a second literature needs, certainly, to know the names of established writers and works in that literature. However, this is not itself a reason for not exploring less well-known texts which may have greater appeal, or have other features which recommend them. It is also quite possible to make a case that some canonical text might be extremely boring to the learner, which is a strong reason for not including it, and might, if it were not so well-established, be thought inappropriate for the non-native student.

4 Selection restricted by syllabus or examining body
v.
free selection of whatever the teacher decides is appropriate.

In theory this is not contentious. Free selection is desirable, and the teacher then chooses items with greater likelihood of appealing to the learner. On the other hand, conservative examining bodies shuffle around a small number of established classics which they have accepted as deserving the attention of all learners. In practice it is not quite like this. Many teachers hold firmly to known (and established) works. It is perhaps not worth making any generalisation here about examining bodies, but fairly frequent change or rotation of texts, and the inclusion of some non-canonical text, is recommended.

5 Related to the country or culture of the reader
v.
unrelated to the culture of the reader: requiring background knowledge of an English-speaking country.

The case for the first item of this pair is that one avoids many of the cultural difficulties of text, which are undoubtedly real and numerous, and in general are proportionate to distance from an English native-speaking location. A cogently argued case has been made by Kachru[1] for much wider recognition of a 'specialized body of English literature which is written by *non-native* users of English' (Kachru's italics). Though the argument is initially for the use of such

1 Braj B. Kachru: 'Non-native Literatures in English as a Resource for Language Teaching' in Brumfit, C J and Carter R A (eds.) 1986 *Literature and Language Teaching* OUP.

text as part of, or at least closely interconnected with, *language* teaching, Kachru does make his position clear as regards the selection of such text for students of literature:

> I don't mean that we should teach exclusively the non-native variety; this would be an extreme position. One has to establish a balance and introduce appropriate proportions (and varieties) of both types.

Of course one may argue that one studies a literature to learn about the culture of the country in which it was written, or, alternatively, as the two are inseparable, the learner must handle cross-cultural difficulties as best he or she can and not try to avoid them. Kachru seems to be less concerned with this point than with the appeal, or at least accessibility, of the text which has a known, home, background. We can scarcely object to this, and we support at all points selection of texts which appeal to learners. The only problem is how to 'balance' the local work with literature in English from elsewhere, though it should be possible to do this through common themes or subject matter (see 3.2 above). The reader/learner, however, needs to be at least aware that the texts he or she has studied may be totally unknown to students of English literature in other countries.

6 Contemporary / 'modern' in terms of literary classification
  v.
  a) not modern, but with no textual difficulties
  b) not modern; features of language markedly different from present day
     English.

The alternatives here are intended not so much as signposts but as warning lights, hopefully to avoid unnecessary difficulties. The implication is that modern literature is closer to the patterns, idiom and discourse style of the language which the student has acquired as language learner. This might be true, though it is not always so. It is more likely to be true for novels, short stories and drama than for poetry, though even for the latter it might be that the difficulty is with 'message' rather than language (consider for example the poem 'Neighbours' in Chapter 1, and in particular the vocabulary of that poem). At the same time there is a corpus of literature which is not modern, but which has few difficulties of language, Wordsworth's *Lyrical Ballads* is an example of this. Conversely, literature of a much earlier period, although otherwise appealing, may be unsuitable because of differences from modern English. In general, then, it should not be selected for study if special language tuition is necessary, or, as might be the case with Chaucer, learners are glossing very large numbers of lexical items.

7 Conceptually (as opposed to linguistically) easy for readers
  v.
  conceptually difficult for readers

This is a corollary of 6 (above), and is also a warning against 'overload', especially in the earlier part of any literature course, where text selection is of greater importance. This also applies to the obvious category of

8 Lengthy text   v.   short text

Thus very careful consideration would be needed before asking non-native students of literature to read George Eliot's *Middlemarch*, simply because it is very long and many students would take a considerable time to read it all. It also seems likely that Shakespeare's *Macbeth* is taught to non-native speakers more frequently than the other tragedies because it is much shorter. However, in considering the selection of extended prose we must decide whether to include

9 Complete work   v.   extract

Though a complete work is frequently set for study, it must be very rare indeed for it to be completely 'taught', that is, that every part of it is read through and commented on in the classroom. Typically, the teacher selects pivotal points of the text, and comments on or asks questions about these. The advantages of this are that the non-native learner is presented with a far wider range of texts than would otherwise be possible, and may hopefully read several of them in complete form because he or she wants to (but consider 1 above – availability), while at the same time he or she is not required to accept a series of approved judgements and comments which frequently accompany a complete work, taught over a period of time and used for essays and written assignments. Extracts from longer poems and drama are also possible. In general, the more extracts the better, though extracts alone are *not* the objective of literature teaching. This then raises the further point of whether the text is

10 Taught for its own sake without overt connection with other texts
    v.
    part of a series of an author or period, with an implied progression from easy to difficult

Clearly, with the first of these alternatives greater experimentation is possible, perhaps with a wider range of techniques, with the second, part has to be related to part and more details of background introduced if the necessary links with other works are to be properly established.

One final point is whether or not the theme is the deciding factor in the selection of a text. This may be expressed as part of the sequence as follows:

11 Selected for theme or subject matter (e.g. youth / death, etc.)
    v.
    selected for genre: poem, sonnet, etc. novel, short story; or for period

In the matter of text selection it is obviously difficult to reconcile all of the above points. Where choice is possible, however, the teacher is well advised to take into account the potential appeal of the text to the learner. It is also clear that consideration of the above issues leads us back to a further polarity of 'breadth' and 'depth' (see 1.3). Choice of texts for study will also express a particular philosophy, either on the part of the teacher or an examining body, concerning the extent to which literary competence is better fostered by reading a few texts *intensively* or more texts *extensively*.

7.1.1
Practical task

Give one hour to conducting a 'market-survey' among a group of learners. Make a list of about ten poems which appear widely in anthologies and which have either been taught, or are known to the learners.

e.g. 'I wandered lonely as a cloud'   by Wordsworth
'Ozymandias'   by Shelley

Ask each individual learner to extend the list by adding personal favourites.
They should also try to include three modern poems.

Divide the group into smaller groups of four or five. Ask each group to
discuss, and reach consensus, on a core of ten poems which they would *teach*
for a poetry course. Group leaders should be prepared to defend their selection
and groups should be instructed to make a 'representative selection'. It is not
necessary to make any rigid interpretation of this phrase, but explain it as
'incorporating poetry of different periods', as 'including one or two longer
poems', and as 'including both narrative poems and lyric poems' (supposing
these terms are already known to the group).

With advanced learners who have read widely, conduct a similar survey
for English prose, with a minimum extract length of 300 words and a maximum
length of any complete short story. The final list of 'core selections' should
include at least two short stories. Again indicate that it should aim at being a
'representative selection'.

7.1.2
Discussion

1 Why does a 'narrowly-based selection' of texts run a risk of not appealing to
the learner/reader? What would you consider a narrowly-based selection?
To what extent do you teach a 'representative selection' yourself?

2 Clarify what you understand by the phrase 'canonical text'. Do you consider
it important that the *teaching* of literature should include canonical text?
What proportion of a whole syllabus should comprise this type of text?

3 The authors imply that there is a case for exploring less well-known texts.
Why? Do you think there is a danger that such texts will not have lasting
appeal? Does this matter?

4 Take the following as a discussion point:
'Tennyson's "Ulysses" is one canonical text which is boring and
impenetrable to most non-native speakers. It would be better replaced by
something less familiar.'
How far do you agree with this comment?
(If you disagree strongly with the statement, and would like to keep this
poem in the course, substitute another well-known text to which you think
learners make little response.)

5 Do you agree that a literary text is inseparable from the culture of the
country in which it was written? Select a text which you consider to be
relatively 'culture free', and another (either British or American) which
presents considerable cross-cultural difficulty.

6 In dealing with prose texts what do you see as the danger of presenting only
extracts, and not a complete work? Do you recommend any special
classroom strategy for presenting extracts? Do you find it particularly
difficult to teach an extract if you (as teacher) have not read the complete
work?

7 Sub-section 11 on p.144 ignores other possible reasons for selection, such as 'teachability', 'appeal when read aloud', etc. What other reasons would you include which are not considered under the headings?

8 What for you are the *five* most important points in text selection, in order of importance? Compare these with colleagues in a group discussion (it is not necessary to reach consensus).

7.2
Simplification and graded readers

7.2.1
The case *for* simplified texts

Learners of a language cannot be expected to read major prose works in the target language when they are still at elementary or intermediate levels. It is for such learners that a very wide selection of readers is available. Many of the titles are classics, and the lists from major publishers are representative enough of the development of the English novel from the eighteenth century to the 1920s, with the addition of spy fiction, science fiction and a few widely popular titles added, to cover the last twenty-five years.

The purpose of these texts is to improve reading skills. The selection of established titles from the literary canon is almost incidental. The principle of selection is perhaps that the work selected has a good story line, and has continued to be enjoyed by readers. There is a chance that the learner has already heard of the title, which is an added incentive to read it. The *Longman Simplified English Series*, which has a wide variety of titles, explains the aim as 'to enable thousands of readers to enjoy without great difficulty some of the best books written in the English language, and in doing so, to equip themselves in the pleasantest possible way, to understand and appreciate any work written in English'. The best books – pleasure and enjoyment – appreciation of other works; it would be difficult for any teacher of literature to object to this.

7.2.2
Simplification and the language learner

On the other hand, the publishers make no mention at all of literature, though presumably there is a direct correlation between 'best books' and literature. Any argument to the effect that a lazy student will read a simplified reader to save him or herself the trouble of reading the original is unproductive; it is equally possible to argue that the simplified version merely whets the appetite for the real thing at an earlier stage than the language learner may otherwise have attempted to read it. But the publishers explain further that the series is planned for readers who are *language learners*:

> There are very few words used which are outside the learner's vocabulary. [A note is given on the number of 'root words' which it is expected that the learner will know.] These few extra words are needed for the story and are explained when they first appear. Long sentences and difficult sentence patterns have been simplified. The resulting language is good and useful English and the simplified book keeps much of the charm and flavour of the original.

The statement that 'the resulting language is good and useful English' may be very true – 'useful' presumably referring to the language learner, and forcing us to accept that some parts of literature, archaisms for example, or the poeticisms of the eighteenth century, are of limited linguistic usefulness. We would argue that in general the study of literature is also greatly useful to the language learner, but that is not the point here. The point is that it is precisely the literature which has been *taken out* of the simplified, or, basal reader, although it could of course be argued that in cases such as that of Lamb in his *Tales from Shakespeare* a new literature has been created.

One main problem then is that of *language*. The literary language which is unique to the original is 'translated' into something else. In translation across languages the translator is faced with the very difficult task of retaining the texture of the original. In the simplification process the writer almost deliberately loses that texture; the 'charm and flavour' of a simplified text are more likely to be the result of setting and character than of language. The lower the level of the simplified reader (i.e. a text which has undergone more drastic simplification, for use with either more elementary learners or younger students) the more 'non-literary' the language is likely to be. Thus shorter sentences, or limited use of dependent clauses, may well occur in literary text (c.f. Hemingway) but not to create the staccato effect of the following:

The date was the 28th of April. It was the early morning. Callao harbour was very busy. The Minister of Marine had ordered a tug to row us out of the harbour. A crowd of people was waiting to watch.

When I arrived, only Herman was there. He was guarding the raft. I got out of the car and jumped on board. Fruit baskets and boxes lay in a heap on the deck. They had been thrown on board at the last moment. In the middle of the heap sat Herman. He was holding a cage; and in the cage there was a green parrot. The bird was a present from a friend in Peru.

"Take care of the parrot for a minute," said Herman. "I want to go ashore and have a drink. The tug won't be here for a long time."

Herman went for his drink, and a few minutes later the tug arrived. A large motor-boat came to tow the raft away from the other boats. The motor-boat was full of officers and sailors. The officers called out some orders; and the sailors then fixed a strong rope to the raft.

"One moment!" I shouted. "It's too early! We must wait for the other men." I pointed towards the city.

But nobody understood. The officers only smiled politely. I untied the rope and threw it into the water. I waved my arms and made signs to the officers. This excited the parrot. The bird opened its cage and escaped. It walked about on the bamboo deck. I tried to catch the parrot. But it called out rude words in Spanish and flew into the cabin. At last, I caught the bird and put it back into its cage.

(from *The Kon-Tiki Expedition* by Thor Heyerdahl *Longman Structural Readers*, Stage 6)

It should be noted that the above is from a 'structural reader' and the students of literature would not be undertaking reading tasks at this level, but it is quoted here to illustrate how simplification, in attempting to deal with the difficulty of dependent clauses, can generate a type of prose which it would be difficult to find elsewhere outside language learning materials. Whatever the necessity for this type of text, it is of limited value as preparation for the study of literature.

7.2.3
A comparative
study: *Adam Bede*
by George Eliot

The following is a more interesting example, and is intended to show the wide divergence of literary from simplified text, and thereby to sound a note of caution:

a)   In the workshop of Mr Jonathan Burge, carpenter and builder, in the village of Hayslope, on the eighteenth of June, 1799, five men were coming to the end of their work for the day.
       The tallest and strongest of them, with black hair, sharp dark eyes, and a pleasing expression of honesty on his large, determined face, was Adam Bede.

       (opening lines of *Adam Bede* by George Eliot, simplified by G. Horsley *Longman Simplified English Series* 1964)

The opening paragraph of the above appers to give an adequate description of the setting, while avoiding the somewhat mannered opening of George Eliot's original:

b)   With a single drop of ink for a mirror, the Egyptian sorcerer undertakes to reveal to any chance comer far-reaching visions of the past. This is what I undertake to do for you, reader. With this drop of ink at the end of my pen, I will show you the roomy workshop of Mr. Jonathan Burge, carpenter and builder, in the village of Hayslope, as it appeared on the eighteenth of June, in the year of our Lord 1799.
       The afternoon sun was warm on the five workmen there, busy upon doors and window-frames and wainscoting. A scent of pine-wood from a tent-like pile of planks outside the open door mingles itself with the scent of the elderbushes which were spreading their summer snow close to the open window opposite . . .

Perhaps the first thing to note is that the original novel of over five hundred pages is reduced in the simplified version to 128 somewhat smaller pages, so clearly simplification, for this novel at least, is also drastic abridgement; there is just no space for the scent of pine wood and the 'summer snow' of the elderbushes. In fact literary figures, such as simile, are also largely removed. Thus, though the sentence monotony of the *Kon-Tiki* example quoted above is avoided, some richness is removed from the text, in terms of literary effect, lexical choice and, inevitably, dialect. Following is the original description of Adam Bede, which should be compared with the second paragraph of a) above.

       In his tall stalwartness Adam Bede was a Saxon, and justified his name, but the jet-black hair made the more noticeable by its contrast with the light paper cap, and the keen glance of the dark eyes that shone from under strongly marked, prominent and mobile eyebrows, indicated a mixture a Celtic blood. The face was large and roughly hewn, and when in repose had no other beauty than such as belongs to an expression of good-humoured honest intelligence.

An examination of the two descriptions reveals the simplified text to be related to the original, but rather as a police identikit picture is related to a high quality portrait. Of course you may argue that some authors seldom give us more than the identikit outlines, and again the short stories of Hemingway come to mind;

the remainder is left for the individual reader to complete for him or herself. Moreover the heavy overlays of the Victorian novel, as exemplified in the description of Adam Bede, are by no means to the taste of all modern readers, and the text may thus have been edited accordingly. A longer example, however, seems to indicate that simplification is not just a way of dealing with long sentences and difficult words, but involves the creation of a whole new sub-text, the only likeness with the original being the close correspondence of the plot.

7.2.4
Adam Bede (2): comparison of the original and simplified versions

The following, a pivotal point of the story, is from Chapter 37 of the 1859 version of the novel:

c)   The good landlady was amazed when she saw Hetty come downstairs soon after herself, neatly dressed, and looking resolutely self-possessed. Hetty told her she was quite well this morning: she had only been very tired and overcome with her journey, for she had come a long way to ask about her brother, who had run away, and they thought he was gone for a soldier, and Captain Donnithorne might know, for he had been very kind to her brother once. It was a lame story, and the landlady looked doubtfully at Hetty as she told it; but there was a resolute air of self-reliance about her this morning, so different from the helpless prostration of yesterday, that the landlady hardly knew how to make a remark that might seem like prying into other people's affairs. She only invited her to sit down to breakfast with them, and in the course of it Hetty brought out her ear-rings and locket, and asked the landlord if he could help her to get money for them: her journey, she said, had cost her much more than she expected, and now she had no money to get back to her friends, which she wanted to do at once.

It was not the first time the landlady had seen the ornaments, for she had examined the contents of Hetty's pocket yesterday, and she and her husband had discussed the fact of a country girl having these beautiful things, with a stronger conviction than ever that Hetty had been miserably deluded by the fine young officer.

"Well," said the landlord, when Hetty had spread the precious trifles before him, "we might take 'em to the jeweller's shop, for there's one not far off; but Lord bless you, they wouldn't give you a quarter o' what the things are worth. And you wouldn't like to part with 'em?" he added, looking at her inquiringly.

"Oh, I don't mind," said Hetty, hastily, "so as I can get money to go back."

"And they might think the things were stolen, as you wanted to sell 'em," he went on; "for it isn't usual for a young woman like you to have jewellery like that."

The blood rushed to Hetty's face with anger. "I belong to respectable folks," she said; "I'm not a thief."

"No, that you aren't, I'll be bound," said the landlady; "and you'd no call to say that," looking indignantly at her husband. "The things were gev to her: that's plain enough to be seen."

"I didn't mean as I thought so," said the husband, apologetically, "but I said it was what the jeweller might think, and so he wouldn't be offering much money for 'em,"

"Well," said the wife, "suppose you were to advance some money on the things yourself, and then if she liked to redeem them when she got home, she could. But if we heard nothing from her after two months, we might do as we liked with 'em.''

I will not say that in this accommodating proposition the landlady had no regard whatever to the possible reward of her good-nature in the ultimate possession of the locket and ear-rings: indeed, the effect they would have in that case on the mind of the grocer's wife had presented itself with remarkable vividness to her rapid imagination. The landlord took up the ornaments and pushed out his lips in a meditative manner. He wished Hetty well, doubtless; but pray, how many of your well-wishers would decline to make a little gain out of you? Your landlady is sincerely affected at parting with you, respects you highly, and will really rejoice if anyone else is generous to you; but at the same time she hands you a bill by which she gains as high a percentage as possible.

"How much money do you want to get home with, young woman?" said the well-wisher, at length.

"Three guineas," answered Hetty, fixing on the sum she set out with, for want of any other standard, and afraid of asking too much.

"Well, I've no objections to advance you three guineas," said the landlord; "and if you like to send it me back and get the jewellery again, you can, you know: the Green Man isn't going to run away."

"Oh yes, I'll be glad if you'll give me that," said Hetty, relieved at the thought that she would not have to go to the jeweller's, and be stared at and questioned.

d) The corresponding simplified version is as follows:

The landlord's wife was astonished when Hetty came downstairs early the next morning, carefully dressed, and looking quite calm. Hetty told her that she felt quite well. She had only been tired after her long journey. She had come to ask about her brother who had run away from home. They thought that he might have gone to be a soldier, and that Captain Donnithorne might know about it, as he had been kind to her brother once. It was a very weak story, and the woman looked doubtfully at Hetty as she told it, but she asked her to sit down and have breakfast with them.

During the meal, Hetty brought out her ear-rings and the locket, and asked the landlord if he could help her to get some money for them. She said that her journey had cost more than she expected, and now she had no money to get back to her friends.

"Well," said the landlord, "we could take them to the jeweller's shop, but he wouldn't give you a quarter of what they are worth. Do you really want to sell them?"

"Oh, I don't mind," said Hetty, "as long as I can get the money to go back."

"And he might think the things were stolen," the landlord went on, "for it isn't usual for a young woman like you to have such fine jewels as these."

The blood rushed to Hetty's face with anger. "I belong to a good, honest family," she said. "I'm not a thief."

"I didn't say that I thought so," said the man, "but I said it was what the jeweller might think, and so he wouldn't offer you much money for them."

"Well," said the wife to her husband, "why don't you lend her some money for these things yourself? Then, if she likes to have them back when she gets home, she can send us the money for them. If we hear nothing from her after two months, we'll do what we like with them."

"How much money do you want to get home with, young woman?" said the landlord at last.

"Three pounds," answered Hetty, thinking of what she had set out with, and afraid of asking too much.

'Well, I'll lend you three pounds," said the landlord, "and if you like to send it back and get the jewels again, you can, you know. The Green Man will still be here."

"Oh yes, I'll be very glad if you'll give me that," said Hetty, and so it was arranged.

As reading material text d) is excellent, and stays remarkably close to the sequence of events of c), *precisely because it is a pivotal point of the novel*. The principal change is that the variety and richness, that is the literariness, of the original have been removed. Incidentally 'variety' and 'richness' are not technical terms, and we make no attempt to make a linguistic analysis of the two texts. But text c) gains authenticity by the use of dialectal forms ('The things were gev to her'), by the insertion of author comment ('I will not say that in this accommodating propositon . . . ') and by a light touch of irony ('It was not the first time the landlady had seen the ornaments . . . ') In 3.5 above, referring to the filming of a literary text, we asserted that the new medium does not distort the literary text, although clearly it creates something quite different from the original. In the above examples the simplification, while much closer to the original, nevertheless distorts it, by generating a product of a uniformity and regularity which is quite unlike the original. It is for this reason that the phrase 'The blood rushed to Hetty's face with anger' stands out in text d); not so much because it is identical with the original, but because the metaphoric texture is severely limited in the simplification.

7.2.5
Conclusions from the foregoing

This extended commentary is included here for one purpose only: to suggest that literature cannot be taught from simplified text. This is not to say that text d) above is 'bad', but that the special purpose rewriting which it has undergone causes it to have a quite different rating on a literary – non-literary cline than the original (see 6.1). This would be even more marked if the process were attempted with a play (unless for comic effect or parody) or a poem, where even the slightest change can distort greatly. On the other hand one use of simplified texts in the teaching of literature is to make a direct comparison, in the manner of texts c) and d) above, just to find out what is 'special' in the literary text. Initially the teacher might ask the students to note, individually, which *is* the literary text, and, discounting length, what makes it so. This can be a most useful exercise, especially where learners have had limited contact with literary text in English, or where their own literature follows widely different conventions.

7.2.6
Practical task

The aim of this task is to make every learner see clearly how simplification changes the texture of any piece of writing. Point out that this is not a judgement of simplification, but that the reader must be aware that he or she is, so to speak, 'buying a different product'. Ask learners to simplify the following, using a much smaller number of words. Do not specify the required number of words, but point out that constructions that they would never use themselves, or that would be uncommon in modern English, must be *either* simplified *or* omitted.

e.g. It was not ill-chosen for such a scene; of a mean description; This ill-omened apparition

As a title to the piece use

A Public Execution

In former times, England had her Tyburn, to which the devoted victims of justice were conducted in solemn procession up what is now called Oxford Road. In Edinburgh, a large open street, or rather oblong square, surrounded by high houses, called the Grassmarket, was used for the same melancholy purpose. It was not ill chosen for such a scene, being of considerable extent, and therefore fit to accommodate a great number of spectators, such as are usually assembled by this melancholy spectacle. On the other hand, few of the houses which surround it were, even in early times, inhabited by persons of fashion; so that those likely to be offended or over deeply affected by such unpleasant exhibitions were not in the way of having their quiet disturbed by them. The houses in the Grassmarket are, generally speaking, of a mean description; yet the place is not without some features of grandeur; being overhung by the southern side of the huge rock on which the castle stands, and by the moss-grown battlements and turreted walls of that ancient fortress.

It was the custom, until within these thirty years, or thereabouts, to use this esplanade for the scene of public executions. The fatal day was announced to the public by the appearance of a huge black gallows-tree towards the eastern end of the Grassmarket. This ill-omened apparition was of great height, with a scaffold surrounding it, and a double ladder placed against it, for the ascent of the unhappy criminal and the executioner. As this apparatus was always arranged before dawn, it seemed as if the gallows had grown out of the earth in the course of one night, like the production of some foul demon . . .

(from *The Heart of Midlothian* by Sir Walter Scott (published 1818)

The rewriting should be done as an assignment outside the classroom. Select one of the better samples and again discuss informally, not just how the message (i.e. the information content) has been changed but also the *effect* or *texture*. Consider particularly adjectives and adjectival phrases, and prompt learners to say which text is more vivid/pictorial/dramatic/interesting, etc. (See also Rewriting 6.2)

One further exercise which can be undertaken either with a class or by teachers working on their own or in a teachers' group is to compare different versions of the same text. Familiar classical and canonical texts such as Jane Austen's *Pride and Prejudice* exist in numerous simplified versions produced by different publishers. The *quality* of the simplified versions varies considerably and it can be instructive to work out the reasons for preferring one version to another. It is worth remembering that – as with all books – there are good, bad and indifferent simplified texts.

| 7.2.7 Discussion | 1 What is your opinion of rewriting a literary work in a vocabulary of say, 1500 words, with perhaps a few more words explained at the bottom of the page? Should simplification be limited to:
a) breaking down long sentences b) rephrasing complex sentence patterns or nominal groups and c) abridgement? |

2 Do you agree that simplified readers 'are generally motivating'? Do you think that they meet the need for 'wider reading'?

3 What do you think the non-native learner misses (if anything) by reading a simplified version of a text rather than the original?

4 Do you see simplification as another form of translation? If so, do you think it is possible to retain the texture of the original in the simplified version?

5 Look again at the first three lines of text a) and the whole of text b) on page 148. Could you argue that there are certain advantages in the three lines from text a), regardless of who the reader is?

6 Do you think it is important to simplify and/or remove dialect forms for all except the most advanced learners. If possible consider your opinion in relation to any work you have read by either Thomas Hardy or D. H. Lawrence. Is dialect a necessary part of the texture of those writers?

7.3 Cross-cultural factors

If people go to another country, particularly one distant from their own, they will inevitably find many differences in language, food, dress and behaviour. A person who finds these differences difficult to adapt to is sometimes said to be suffering from 'culture shock'. Something of the same problem can occur when reading a text in another literature. The text describes, or is the setting for, a whole series of features which are very different from one's normal everyday experience. You do not normally suffer 'culture shock' from reading. You must however think your way into another culture. You must 'cross' cultures. As there is no readily available noun in English for this we will describe it as 'cross-cultural adaptation'.

Normally the author and reader share some knowledge which is hinted at in the text but not explained or commented on. The non-native speaker may see it as a difficulty, or, possibly, may fail to notice it altogether. In cases where the text is totally integrated with a whole range of features, social (as with the novels of Charles Dickens), historical (as with the poetry of the First World War) or personal (as in the stories and novels of Joseph Conrad), we are concerned with 'background' (see 6.6). While it is possible to read these texts without background knowledge, it seems certain that it would be an 'incomplete' reading. Lack of background where background is needed is perhaps among the first reasons for putting a text aside and not continuing to read.

There are, however, many texts which do not need an extensive background, but which nevertheless reveal points which are curious, inexplicable at first sight and potentially difficult for non-native readers because they have nowhere to turn for explanation. For the teacher there is no way to prepare the learner for all possible cross-cultural implications, although for a particular text some explanation in advance of the reading or teaching would undoubtedly be helpful.

One thing which the teacher can do is to 'present' an occasional text for its cross-cultural implications. This means a teacher-centred but interactive lesson, with low-order and higher-order questions directed solely to the points arising from that text. The aim of the lesson is to develop *awareness*, and to increase learner preparedness for the kinds of points which may occur in any text.

The following example is the first paragraph of the short story *The Obelisk* by E. M. Forster.

> Ernest was an elementary schoolmaster, and very small; it was like marrying a doll, Hilda sometimes thought, and one with glass eyes too. She was larger herself: tall enough to make them look funny as they walked down the esplanade, but not tall enough to look dignified when she was alone. She cherished aspirations; none would have guessed it from her stumpy exterior. She yearned for a trip in a Rolls Royce with a sheikh, but one cannot have everything or anything like it, one cannot even always be young. It is better to have a home of one's own than to always be a typist. Hilda did not talk quite as she should, and her husband had not scrupled to correct her. She had never forgotten – it was such a small thing, yet she could not forget it – she had never forgotten that night on their honeymoon when she had said something ungrammatical about the relative position of their limbs.

We believe that there might be problems with this paragraph for some non-native readers. One problem is related to the social status of Hilda and Ernest, and the particular sociological relationship of which the author, E. M. Forster, is very conscious. We should mention, however, that it is in the nature of literary text to provide this sort of detail in small increments, and it is thus possible that if students of literature read the whole story carefully, they would have as much information as they needed to understand it, by piecing together bits of information from different parts of the story.

With non-native speakers, a teacher is very unlikely to reveal the particular points the author is making by asking 'open' or high-order questions of the type: 'What do we know of the social background of Ernest and Hilda?' or 'What sort of person is Hilda?'

The following is a question sequence for manipulation by the teacher. If some of the questions are altogether too low-order for the learners they should of course be omitted. Moreover, the sequence does not take account of possible answers, which may make some of the questions redundant. Consider the following, and suppose the questions elicit partial responses and the teacher collates and summarises these at a) – e):

Look at line 4. What is an 'esplanade'?
Why are Ernest and Hilda walking there?
How often do they walk there?

a) So they are on holiday. They are at the seaside and they go there only for a week a year.

What is a Rolls Royce?
Why does Hilda want a trip in one?

Why does she want a trip in one *with a sheikh*?
Has she any hope of taking a trip in a Rolls Royce with a sheikh?
What does the author mean by 'her stumpy exterior'?
Would you say then that Hilda is a dreamer, a romantic?
How old do you think she is, by the way?

b) OK. Hilda has a rather dull existence as a housewife, and she creates a fantasy world for herself.

What is Ernest's job?
How big is he?
Would you agree that in general he does not command much respect, either for his job or his appearance?
How does he try to compensate for his deficiencies?
How does Hilda feel when he corrects her?
Why would the incident on their honeymoon be particularly unkind, humiliating, for Hilda?

c) Ernest then is in no way a 'big' man, but he likes to assert himself with his wife, who is not very well-educated.

What was Hilda's job, by the way?
Is she still a typist?
Why did she give it up?
Does she regret having given it up?
Is she happy?

d) Hilda realises that looking after her husband is better than being a typist. But it is an unexciting life, and Ernest is neither charming nor considerate. And a prediction (see 2.5):

e) Hilda is ready for adventure and excitement, especially sexual excitement.

Of course e) above is not part of the socio-cultural background which we have constructed from the question sequence, and belongs more properly to the narrative as a whole. The remainder, however, (which it is not necessary to accept as a 'correct' reading of the text, but which seems to us reasonable) is a reconstruction from the words 'esplanade', 'Rolls Royce', 'schoolmaster', 'typist' and a small number of other words. In this text, but not necessarily in the lexicon as a whole, they carry cultural associations. Collectively they provide a detailed cultural reference, which the author does not intend to make absolutely explicit. He relies on the reader to reconstruct the relationship between Hilda and Ernest and the social ambience which affects their lives, from the opening proposition: 'Ernest was an elementary schoolmaster', and thereafter from a number of small increments or hints. For native speakers of English who have lived all their life in England none of this presents a problem. For an American or Australian the situation is not identical, but they may recognise a period flavour about it (that is, Ernest and Hilda were at the seaside in, say, 1910) and make the cross-cultural adaptation. For a reader whose reading proficiency is good, but who lives in a society where elementary schoolmasters are highly respected, and where women have a duty to stay at home and look after their husbands and should not 'cherish aspirations', the story reads somewhat differently. Cross-cultural adaptation is necessary. You need to know what a Rolls Royce is, and why Hilda wants to ride in one.

As with acquiring vocabulary, there is no way in which the teacher can present all of it, or equip a student of literature for all eventualities. A 'pre-teach' session is useful for a text which carries either numerous or obscure cross-cultural references. A question sequence as illustrated above, for an in-depth study of multiple features, is a sound preparation for the cross-cultural adaptation which is a necessary part of much literature study and reading. Note: A work of fiction which offers multiple features for cross-cultural adaptation and comment is *An Artist of the Floating World* by Kazuo Ishiguro (1986). The English or American reader would immediately recognise a 'strangeness' in the behaviour of the child, and the politeness/courtesy practice, though a question sequence as above may be necessary to reveal all details of the 'alien' culture.

7.4
Literatures in English

There are literatures in English which require of non-native speakers less cross-cultural adaptation of the kind described in the previous section. Indeed, some very distinguished examples are of text written in English in the environment in which learners are themselves situated. This raises immediate questions for curriculum development: Should literature in English be the first literature with which certain students in certain cultural contexts have contact? What place and what priority should such texts be accorded within the general literature curriculum? What are the implications of the existence of such writing for the integration of language and literature in the curriculum?

Many teachers of literature prefer the term 'literature in English' as a general term to 'English literature'. English literature carries very specific associations of literature written by authors of English nationality usually (though not necessarily) within the geographical confines of Great Britain. There is no doubt that English literature is one of the great world literatures and represents a very rich tradition, but the term 'English literature' is rather narrow, exclusive and ethnocentric. 'Literature(s) in English' includes the considerable diversity of literature produced *in the English language* not only in the more obvious context of American literature, but also literature in the following contexts: Australia, Canada, New Zealand, South Africa. It also includes a growing and important body of work produced in countries where English is an institutionalised second language or where it is a foreign language but carries important social and cultural functions within a society. Such literatures in English include work produced by writers in Nigeria, Kenya, India, the Phillipines, the Caribbean, Malaysia and Singapore. In these latter countries the creative writer may not be writing in his or her mother tongue but has chosen English as a medium for creative expression. Although normally excluded from courses in English literature, it is worth noting that contributions to literature in English by writers whose first language is not English, number in their ranks those who have won or been short-listed for prestigious international literary prizes. Examples from the last ten years include.

Wole Soyinka (Nigeria) – Nobel Prize for Literature
V. S. Naipaul (India/Caribbean) – Booker Prize for Literature
Chinua Achebe (Nigeria) – short-listed for the Booker Prize
Anita Desai (India) – short-listed for the Booker Prize
R. K. Narayan (India) – Whitbread Award for Fiction

Other writers recognised to have made major contributions to world literature in English include: Lloyd Fernando (Malaysia); Ngugi Wa Th'ongo (Kenya); Raja Rao (India) and Nick Joacquim (The Phillipines).

7.4.1 Writing and the English language

In this connection it is valuable to explore *why* such writers choose to adopt English as a literary medium. With two or three potential languages available to them a choice is clearly possible and is seen by most writers as necessary. Most writers are faced, too, with the fact of English being a colonial language – the language, that is associated with an occupying power, even if their nation has been, as in the cases of Nigeria, Kenya, India, etc., long since independent of Britain. Listed below are some of the main factors determining the choice of English as a medium of creative expression:

a) English is a world language. The choice of English gives access to an international readership.

b) Nationally and regionally, too, English is a language which allows communication between different ethnic groups. Thus English is generally seen as the natural language for African literature. Within the different countries of a continent, too, English can be seen as a paradoxically 'neutral' language, in so far as the choice of English does not privilege any one ethnic or tribal or language group. In a multilingual society such as India or Kenya or Singapore, English is an institutionalised language of government, the legal system, etc. precisely because to have privileged one of the countries' many other languages would have led to severe problems. The instance of literary English is a not dissimilar one.

c) Because English is associated with a colonial power and with oppression, there is a considerable challenge to the writer to decolonise both the language and the ideologies which accompany the language. There is a challenge to make the language his or her own and to serve as an expression of specifically African or Asian identity. Major African writers such as the Nobel Prize winner Wole Soyinka have advocated Swahili as the language of African literature; others such as Ngugi Wa Th'ongo have written in local languages such as Kikuyu as a way of contacting ordinary, less well-educated people. Others continue to advocate the creative development of different national varieties of English.

d) There is a long tradition of literature in English which provides a source for creative utilisation of the kind not normally available within a local language.

7.4.2 Varieties of English: varieties of literature

The choice for the writer, as presented above, between English or local language, is of course not in all cases as straightforward as may appear. Such a clear and unequivocal choice presupposes an English which is not only international but also uniform and homogenous. For many writers there is a further choice: between British and American English (the standard language norms of native speakers) and local Englishes in the sense, for example, of Singapore English, Fillipino English or Nigerian English.

Here is an example of a poem written in a version of English which is conveniently called a local or 'new' English:

> I am standing for peace and non-violence,
> Why world is fighting fighting
> Why all people of world
> Are not following Mahatma Gandhi,
> I am simply not understanding.
> Ancient Indian Wisdom is 100% correct.
> I should say even 200% correct.
> But Modern generation is neglecting –
> Too much going for fashion and foreign thing.
>
> Nissim Ezekiel, 'The Patriot',
> *Very Indian Poems in Indian English*

The poem contains non-standard linguistic features such as: the use of a present progressive in contrast with a simple present in standard English; the omission of articles; the use of a singular in place of a standard English plural. However, the term 'non-standard' is a potentially dangerous one, for it may suggest that this version of English is somehow incorrect or at least inferior when it is, in fact, a perfectly legitimate form of international English. Indian English is one of many international Englishes and is a variety chosen as a creative medium by some Indian writers in preference both to local Indian languages and to 'standard' versions of British and American English. It is a variety of English in its own right and will be familiar to many Indian readers, thus imparting to the text a very particular identity and character.

What are the curriculum issues raised by such literatures, particularly in the context of learning English as a second (normally) or foreign language, in those countries where there is a strong tradition of these literatures in English?

There are a number of factors which will influence the inclusion of literatures in English in the 'English' literature curriculum:

a) The language will be familiar to learners within the culture or nation in which the literature is produced. It is likely, too, that the topics or treatment of content in the texts will involve expression of local viewpoints, attitudes and identities. Such texts are, therefore, likely to be more *accessible* to learners in such contexts. A case could, therefore, be made for local literature being among the *first* literary texts read in English.

b) Such texts will be likely to be *less* accessible in cultural and linguistic terms to speakers of other Englishes. But the inclusion of a variety of literatures in English can do much to

   i)   modify the notion of a single canon of texts;

   ii) help students appreciate the concerns of a wider range of cultures than the predominantly anglocentric Euro-American oriented concerns of standard canonical literature;

   iii) foster appreciation of different varieties of language, each with different values and socio-cultural functions, in creative contact with one another. In this connection it should be remembered that 'new Englishes' are primarily marked in spoken forms, and that there is much greater convergence to norms of 'standard' British or American English in written forms.

c) There is likely to be greater involvement on the part of readers with environments with which they can more easily identify. 'New' literatures develop most rapidly in those countries which exist in a post-colonial context. There are numerous such countries in the world and English teaching normally has a high profile in these situations. Rich opportunities exist, therefore, for locally relevant integrated language and literature work.

7.5
Issues in the testing of literature

It is often argued that literature classes should not result in examinations, for literature is a subject where the students' capacities for reading may only emerge over a period of years and after re-readings of texts have occurred. However, examinations there are, passes or fails are important, and the existence of examinations can serve to institutionalise and, in the case of teachers of English as a second language, focus attention on, an area of English which until recently was considered marginal to the more instrumental purposes of language learning. Among other developments in recent years in theory, practice and materials at the interface of language and literature teaching, the existence of 'set texts' in University of Cambridge examinations (optionally at First Certificate and Proficiency, as part of 'composition', and as a separate Diploma paper) may have done most to re-establish the place of literature in the language curriculum.

Our purpose here is to explore the nature of examinations in literature, especially in terms of question types, and to argue that greater flexibility and imagination will be required if recent advances in integrated language-based approaches to literature are to be built on. We begin with an attempt to characterise some prevalent design characteristics of literature examination questions in different parts of the world.

Paraphrase and context

In such questions candidates are presented with extracts from texts they have studied. The extracts are normally pivotal to the text and candidates can be invited to say what is pivotal about them in terms of the structure, normally either of plot or character, of the whole. Such questions are sometimes called 'context' questions and modified versions may also ask for details of what 'happens' just before or after the scene extracted. Equally common is the requirement to paraphrase the extract in the form of a commentary on its particular significance. Rather less commonly, students can be asked to identify particular tropes; that is, isolate from the text examples of metaphors, similes or other rhetorical features. Such naming of the parts of a text is not necessarily accompanied by any requirement to analyse their significance or evaluate their local effectiveness.

Describe and discuss

In our observation such questions are the most common type. A general essay is invited from candidates in which they have to comment on what happens to a character with some discussion of reasons or motives for an action(s). Such questions are common in University of Cambridge First Certificate examinations. Here are two representative examples.

> 'Describe Snowball and explain what happens to him.'
>
> (Cambridge First Certificate, June 1987)
> (George Orwell, *Animal Farm*)

> 'What does Mrs Birling find out about her son, and what are her feelings about this?'
>
> (Cambridge First Certificate, December 1986)
> (J.B. Priestley, *An Inspector Calls*)

The questions are related to the paraphrase and context questions and, although there is a more varied range than we have suggested, there is a standard format. The format extends into Cambridge Proficiency level examinations which also contain a relatively high proportion of descriptive and plot-based questions. In all cases an essential element is the retrieval of information from the text – a process which advantages students with good memories.

Evaluate and criticise
These types of questions tend to be directed at rather more advanced level students. They normally require a more critical stance from the candidate and sometimes invite evaluation of the relative success the writer has in conveying a particular scene or idea or character. As in the case of 'describe and discuss' questions, the focus is on plot and character. Here are two more representative examples:

> 'Illustrate from the stories how Lawrence's attitude to his characters is often a mixture of ridicule and compassion.'
>
> (Cambridge Proficiency, December 1987)
> (D. H. Lawrence, *Selected Tales*)

> 'Describe the ways in which the other members of the Rice family struggle to cope with their feelings of failure and loss.'
>
> (Cambridge Proficiency, June 1987)
> (John Osborne, *The Entertainer*)

There is a strong psychological orientation to such questions with students asked to consider characters in plays, novels and even poems as complete psychological entities whose behaviour and motivations can be explored in the light of a common sense knowledge of human nature. Occasionally, essays are elicited in which texts are viewed as sources of moral, religious or sociological ideas, but these are less common.

Not unexpectedly, preparation for such examinations is supported by a minor industry producing slim books which advise students how to pass the questions on the set book. Most typically, context questions are spotted and suitable paraphrases provided to be learned; or plot and character behaviour summaries are provided for purposes of subsequent retelling, usually together with a set of past or predicted questions; or extracts from eminent literary critics are supplied in order to prepare for questions which elicit a more evaluative commentary, and once again the students can digest these comments and either quote them or pass them off as their own opinions. In more senses than one such cribs are indispensable.

The conventional nature of such question types raises a number of issues concerning exactly what is being tested in literature examinations. First, in many examinations students are rarely encouraged to read a text closely; instead there is what Short and Candlin characterise as a 'flight from the text', a flight from the text as a formal, linguistic and aesthetic artefact into the text as a sequence of events or a set of behaviours. Second, such questions prompt a further question of whether the information required from the candidate would not just as easily be obtained from a translation or from a simplified version of the text. Thirdly, what kind of literary competence is illustrated by discursive essays in which some candidates retell plots and formulate second-hand judgements? And why is the essay format so exclusive a mode of assessment?

Of course it is also necessary to link these general tendencies to the very different teaching situations around the world, for such situations also determine how and why literature is taught and examined. For example, in some countries it is taught mainly to native speakers within cultural contexts in which the students themselves live. In other countries (e.g. Singapore and Kenya) literature in English is taught to bilingual or second language learners in a context in which English has institutionalised status and may or may not have been the language of a former colonising culture. In other countries literature in English is taught in the context of advanced courses in English as a foreign language. Each of these contexts will of course necessitate different priorities in terms of what counts as literature in English and in terms of which models are oriented towards. It is also necessary to link discussion of these contexts to different models of literature teaching (1.1) and to related pedagogic practices.

However, the argument which we have consistently advanced in this book for fuller consideration of language-based approaches is not without relevance here. In each of the contexts outlined in the preceding paragraph we would argue that language-based work is highly germane both for developing sensitivity to literary text, for developing interpretive skills and for developing language competence. And if such approaches are argued to be relevant to literature teaching, then they must also be taken proper account of in examining and assessment procedures.

7.5.1
Language-based tasks

A principle of testing is that we should test what has been taught. If we have been teaching to a generalised method that draws attention to the different levels of language in a literary text, and how they work together to express or symbolise the content or propositions of that text, then it is that which we should test. This applies equally to a text studied previously in the classroom and to an 'unseen' text. The fact that texts are unseen does not matter, as long as they do not contain a large number of archaisms, or other unexpected difficulties (which could include cultural difficulties) and that the features to be noted have been met in other texts.

If a poem has not been studied previously, a wide range of questions can be generated, including who the speakers are at various points of the poem and what the generalised proposition or 'message' contained in it is. Clearly, if it has not been studied, the whole poem must be presented. If it *has* been studied, and supposing learners have been taught to look at the *language* of the literary text, they can be invited to comment on the use and success of any features of *shape, lexis, syntax* (or other features) which make the language 'special' or deviant in a given section. This type of question demands a reasonably advanced knowledge of how various features of language work together in literary text, while requiring very little writing and none of the general discussion of the literary essay. (Note that the word 'deviant' is a useful item in this area of teaching/testing.)

Consider the following as an item to be tested in this way:

They leave their trenches, going over the top,
While time ticks blank and busy on their wrists
And hope, with furtive eyes and grappling fists,
Flounders in mud. O Jesus, make it stop!

(Siegfried Sassoon)

In dealing with prose text, slightly different criteria are the focus of attention. These might include sentence length, lexis and syntax, while clearly rhyme, or other poetic features, do not apply. The question type, 'Comment on features . . . ' remains the same. Consider the following text as a sample:

Mr Sniggs, the Junior Dean, and Mr Postlethwaite, the Domestic Bursar, sat alone in Mr Sniggs' room overlooking the garden quad at Scone College. From the rooms of Sir Alastair Digby-Vane-Trumpington, two staircases away, came a confused roaring and breaking of glass. They alone of the senior members of Scone were at home that evening, for it was the night of the annual dinner of the Bollinger Club. The others were all scattered over Boar's Hill and North Oxford at gay, contentious little parties, or at other senior common-rooms, or at the meetings of learned societies, for the annual Bollinger dinner is a difficult time for those in authority.

It is not accurate to call this an annual event, because quite often the Club is suspended for some years after each meeting. There is tradition behind the Bollinger; it numbers reigning kings among its past members. At the last dinner, three years ago, a fox had been brought in in a cage and stoned to death with champagne bottles. What an evening that had been! This was the first meeting since then, and from all over Europe old members had rallied for the occasion. For two days they had been pouring into Oxford: epileptic royalty from their villas of exile; uncouth peers from crumbling country seats; smooth young men of uncertain tastes from embassies and legations; illiterate lairds from wet granite hovels in the Highlands; ambitious young barristers and Conservative candidates torn from the London season and the indelicate advances of debutantes; all that was most sonorous of name and title was there for the beano.

(from *Decline and Fall* by Evelyn Waugh)

7.5.2
Literary tasks

We retain the word 'task', in the sense of something which has to be done as part of a routine, because we recognise the necessity for testing. On the other hand, in any examination context it is not easy to invent tasks, apart from the essay, which almost certainly accounts for its widespread use. It is of course possible to devise more specific questions than the type generally given for essays, with the aim of eliciting a detailed engagement with the text rather than a second-hand discussion, and the examinee's own view rather than someone else's, for example:

> The voice of my education said to me
> He must be killed,
> For in Sicily the black, black snakes are innocent, the gold are
>   venomous.
>
> And voices in me said, if you were a man
> You would take a stick and break him now, and finish him off
> But I must confess how I liked him,
> How glad I was he had come like a guest in quiet, to drink at
>   my water-trough
> And depart peaceful, pacified, and thankless,
> Into the burning bowels of this earth?
>
> Was it cowardice, that I dared not kill him?
> Was it perversity, that I longed to talk to him?
> Was it humility, to feel so honoured?
> I felt so honoured.
>
> (from 'Snake' by D. H. Lawrence)

a) Explain, in a few sentences, the *situation*.
   (Where is the poet? What has happened?
   Why is it important to describe the event?)
b) What is the *message* of the poem, and particularly of the above lines? Do you think the message is in any way unusual? Are you convinced by what the poet says?

This clearly requires competence in writing, but less so than the essay. Some idea of 'what is going on' in the literary text is required, but the questions are more 'open' than mere information-retrieval questions.

Cloze, though a widely recognised test of reading skill, is not satisfactory as a literary task. If the text has already been studied it is only a test of recall. If the text has not been studied, cloze does not, as a task, take account of the polysemic nature of literary text, unless the learner is also asked to comment on the merits of a number of words and decide which is best, which would be a very unwieldy type of examination question. This of course does not detract from the possibilities of cloze as a teaching device in the literature class.

Explanation of literary 'tropes' is also a long established testing practice. If used, examinees should be asked to comment on the impact and originality of the trope, rather than simply glossing it, and should never be asked (for example) to 'find the metaphor in stanza 3'. All exercises related to literary tropes combine language and literature, however consciously literary the trope may be e.g. 'My soul is an enchanted Boat/Which like a sleeping swan, doth float' (Shelley).

Paraphrasing is similarly established, and was mentioned above in the case for not testing. Its weakness is that it asks the examinee to translate the literary text into something else which is not literature. In doing so we run the risk of wiping out any evidence that the learner saw anything special in the literary artefact originally, or, to use a more elevated phrase, that he or she was 'moved by it'.

On the other hand, question types deriving from 'reader's theatre' (see 6.5) do seem to require a genuine interpretation of text, while avoiding the conventionalised format of the essay. For example:

Look at these lines from Harold Pinter's play *Last to Go*.

Man:	You were a bit busier earlier.
Barman:	Ah.
Man:	Round about ten.
Barman:	Ten, was it?
Man:	About then.

a) Write a paragraph on how you would produce this play. (You may include *manner of speech, clothes, anything on the stage, lighting, movement, position on stage* or any other features.)

b) Why does this text seem *unlike* literature, at least at first reading?

The problem with this is the difficulty of marking it, because it is highly subjective, though it could be argued that this is no more so than the essay. It is perhaps most 'creative' as a test type when the text has been studied in class but *not* through a 'reader's theatre' process.

One further type of question is to ask examinees to make a number of statements about a text (a poem, an extract from a prose work or play, but not a complete book, where the statements would be too generalised to have any validity), as in a *ranking* exercise, and then to defend the statement which they believe best summarises the whole. This is demanding, as the statements relating to the text must all be reasonable and must not approximate to the 'distractors' of multiple choice testing. This type of exercise needs to have been practised in class work so that students have become accustomed to it.

7.5.3
More question types

Rewriting is a legitimate and useful form of test question, though normally only with texts which have been studied in some detail in the classroom (by whatever process, and whether student-centred or not). The combined skills required are the recognition of what is specifically literary in the original and the 'translation' (or omission) of literariness into some other form; the recall or retention of information from the original, perhaps with a prompt; and, thirdly, the ability to write in an approximation to another register. Suppose the following is the cue or prompt:

Of course she had read novels about the Malay Archipelago and she had formed an impression of a sombre land with great ominous rivers and a silent, impenetrable jungle.

(from *The Force of Circumstance* by W. Somerset Maugham)

The task would then be to write a promotional item for Malaysia, using as much of the original information as possible, which would involve recall. It would then be necessary to mention the land, the rivers and the jungle, but *not*, respectively, as 'sombre', 'ominous' or 'impenetrable' which clearly do not promote. Beyond that, reasonable accuracy and simplicity in the rewriting are more important than absolute authenticity, as the answer is not of course intended for publication. A more complete test item might be as follows:

> As we pulled across her stern a slim dart of fire shot out viciously at us, and suddenly she went down, head first, in a great hiss of steam.

This is an extract from Conrad's story *Youth*. The name of the ship is the *Judea*.

Rewrite the incident as a short newspaper report under the following headline. Use as much of the *information* (everybody was saved, sank in the night, etc.) of Conrad's text as you can remember, but not the literary language:

SHIP SINKS IN GULF OF THAILAND

Note that this type of question involves recall, but without extensive memorisation of text, which would be necessary to answer the following type of question:

'What is there in the scene in which Romeo and Juliet first meet that gives it dramatic excitement? How are both the situation and feelings of Romeo and Juliet made specially intense by particular words and phrases?'

(Question from the sample paper of the General Certificate of Secondary Education, quoted in an article by Margot Norman, writing on this examination for native speaker students, aged about 16, in an article in *The Daily Telegraph* 26 February 1988. According to the writer relatively few students were able to answer the question satisfactorily.)

There are, of course, differences other than the need for memorisation which separate this question from all other types we have suggested, foremost among them being the implied value judgement of 'dramatic excitement'. By no means all non-native speakers, and perhaps not all native speakers, can be expected to recognise the dramatic excitement, in which case they have little chance of answering the question. This, however, should not be a reason to avoid the study of literature; the excitement may come much later. This is a warning to avoid at all cost the question which quotes an extract and then asks learners 'What do you most enjoy in this fine piece of writing?'

Where learners have been studying prose extracts, a different type of question is possible. It is fairly elementary, it is linguistically oriented, and it deals with theme, though very much at the level of intensive text study, rather than extensive reading. The sample text used here is the same as for the rewriting above. A possible rubric might be:

'Trace the themes of fire, darkness and the sea in the following text'

or, at a slightly higher level:

'What are the themes in the following text, and how are they interrelated?'

> 'Between the darkness of earth and heaven she was burning fiercely upon a 5
> disc of purple sea shot by the blood-red play of gleams; upon a disc of water
> glittering and sinister. A high, clear flame, an immense and lonely flame,
> ascended from the ocean, and from its summit the black smoke poured

continuously at the sky. She burned furiously; mournful and imposing like a
funeral pile kindled in the night, surrounded by the sea, watched over by the   10
stars. A magnificent death had come like a grace, like a gift, like a reward to
that old ship at the end of her laborious days. The surrender of her weary
ghost to the keeping of stars and sea was stirring like the sight of a glorious
triumph. The masts fell just before daybreak, and for a moment there was a
burst and turmoil of sparks that seemed to fill with flying fire the night   15
patient and watchful, the vast night lying silent upon the sea . . .

The answer, according to what has been previously established by the teacher,
may be either a word set, or a 'map' on the text itself (which can be difficult to
grade), or a commentary, the latter moving again to more extended writing.
     We do not suggest that we have by any means exhausted either question
types, or the subject of testing literature. We have argued, however, that
a) many literature examinations operate according to somewhat rigid formulae
b) that such formulae may run counter to and not effectively assess the kinds of
capacities and literary competence teachers may want to develop in their
students c) that typical literature examination questions do not reflect
integrated language and literature work d) that language-based approaches
used in the integrated language and literature class can be adapted to foster
more activity-centred examination questions directed towards students' own
personal responses to and readings of literary texts.

7.5.4
Practical task

Devise a 'bank' of test questions for the following (somewhat unusual, and
certainly unfashionable) Victorian poem. Question types should include:
a) recall, 'information retrieval', assuming the poem has been studied but is
    not reprinted on the examination paper
b) comprehension, interpretation, for both intermediate and advanced
    learners
c) 'translation'/paraphrase for learners of a stated language competence and
    literary experience
d) language features, especially lexis and word order
e) theme, message, proposition
f) rewriting (letter of condolence, obituary. See 6.3)
g) background – questions which relate to any social or religious features
    implicit in the poem (for advanced learners)
h) video production (see 3.5) – state the learner group
i) commentary, related to poetic features, especially rhyme, sound patterns
    and tropes (see 6.2)
j) *for advanced learners:*
    i) evaluation, but designed to make the learner see the text as a statement
        of faith, devotion, sincerity
    ii) evaluation, but designed to invite criticism of sentimentality, morbid
        obsession, etc., and to say why such a poem is unlikely to be written in
        the 1990s.

Give precise instructions for all questions.

Barbara

On the Sabbath-day
Through the churchyard old and gray,
Over the crisp and yellow leaves I held my rustling way;
And amid the words of mercy, falling on my soul like balms;
'Mid the gorgeous storms of music – in the mellow organ – calms,
'Mid the upward-streaming prayers, and the rich and solemn psalms,
I stood careless, Barbara.

My heart was otherwhere,
While the organ shook the air,
And the priest, with outspread hands, bless'd the people with a prayer;
But when rising to go homeward, with a wild and saint-like shine
Gleam'd a face of airy beauty with its heavenly eyes on mine –
Gleam'd and vanish'd in a moment – O that face was surely thine
Out of heaven, Barbara!

O pallid, pallid face.
O earnest eyes of grace!
When last I saw thee, dearest, it was in another place.
You came running forth to meet me with my love-gift on your wrist:
The flutter of a long white dress, then all was lost in mist –
A purple stain of agony was on the mouth I kiss'd,
That wild morning, Barbara.

I search'd, in my despair,
Sunny noon and midnight air;
I could not drive away the thought that you were lingering there.
O many and many a winter night I sat when you were gone,
My worn face buried in my hands, beside the fire alone –
Within the dripping churchyard, the rain plashing on your stone,
You were sleeping, Barbara.

'Mong angels, do you think
Of the precious golden link
I clasp'd around your happy arm while sitting by yon brink?
Or when that night of gliding dance, of laughter and guitars,
Was emptied of its music, and we watch'd through lattice-
    bars
The silent midnight heaven moving o'er us with its stars,
Till the day broke, Barbara?

In the years I've changed;
Wild and far my heart has ranged,
And many sins and errors now have been on me avenged;
But to you I have been faithful whatsoever good I lack'd;
I loved you, and above my life still hangs that love intact –
Your love the trembling rainbow, I the reckless cataract.
Still I love you, Barbara.

Alexander Smith

Questions for discussion

1 Examine the following statement (a) by the Nigerian novelist Chinua Achebe in the light of the extract (b) below from his novel *A Man of The People*. Pay attention to the following questions:

   i)   How and for what purposes does Achebe use different varieties of standard and Nigerian English?

   ii) What do such uses reveal of the character of the Minister and the attitude to him of the narrator?

   iii) Does Achebe succeed in imparting to the reader distinctly African values as a result of a juxtaposition of different Englishes. Is there a use of English 'altered to suit its new African surroundings'?

a)   So my answer to the question, Can an African ever learn English well enough to be able to use it effectively in creative writing? is certainly yes. If on the other hand you ask: Can he ever learn to use it like a native speaker? I should say, I hope not. It is neither necessary nor desirable for him to be able to do so. The price a world language must be prepared to pay is submission to many different kinds of use. The African writer should aim to use English in a way that brings out his message best without altering the language to the extent that its value as a medium of international exchange will be lost. He should aim at fashioning out an English which is at once universal and able to carry his peculiar experience . . . . It will have to be a new English, still in full communion with its ancestral home, but altered to suit its new African surroundings.

(from 'English and the African Writer' in *Transition* 1965)

b)   Changing the subject slightly, the Minister said 'Only teachers can make this excellent arrangement.' Then turning to the newspaper correspondent in his party he said, 'It is a mammoth crowd.'

The journalist whipped out his note-book and began to write . . .

We had now entered the Assembly Hall and the Minister and his party were conducted to their seats on the dais. The crowd raised a deafening shout of welcome. He waved his fan to the different parts of the hall. Then he turned to Mr Nwege and said:

'Thank you very much, thank you, sir.'

A huge, tough-looking member of the Minister's entourage who stood with us at the back of the dais raised his voice and said:

'You see wetin I de talk. How many minister fit handswer *sir* to any Tom, Dick and Harry wey senior them for age? I hask you how many?' . . .

The Minister's speech sounded spontaneous and was most effective. There was no election at hand, he said, amid laughter. He had not come to beg for their votes; it was just 'a family reunion—pure and simple.' He would have preferred not to speak to his own kinsmen in English which was after all a foreign language, but he had learnt from experience that speeches made in vernacular were liable to be distorted and misquoted in the press. Also there were some strangers in that audience who did not speak our own tongue and he did not wish to exclude them. They were all citizens of our great country whether they came from the highlands or the lowlands, etc. etc.

At the end of his speech the Minister and his party were invited to the Proprietor's Lodge—as Mr Nwege called his square, cement-block house. Outside, the dancers had all come alive again and the hunters—their last powder gone—were tamely waiting for the promised palm-wine. The

Minister danced a few dignified steps to the music of each group and stuck red pound notes on the perspiring faces of the best dancers. To one group alone he gave away five pounds.

The same man who had drawn our attention to the Minister's humility was now pointing out yet another quality. I looked at him closely for the first time and noticed that he had one bad eye—what we call a cowrieshell eye.

'You see how e de do as if to say money be san-san,' he was saying. 'People wey de jealous the money gorment de pay Minister no sabi say no be him one de chop am. Na so so troway.'

Later on in the Proprietor's Lodge I said to the Minister: 'You must have spent a fortune today.'

He smiled at the glass of cold beer in his hand and said:

'You call this spend? You never see some thing, my brother. I no de keep anini for myself, na so so troway. If some person come to you and say "I wan' make you Minister" make you run like blazes comot, Na true word I tell you. To God who made me.' He showed the tip of his tongue to the sky to confirm the oath. 'Minister de sweet for eye but too much katakata de for inside. Believe me yours sincerely.'

'Big man, big palaver,' said the one-eyed man.

(from *A Man of the People* by Chinua Achebe)

Would you include such an extract, or the novel itself from which the extract is taken, in your own literature syllabus? If you would not, give particular reasons why? If you would include such texts and you do not live and teach in West Africa, what would you need to overcome? To what extent could the following language-based teaching strategies be employed:

i)   rewriting (pp. 116–121)
ii) jigsaw reading (pp. 71–75) – with jumbled paragraphs
iii) character grids (pp. 67–69)
iv) cloze (pp. 80–81) – with, for example, characters names deleted but with a completed grid for guidance and the task of assigning the character to the speech.

Note: This passage is discussed in detail in Traugott, E and Pratt, M L 1980 *Linguistics for Students of Literature* Harcourt Brace Jovanovich Chapter 9.

2 Discuss the relevance of the following examination paper (University of Cambridge First Certificate) to the teaching of literature in English in the teaching situation with which you are most familiar. If the questions are relevant write a paragraph clearly stating your reasons. If the questions are not relevant or run counter to your normal teaching practices give reasons why and rewrite the questions substituting new texts if necessary.

First Certificate in English

J.B. PRIESTLEY: An Inspector Calls

What evidence is there to suggest that the Inspector is no ordinary policeman? Who do you think he is?

GEORGE ORWELL: Animal Farm
Describe Snowball and explain what happens to him.

Zero Hour (Cambridge University Press)

What do you think of the way in which parents behave towards their children in one or more of these stories?

© University of Cambridge Local Examinations Syndicate 1987

5   Based on your reading of one of these books, write on one of the following.
J.B. PRIESTLEY: An Inspector Calls
What does Mrs. Birling find out about her son, and what are her feelings about this?

GEORGE ORWELL: Animal Farm
How does trying to build the windmill change the lives of the animals?

PETER DICKINSON: The Seventh Raven
Describe the character of Mrs. Dunnitt, and the part she plays in the story.

© University of Cambridge Local Examinations Syndicate 1986

3 The following questions are extracted from a recent text book *Openings* by Brian Tomlinson Lingual House, 1986. In the light of discussion in this chapter evaluate the questions. The passage, to which the questions relate is extracted from a poem in English 'Song of Lawino' by the Ugandan poet Okot P'Bitek.
a) Write a paragraph or two giving your reactions.
b) How appropriate would it be for any of the questions 5a)–e) to be set as examination questions?

My Name Blew Like a Horn
Among the Payira

1 You are going to listen to your teacher reading part of a poem called 'Song of Lawino'. In this poem a Ugandan wife complains about the treatment she gets from her husband.

   Before you listen to the poem, form groups and note down:
   a) what you think a wife in your country might complain about;
   b) what you expect the Ugandan wife to complain about.

2 Listen to your teacher reading an extract from 'Song of Lawino' and as you listen, try to imagine what Lawino and Ocol look like, and to decide whether Lawino's complaints are justified.

3 In groups, answer the following questions:
   a) What does Lawino complain about?
   b) Do you think her complaints are justified?
   c) Why do you think Ocol treats Lawino as he does?
   d) What problems of Third World countries are illustrated in the poem?

4 Read the extract from 'Song of Lawino' and as you read, check your answers to 1b) and 3 above.

5 Choose *one* of the following activities and then work individually, in pairs or in groups, as appropriate.
   a) Mime the poem as it is read aloud by one of the group.
   b) Draw a series of pictures to illustrate the poem.
   c) Write a short extract from the 'Song of Ocol'.
   d) Write a scene from a play about Lawino and Ocol.
   e) Write a poem or story about yourself in which you complain about aspects of your present condition and look back to a time when things seemed better.

   When you have finished, get an individual, a pair or a group to look at what you have produced and to help you to make it better.

My Name Blew Like a Horn
Among the Payira

Okot P'Bitek

I was made chief of girls
Because I was lively,
I was bright,
I was not clumsy or untidy,
I was not dull,
I was not heavy and slow.

I did not grow up a fool
I am not cold
I am not shy
My skin is smooth
It still shines smoothly in the moonlight.

When Ocol was wooing me
My breasts were erect
And they shook
As I walked briskly.
And as I walked
I threw my long neck
This way and that way
Like the flower of the *lyonna* lily
Waving in a gentle breeze.

And my brothers called me *Nya-Dyang*
For my breasts shook
And beckoned the cattle,
And they sang silently:
Father prepare the kraal,
Father prepare the kraal,
The cattle are coming

I was the Leader of the girls
And my name blew
Like a horn
Among the Payira.
And I played on my bow harp
And praised my love.

Ocol, my husband,
My friend,
What are you talking?
You saw me when I was young.
In my mother's house
This man crawled on the floor!

The son of the Bull wept
For me with tears,
Like a hungry child
Whose mother has starved long
In the simsim field!

Every night he came
To my father's homestead
He never missed one night
Even after he had been beaten
By my brothers.

You loved my giraffe-tail bangles.
My father brought them for me
From the Hills in the East.

The roof of my mother's house
Was beautifully-laced
With elephant grass:
My father built it
With the skill of the Acoli.

You admired my sister's
Colourful ten-stringed loin beads;
My mother threaded them
And arranged them with care.

You trembled
When you saw the tattoos
On my breasts
And the tattoos below my belly button;
And you were very fond
Of the gap in my teeth!

My man, what are you talking?
My clansmen. I ask you:
What has become of my husband?
Is he suffering from boils?
Is it ripe now?
Should they open it
So that the pus may flow out?

I was chief of youths
Because of my good manners.
Because my waist was soft.
I sang sweetly
When I was grinding millet
Or on the way to the well
Nobody's voice was sweeter than mine!
And in the arena
I sang the solos
Loud and clear
Like the *ogilo* bird
At sunset.

Now, Ocol says
I am a mere dog
A puppy,
A little puppy
Suffering from skin diseases.

Ocol says
He does not love me any more
Because I cannot play the guitar
And I do not like their stupid dance.
Because I despise the songs
They play at the ballroom dance
And I do not follow the steps of foreign songs
On the gramophone records.
And I cannot tune the radio
Because I do not hear
Swahili or Luganda.

4 The following syllabus is one designed for first year undergraduate students of English language and literature at an Egyptian university. Would such a syllabus be appropriate in the context in which you teach? What do you see as the advantages and disadvantages of such a syllabus?

Module One : The Middle Ages   (6 hours)
                                      i.e. 3 weeks

1 Introductory reminder of the relationship between literature and culture. Reference to social history, political history, economic history, the other arts, the state of language, etc.

2 *England at the beginning of the Middle Ages*
Text (1) p.p. 39–45

Main points : The Norman conquest
The feudal system
The Domesday Book
The Church : its architecture and
sphere of influence

Aids : Student handout
Visual(s) of church architecture
e.g. a Norman nave
a stained glass window
Audio: Excerpt from "The Middle Ages"

3 *England in the later Middle Ages*
Text (2) p.p. 72–80

Main points : The Language
Geoffrey Chaucer
The Wars of the Roses

Aids : Student handout
Audiovisual : Videotape of *Sir Gawain and the Green Knight* in the British Council's "Telling Tales" series. This is a 14th century poem which tells a story containing many traditional elements and the support material provided with the British Council videotape provides an introduction to the mediaeval period, e.g. the people and their dress, the musicians, dancing, fencing and other games, the food and decorations, celebrations, etc.

Reference: *A Concise History of England* – F. E. Halliday
Published : Thames & Hudson

Discussion

1 Would you agree that literature teaching might have a greater impact on a larger number of learners if it were possible to avoid testing?

2 How important do you think it is to test *plot* or *narrative* for a play, short story or novel? For what level of learner might this type of question become unnecessary?

3 In your experience, is it true to say that 'the more discursive the essay type the less it seems to be concerned with the text itself'?

4 If you ask learners to state the 'proposition' or 'message' of a poem what are you in fact testing? Do you consider such questions 'closed' or 'open'?

5 In your own teaching situation are learners able to 'comment on' features of lexis and syntax in a literary text? What sort of pre-training do you consider necessary for learners to be able to do such tasks? Do you believe that the study of a second literature should include some 'language based' work of this type?

6 Look again at the two part question on Romeo and Juliet, from the General Certificate of Secondary Education (p.104). In what way is this question type *different* from other question types discussed in this section? Do you consider it suitable or unsuitable for your own learners?

7.6
Conclusions; and a note about class size

The only main conclusion to this last section is that no real conclusions can be drawn. The examining of students on literature courses in not especially sophisticated and is in need of careful revision and reformulation. In many respects modes of testing have fallen behind developments in classroom practice and that is always a recipe for cynicism or at best demotivation among teachers and students. Especially in the context of second and foreign language teaching it is, in our view, necessary for literature examinations to become more language-based. A recent publication which will enable you to continue to explore some of the questions raised in this chapter is *Teaching Literature for Examinations* by Robert Protherough Open University Press, 1986.

The only conclusion to be drawn from this discussion of issues in the design and practice of a literature curriculum is that it is difficult to draw general conclusions when literature is taught in so many different contexts and in relation to different objectives. We are conscious, too, that we have omitted consideration of many other issues pertaining to the literature curriculum and its associated syllabi. For example, *class size* is a key factor and needs to be added to our list of 'criteria':

large classes ◄————————————————► small classes

Large classes, which in some contexts involve hundreds of students, obviously have implications both for text selection and for methodology. It could be that with large classes, intensive, text-based study becomes more difficult and transmissive information-based survey courses represent an easier alternative. We have also not devoted much space to teaching texts from world literatures in translation.

literature in translation ◄————————————► only 'authentic' texts in English (or the target language)

This prompts the question of whether major writers such as Dostoevsky should be included in the English syllabus. A further question is that of the relationship between literature and *other media*:

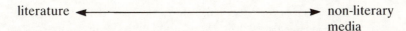

literature ◄──────────────────────► non-literary
                                        media

The question here is one of the extent to which it is useful or feasible to study literary texts in relation to other media. For example, viewing a film or video of a novel. Further questions are also prompted by courses which include a higher proportion of film and video material on the assumption that the ability to acquire *televisual literacy* – to see through and interpret the visual *and* linguistic message – is to be the most important of capacities to develop for the future. Readers will also be able to suggest further curricular clines.

   Our conclusion does perhaps reinforce above all the importance of where possible seeing curriculum design in terms of clines. There are curricular constraints of all kinds, such as prescribed texts, administrative limitations, such as class sizes, as well as ideological and cultural patterns which affect, for example, the nature of the relationship between teaching methodology, text and student. We hope to have demonstrated in this chapter, however, that clines are preferable to prescriptions and that teachers should always, under whatever constraints, attempt to negotiate their way through a literature curriculum. This will, in our view, better enable them to continue to ask what to teach, for how long, in what way and why.

8

Theories of reading

**8.0
Introduction**

During the nineteen eighties there has been a considerable growth of interest in theories of literature or in what is more generally termed literary or critical theory. Such interest has polarised debate concerning the teaching of literature in a number of universities, mainly in Europe and North America. In certain cases the debate has even acquired a certain notoriety, the most marked instance being the 'MacCabe affair' where a young lecturer with strong teaching and research interests in contemporary literary theory was refused tenure by the English department at the University of Cambridge, allegedly because such concerns were seen to be irrelevant to the teaching and study of English literature. Colin MacCabe subsequently became Professor of English at the University of Strathclyde and developed courses which parallel other courses in British universities such as Cardiff, Sussex, Nottingham and Southampton, where students engage in issues of literary theory and undertake courses in reading texts which are informed by recent work in critical theory. The development of critical theory in university courses has considerably expanded the horizons of English studies and has in turn been reflected in international conferences, important publications such as the Methuen/ Routledge *New Accents Series* (edited by Professor Terence Hawkes), journals such as *Textual Practice* and introductory guides to the field which explicate recent developments. An example of this explosion of interest can be provided by the estimated 70,000 copies of Terry Eagleton's *Literary Theory* (Blackwell, 1983) which have been sold since its publication – sales far in excess of the norm for an academic book.

It is, of course, impossible to represent in a book such as this, the range and depth of the field of literary theory and interested readers are encouraged to consult the titles suggested in our bibliography. In this chapter a necessarily selective approach is, therefore, taken. We select only those theories of literary text study which we consider to be particularly important and relevant to the study of literature; and we discuss in detail only those which we believe to be most relevant and enabling for the teaching of literature in a second or foreign language. For example, we give attention to feminist theories of literature for the simple reason that many students and teachers of literature throughout the world are women and therefore read and interpret texts as women. We also devote attention to colonial discourse and to literatures in English because of the undoubted importance of such issues to the study of literature in many post-colonial nations in many parts of the world. Additionally, theories of interpretation are important in our view. We have advocated that a high priority be given to language-based, student-centred approaches to literature teaching in this book, and the implications of such approaches are that the 'position' of the reader/interpreter will be an important factor and that the role of language in interpretation cannot be ignored.

The main areas in critical theory can be divided into three phases:

a pre-structuralist phase
a structuralist phase
a post-structuralist phase

A pre-structuralist phase will be the most familiar. It is a way of referring to the establishment of literary critical procedures in the early part of this century and is closely associated with the growth of literary studies as a discipline. In many respects it represents a challenge to older forms of historical or philological scholarship. For many students and teachers of literature it still represents the standard approach to the critical reading of texts. A pre-structural approach underlies the main orientation of this book. The structuralist phase was particularly dominant during the 1950s and 60s; the post-structuralist phase has been dominant during the late 1970s and 80s. It should be pointed out, however, that many of the relevant theories originated in Eastern Europe and in France, and that neither structuralist nor post-structuralist phases have had any serious impact on literary studies elsewhere in the world until the last ten to fifteen years. It is important to recognise that these three phases are less distinct than this account or the diagram on the following page indicate, and that there are, of course, in actual critical practice several areas of overlap between the phases.

A key characteristic of literary/critical theory is the posing of fundamental questions about the nature of literature and about the processes involved in reading and interpreting texts. Here are some examples:

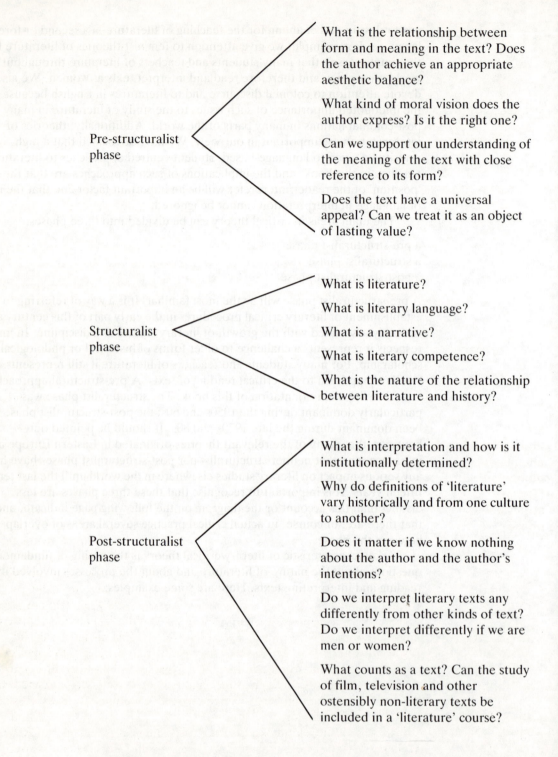

Pre-structuralist phase

What is the relationship between form and meaning in the text? Does the author achieve an appropriate aesthetic balance?

What kind of moral vision does the author express? Is it the right one?

Can we support our understanding of the meaning of the text with close reference to its form?

Does the text have a universal appeal? Can we treat it as an object of lasting value?

Structuralist phase

What is literature?

What is literary language?

What is a narrative?

What is literary competence?

What is the nature of the relationship between literature and history?

Post-structuralist phase

What is interpretation and how is it institutionally determined?

Why do definitions of 'literature' vary historically and from one culture to another?

Does it matter if we know nothing about the author and the author's intentions?

Do we interpret literary texts any differently from other kinds of text? Do we interpret differently if we are men or women?

What counts as a text? Can the study of film, television and other ostensibly non-literary texts be included in a 'literature' course?

Even from this oversimplified account we can see that literary theory considers both the instrinsic and extrinsic relations within which literature exists. But the fundamental questions which are posed within literary theory constitute a *challenge* to ways of reading and teaching literature which have been prominent in this century and which continue to be prominent in many institutions internationally. In other words, a challenge is posed both to ways of close reading and to the place of background information in the reading of literature. For example:

Existing pre-structuralist model	*Challenge to assumptions*
e.g. Text intrinsic, close verbal study.	What *is* literary language? How is it different from other kinds of language? Can we discuss narratives without an explicit account of the formal components of narrative organisation?
e.g. Extrinsic, contextual 'background' study. The philosophical and cultural assumptions of liberal humanism.	Does it matter if we know little about the author of a literature text?
	How is the representation of women in the text managed? Does our interpretation of the text differ if we are men or women? Are there universal meanings? Can texts be interpreted independently of political ideologies? Whose account of relevant background do we study?

**8.1
Practical criticism and liberal humanism (The pre-structuralist phase)**

Practical criticism (also known as new criticism) is a strategy of close verbal reading of texts. It is at the core of pre-structuralist criticism. The aim is to explore the relationship between *what* is said in a literary text and *how* it is said. According to many practical critics, the *what* and the *how* will be mutually supportive in literary texts and attention is therefore devoted to showing how different formal techniques of writing serve to underscore or 'express' meaning. There is normally discussion of the *tone* of the writing, that is the appropriateness of the disposition of patterns of language (especially sound patterns) to the subject matter, for the tone of the text should bear an organic relation to the content of the whole work. And there is also normally consideration of the *balance* achieved in the text. Great writers do not present arguments for a particular point of view, for that is the remit of the politician or journalist; instead they rather seek to resolve opposing points of view into an aesthetic balance. This artistic integrity results from the ability to balance discordant ideas and to present them in a formally and linguistically controlled way to the reader. At the same time an attendant vision of balance and order, in which extreme or opposing views are reconciled, represents an expression of liberal humanist ideology.

In America this kind of criticism is associated with the names of Rene Wellek, Cleanth Brooks, John Crowe Ransome and Robert Penn Warren; in Britain the most prominent name is that of F. R. Leavis who practised close verbal readings of both poetry and fiction and for whom 'balance', 'integrity' and 'tone' were always profoundly a matter of *moral* vision on the part of the writer. (Other influential British critics in this tradition are I. A. Richards and L. C. Knights.)

Practical criticism has been a very influential practice in the teaching of literature in many parts of the world. For many teachers and students it has provided a counterbalance to a more historically-based or survey approach to the study of literature. Although it is a pedagogical approach which works best with small groups where there can be intensive question and answer sessions, close reading can be demonstrated by the teacher in more formal contexts such as a lecture, where the teacher can present his or her own close reading of a text. As we hope to show, practical criticism can be a valuable approach to the words on the page and to the verbal particularities of specific texts. It is, however, a practice which has certain pedagogic weaknesses. It is also a practice whose foundations have been fundamentally challenged by much work in contemporary critical theory.

We begin this section by examining a short narrative by the American novelist and short story writer Ernest Hemingway.

The first matador got the horn through his sword hand and the crowd hooted him out. The second matador slipped, and the bull caught him through the belly and he hung on to the horn with one hand and held the other tight against the place, and the bull rammed him wham against the barrier and the horn came out, and he lay in the sand, and then got up like crazy drunk and tried to slug the men carrying him away and yelled for his sword, but he fainted. The kid came out and had to kill five bulls because you can't have more than three matadors, and the last bull he was so tired he could hardly get the sword in. He could barely lift his arm. He tried five times and the crowd was quiet because it was a good bull and it looked like him or the bull and then he finally made it. He sat down in the sand and puked and they held a cape over him while the crowd hollered and threw things down into the bull-ring.

As we have pointed out, an aim of much practical criticism would be to undertake a *close reading* of this text. Normally, this close reading would be carefully regulated by the teacher who would prompt consideration of some of the following features:

How does the writer's choice of language express the meanings of the narrative? (form and meaning; expression)

What is the tone of the writing? (tone; feeling)

Is there a *balance* to the text, (balance; integrity)
(i.e. a balance between the text's form
and the integrity of the writer's vision;
a balance in that the writer *resolves*
opposing ideas or positions in his
world view.)

Among the 'answers' to these questions which the teacher is trying to elicit will be responses to the following textual features:

the effect of the repetition of the conjunction *and*; the particular tone it communicates;

the effect of point of view in the story; what is revealed by the narrative being written entirely in the third person; the relationship between point of view and the meaning of the story.

the tone of items such as 'slug'; 'hooked'; 'belly'; 'puked'; 'hollered'; the closeness of these words and other features of the story to the *spoken* language; the effect of a corresponding gain in immediacy.

One conclusion to be drawn is that there is no clear resolution to the action, no overt moral to be extracted; the author presents the narrative *impersonally* and seemingly without judgement or evaluation. There is little evidence of balance between opposing ideas, little effort at resolution on the part of the writer and no obvious connection between the point of view adopted and the potential meaning of the narrative.

One of the advantages of this kind of practical critical exposition is that students' attention is directed towards certain textual features, and that they are thus prompted to think about the *how* as well as the *what*, about the form of the text as well as what it says. This kind of close reading contrasts with the overall survey mention of texts and writers in which a range of texts is set against the context of general historical, socio-cultural or literary developments.

A pedagogical disadvantage, however, is that there is no clear *method* to practical criticism. It is hard to discern *how* students come to learn how to recognise tone, or work out for themselves the relationship between narrative form and literary meaning. It is likely that practical criticism teaching procedures are tightly controlled by the teacher, either in the form of directed questions accompanied by teacher-led commentary, or in the form of a demonstration exposition in a lecture or seminar. There are few explicit procedures presented which students can discover and implement for themselves, and one result is that students may resort to learning critical insights at second hand either from the exposition of their teacher or from recommended books of criticism. They may thus come to learn the judgements required of them or at least learn to play a critical game sufficiently well to pass an examination. Of course, the brightest and most capable students develop independent critical skills and acquire an impressive literary competence, but there are many others who only go through the motions, pass examinations but never take any active critical interest or engage in reading literature for themselves. One view which is regularly expressed is that practical criticism is best suited to mother tongue literature classes, whereas language-based approaches are better suited to contexts in which literature is read in a second or foreign language, though others would point to the growing employment of language-based and stylistic procedures in mother tongue literature classes too.

8.1.1
Stylistics and
language-based
approaches

Stylistics shares a number of presuppositions with practical critical approaches in that both are directed to a close, detailed consideration of the verbal structure of texts although there is less concern with an evaluation of texts. The aims and procedures of stylistics have been discussed at 2.8 and 6.4 and there are numerous examples of pre-stylistic language-based teaching procedures throughout the book. From this we hope that the differences between these approaches and those associated with practical criticism will be apparent. The main orientation of stylistics and of language-based approaches remains pre-structuralist.

Here are some language-based approaches which we suggest may be appropriate to a teaching of the Hemingway story. Such approaches aim to offer a more systematic discovery procedure, more explicit attention to language, to be more activity-centred, and to allow students greater pedagogic space to work on and work out what the text might mean to them:

1 **a text-completion exercise** in which students are invited to a) select a title for the story b) supply a *coda* in which the point of the narrative is evaluated for the reader. Both activities require interpretation on the part of the student or group/pair working on the exercise.

2 **a prediction exercise** in which students are invited to anticipate the events befalling the third matador after reading the outcomes affecting the first two matadors.

3 **a cloze activity** in which, prior to reading, words which have (in the judgement of the teacher) a key structural role in signification are deleted and a list of alternatives is presented to students for substitution. One example here might be the words *hooted* and *puked*. Examination of alternatives and of the choices actually entered into by the author present interesting opportunities on the part of students for involvement with the text.

4 **a jumbled sentence activity** in which students are invited to recombine the markedly co-ordinating conjunction-bound style of the story into short main clauses. The effects of deleting the *and* conjunction are examined and explored by comparison with the text which Hemingway produced.

5 **re-writing exercises** which involve either a shift in point of view or a 're-registration' in which the story is re-written in a style designed to serve different and contrasting registerial functions. For example, students could be invited to re-write the story from the point of view of the boy matador or from the 'position' of either of the two matadors who have failed in the earlier attempts. Re-registration activities can involve the student in producing alternative, contrasting but thematically related texts such as writing a newspaper report of the bullfight, or designing an itinerary for a visit to a bullfight such as may appear in a holiday brochure or an historical account of the signficance of bullfighting in Spanish culture. In all such exercises, the aim would be to draw attention to the specifically literary qualities of the Hemingway piece and to explore how language is used for purposes of narrative shaping.

8.2
Narrative models   Language-based approaches to literary texts aim to supply awareness of the way language works in specific texts. Theories of reading literature, especially those associated with its structuralist phase, also demonstrate that literature comprises specific *structures*, or patterns of formal organisation which inform literature, which correspond to those established in other texts, literary and

non-literary, and which have to be internalised, often as a result of direct teaching, in order for literary competence to be developed.

One of the most important of these structures is *narrative* structure and much work in literary theory has concentrated on describing the linguistic and semantic organisation of narrative. Research into narrative structure has demonstrated that there are three main components in a well-formed narrative:

Setting
Complication
Resolution

Setting refers to the *when, where, who* and *in what circumstances* of narrative, referring the reader or listener of a narrative to the relevant characters, their background to the physical and temporal settings for their actions and to the reasons for the initial narrative incitement. *Complication* refers to the plot of the narrative, marked by a series of events in temporal sequence, usually resulting in some kind of problem. The *resolution* is the part of the narrative concerned with the outcomes of the plot and how the main characters are affected. To these categories can be added an *abstract* (found in titles to stories, or in the prefaces common in jokes ('did you hear the one about . . . ?') and a *coda* or *evaluation* (see 8.1.1 above) in which the particular 'point' or moral of the story is pointed up.

As far as the Hemingway narrative is concerned, such a framework supplies some basic awareness and some terms which help us to begin talking about the text, its particular structure and the relationship between the way it is written and the kind of meanings it conveys. For example, there is a lack of evaluation and no abstract to this story (it has no title) and even the *resolution* only 'resolves' things on the plane of mere action as we learn little of the boy's state of mind. It is in more senses than one a minimalist narrative, and as with many narratives written during the modernist period (approximately 1900–1930 in Western Europe and North America) is essentially indeterminate. It does not have a proper ending in which events are resolved and presented to the reader in the form of some kind of moral judgement. In terms of practical criticism the text lacks an appropriate sense of aesthetic balance. On one level, the structural indeterminacy parallels a sense that the boy (the 'kid' matador) does not know whether what he has 'achieved' is positive or negative; on another level, it may embody a sense of confusion and uncertainty. Structural description of narrative may, however, enable us to talk explicitly about narrative form, and tied to language-based approaches provides access to the text for students in a way not normally allowed by the techniques or procedures of practical criticism.

8.3
The death of the author

One of the objections raised against structuralism by traditional literary critics is that it takes the *life* out of literary appreciation. Instead of being concerned with how a literary text renders an author's experience of life and allows us access to human meanings, the structuralist is only interested in mechanical formal relationships, such as the components of a narrative, and treats the literary text as if it were a scientific object.

Modern literary theorists would in turn challenge these assumptions as being in themselves partial and limited. Much traditional criticism could be said to be *liberal humanist*, originating from a balanced position of moderation and commitment to an essentially unchanging order of things. Such a philosophy will scrutinise texts for expressions of an unchanging view of human life and feeling. Its proponents will therefore seek the 'felt life' in the expression of an author and explore how the author's use of technique services such expression. Those writers are preferred who can resolve tension and conflict into a balanced moderate position and who can in the process release meanings which are not bound by any particular time or place but are *universal* in import. At the centre of this philosophy is the *author*. The great author transcends the particulars of his or her own life and history and speaks to us across time and space in terms we can understand because we are human. Modern literary theorists argue that the value attached to this kind of writing and to the author who produces it is itself a theory of literature which can be challenged and shown to be limited to a particular critical practice. Critical practices change from one period of history to another. This particular critical practice is, though still powerful at the present time, limited to a view of literature (and literature teaching) prevalent in the period from 1940–1980 and is gradually being replaced by other theories of literature and literature teaching. One particular challenge to this orthodoxy comes in the form of assertions of the 'death of the author'.

The author is powerful within many literary cultures and appears in many institutionalised forms. For example:

English Poetry from Hardy to Larkin	(an option course for undergraduate English students)
The Auden Generation	(a book title)
The James Joyce Quarterly	(an academic journal)
The Life and Works of John Donne	(a course or a book or a lecture title)

An outcome of this is that what an author says about his or her own work is recorded, stored and often used to bolster criticism of that author's work. Writers themselves unite their person and their work through letters, diaries, memoirs, etc. Readers are trained and taught to take very seriously the statements made by an author.

French literary theorists such as Roland Barthes and Michel Foucault in particular have argued for the death of the author. They make two main points:

a) That the notion of 'the author' is a construction of a bourgeois capitalist phase in Western European and North American history. They point out that before the Renaissance these same societies favoured the anonymity of the author, and that in many societies in different parts of the world the idea of the author has not even been born, since literature is created anonymously or in a group or by the means of oral transmission from one group of people to another.

b) that the notion of the author serves to minimise the role of the reader and to constrain interpretation. The reader has to interpret the text within the limits set for it by the author.

The following extract from a famous essay by Roland Barthes entitled 'The Death of the Author' concludes with a statement much quoted within the context of modern critical theory:

'The birth of the reader must be at the cost of the death of the author.'

> No doubt it has always been that way. As soon as a fact is *narrated* no longer with a view to acting directly on reality but intransitively, that is to say, finally outside of any function other than that of the very practice of the symbol itself, this disconnection occurs, the voice loses its origin, the author enters into his own death, writing begins. The sense of this phenomenon, however, has varied; in ethnographic societies the responsibility for a narrative is never assumed by a person but by a mediator, shaman or relator whose 'performance'—the mastery of the narrative code–may possibly be admired but never his 'genius'. The author is a modern figure, a product of our society insofar as, emerging from the Middle Ages with English empiricism, French rationalism and the personal faith of the Reformation, it discovered the prestige of the individual, of, as it is more nobly put, the 'human person'. It is thus logical that in literature it should be this positivism, the epitome and culmination of capitalist ideology, which has attached the greatest importance to the 'person' of the author. The *author* still reigns in histories of literature, biographies of writers, interviews, magazines, as in the very consciousness of men of letters anxious to unite their person and their work through diaries and memoirs. The image of literature to be found in ordinary culture is tyrannically centred on the author, his person, his life, his tastes, his passions, while criticism still consists for the most part in saying that Baudelaire's work is the failure of Baudelaire the man, Van Gogh's his madness, Tchaikovsky's his vice. The *explanation* of a work is always sought in the man or woman who produced it, as if it were always in the end, through the more or less transparent allegory of the fiction, the voice of a single person, the *author* 'confiding' in us.
>
> (from 'The Death of the Author' by Roland Barthes from *Manteia V* 1968 Basil Blackwell Ltd.)

In other words, if we accept the death of the author or at least if we accept that the author's control over the text is limited, then the text is available for more plural interpretation; readers are at liberty to read more meanings more variously and according to their own predilections, ideologies, political convictions and so on. In classroom terms, theorists such as Barthes would argue, the student is freed to read more into a text without feeling constrained to take into account what an author or a teacher teaching 'the life and works of the author' may limit it to mean. The birth of the reader must be at the cost of the death of the author.

One example of the kind of issues in interpretation raised by author-centred criticism and by attempts to deconstruct such criticism might be given as follows: what would be the effect on our interpretation of the Hemingway story if Hemingway himself had written in a letter to his publisher that he intended his story to have a political message? The bullfight symbolises the kind of ritualistic violence encountered daily during the Spanish Civil War and increasingly so by children. The boy represents the sudden maturity forced upon children who were 'used' by the Republican forces as they became desperate owing to the deaths of many adult soldiers.

We should consider this hypothetical situation and examine the kinds of processes of interpretation such information would promote. We should also consider whether students are advantaged by *not* having such information because it may limit their capacity and motivation to work out their own meanings from this story.

Another consideration is whether male and female students interpret the story differently. It can be argued that this is a male-centred story with exclusively male characters and even a masculine language of basic demotic speech ('puked', 'hollered') which could suggest a story written for men and from which women readers are excluded or marginalised. This topic is the subject of our next section.

Questions for discussion

1 Select five narratives which you teach regularly. (These can be either stories or narrative poems.) How many of them are standard, unmarked narratives in so far as they have a *setting, complication* and *resolution.* How many contain a *coda?* Do you teach narratives which lack a *resolution* and/or *coda?* If so, why? If not, why not?

2 In your teaching of poetry how often do you find yourself using terms such as 'practical critical balance', 'harmony', 'resolution' and 'wholeness' or 'completeness'? Do you value poems which do not conform to such aesthetic notions?

   What are the implications of your preferences for what your students view as successful poems?

3 Would you accept that reading, interpreting and teaching literature can or cannot be connected with ideological positions? To what extent do you consciously or unconsciously convey a liberal humanist ideology in:
   a) the texts you teach and the critical aesthetic terms you use?
   b) the use of group work in which participants are invited to reach consensus?
   c) the practice of certain methodological procedures of discussion such as 'forum' or related practices (see 6.7)?

   What definite advantages do you see in teaching strategies which support a liberal humanist approach to literary study?

4 Examine your notes or handouts or teaching materials on the texts you teach. What proportion of your notes are devoted to:
   a) the life of the author?
   b) what the author said about his or her work?
   c) what the critics have said about an individual author?

   Do you accept that your class discussion of these texts will be limited by such information? What would be lost (if anything) if you did not have such information?

8.4 Reading as a woman

It's queer how out of touch with truth women are. They live in a world of their own, and there has never been anything like it, and never can be. It is too beautiful altogether, and if they were to set it up it would go to pieces before the first sunset.

Some confounded fact we men have been living contentedly with ever since the day creation would start up and knock the whole thing over.

(from *Heart of Darkness* by Joseph Conrad)

One does not have to be a feminist to recognise that language is man-made. The power of men within social and institutional structures is reflected in the ways in which even the word man is institutionalised within key phrases in the English language which are encountered in daily social uses. For example: *odd-man-out; the man in the street; the average man; man hours; manslaughter; man-made; overmanning; manhandle;* and so on. Male dominance is also regularly encoded in grammatical patterns such as:

The student who takes these examinations will find that he needs to prepare well.

which deletes the possibility of students being female or rather which assumes *male* as the normal or unmarked feature. When opposed semantically to male it is noticeable too how a female term will also attract negative or unflattering associations. In the following oppositions, for example, the female term contracts extra connotations of sexual promiscuity which do not attach to the male term:

Sir   Madam   (+ owner of a brothel: procuress)
Master   Mistress   (+ an adulterous lover)
Lord   Lady   (+ prostitute 'lady of the night')

Reading texts as a woman is an experience in which one finds a particular kind of role or position constructed in and through the language system. Many students of English literature are women, and it is important that they read with an awareness of how they are positioned. Feminist movements within modern literary theory serve to challenge the orthodox or stereotype role created for them.

There is insufficient space in this section to illustrate any critical theory in detail but two brief examples may serve to show what is involved in reading with a feminist critical awareness. Necessarily much feminist theory has been concerned with the way female characters are presented in drama and fiction and with challenging the points of views of authors and critics (usually male). In the following poem reading as a woman involves a consideration of linguistic choices and of how these embody a particular view of women and of women as a subject for poetry.

A Song

Aske me no more where Jove bestowes,
When June is past, the fading rose:
For in your beauties orient deepe,
These Flowers as in their causes sleepe.

Aske me no more whither doe stray
The golden Atomes of the day:
For in pure love heaven did prepare
Those powders to inrich your haire.

Aske me no more whither doth hast
The Nightingale when May is past:
For in your sweet dividing throat
She winters and keepes warme her note.

Aske me no more where those starres light,
That downewards fall in dead of night:
For in your eyes they sit, and there,
Fixed become as in their sphere.

Aske me no more if East or West,
The Phenix builds her spicy nest:
For unto you at last shee flies,
And in your fragrant bosome dyes.

Thomas Carew (1595–1639)

Here one of the points made by reading approaches from a feminist perspective would be that the woman, to whom the 'song' is addressed, is constructed not as a whole but rather as a collection of parts. The woman is described in terms of 'haire', 'throat', 'eyes', 'bosome', that is, in terms of parts of the body. The effect may be said to be a depersonalising one, relegating the view of the loved woman to a list of physical features or attributes when the aim is to try to bestow praise. The view of woman here is a conventional one and, feminists point out, has become conventionalised so that it is now a standard common sense view in popular fiction (especially romances), in advertisements and even to some extent in the language of today (e.g. 'an old bag', 'a blonde', 'a bit of skirt', etc.)

Here is another representation of a woman in a poem. The angle of representation in this case is different and involves metaphors and analogies which may appear unusual at least on first reading:

Her lips are red hot
Like glowing charcoal,
She resembles the wild cat
That has dipped its mouth in blood,
Her mouth is like raw yaws
It looks like an open ulcer
Like the mouth of a fiend.
Tina dusts powder on her face
And it looks so pale.
She resembles the wizard
Getting reading for the midnight dance
She dusts the ash-dirt all over her face.
And when a little sweat
Begins to appear on her body
She looks like the guinea fowl!

Here two woman are compared but neither seems to be represented in the kinds of eulogistic terms of Carew's 'Song' (above). Two contrasting types emerge: one more traditional and compared to more elemental natural things (charcoal, blood, the wild cat, raw yaws, an ulcer), the other more artificial, and whose actions are analogised to or described with reference to those transient, less elemental things (powder, ash-dirt, the guinea fowl, the wizard). The overall intention here appears to be to produce distinctly unflattering pictures.

The poem is written by Okot P'Bitek, a Ugandan whose chosen linguistic medium is English (see 7.5.4). P'Bitek is the author of two of the best known African narrative poems in English *Song of Lawino* and *Song of Ocol*. One of the recurring themes of P'Bitek's poetry is the opposition between traditional and indigenous African cultures and the culture imported into Africa by Western European and American colonisers and usually left behind in a post-colonial situation by means of aid programmes. In the above poem, which is in fact an extract from the much longer *Song of Lawino*, P'Bitek juxtaposes in the actions of the two women two opposing cultures: the traditional Acoli woman who has no knowledge of Western modes of behaviour and a woman who imitates foreign customs, here in particular in the wearing of make-up. Both are rivals for the narrator's affections.

The poet achieves some success in putting before the reader some of the dilemmas of identity faced in a situation where choices are polarised between different life-styles and cultures. But the narrative perspective is a man's perspective and the particular situation dramatised is that of two women competing for a man's interest. Reading the text from a differently 'gendered' perspective may point to the following: how the text oversimplifies the position by a process of caricature and by viewing the women as, as it were, in the grip of cultural forces they do not fully understand; by narrating from an exclusive 'male' position which allows no insight into the women's own feelings or viewpoints; by selecting poetic comparisons and analogies which reduce and demean the respective identities of the two 'opponents'.

The two examples considered in this section illustrate how *all* readers need to be alert to male-centredness. Often readers are not particularly alert to the ways in which women are 'represented' by male writers and it is important to challenge and deconstruct any assumption that a masculine point of view is a normal or naturalised one.

In the following section another critical perspective is examined: in this case it is the assumption that the normal naturalised view of the world in developing countries is one which is Western European and capitalist in terms of race and ideology.

8.5 Reading in a post-colonial situation

Reading as a woman can frequently involve reading from a marginalised position. The situation has given rise to feminist critical theory, fuller attention to writing by women and to university and college courses which examine the representation of women in literature. Reading in a post-colonial situation creates parallel positions for the reader. In any country newly independent from colonial rule the literature studied can, for example, continue to be that produced by the colonising people. In a country such as Kenya, for example, British English literature continued to dominate the literature curriculum through the nineteen seventies even though independence was granted to Kenya in 1961, and it is only in the last few years that significant changes have occurred in the selection of texts set for study. The result is, of course, that the reader in such a context feels marginalised and that his or her interests are remote from those central to many of the texts studied. These issues here are greater than those examined at 7.3 where cross-cultural reading difficulties were explored. According to literary theorists there is a more fundamental encounter with what has been termed *colonial discourses*.

Work on colonial discourse is largely associated with the name of the literary theorist Edward Said. There is insufficient space for us to explore his ideas here, but in a ground-breaking book entitled *Orientalism*, published in 1976 he shows how Western scholars and writers in the tradition of Western literature have constructed an image of the Orient as peopled by lazy, deceitful and irrational individuals. Said deconstructs this image as untrue, and shows it to be a historically constructed discourse of the West and thus limited and partial.

> As momentous, generally important issues face the world—issues involving nuclear destruction, catastrophically scarce resources, unprecedented human demands for equality, justice, and economic parity—popular caricatures of the Orient are exploited by politicians whose source of ideological supply is not only the half-literate technocrat but the superliterate Orientalist. The legendary Arabists in the State Department warn of Arab plans to take over the world. The perfidious Chinese, half-naked Indians, and passive Muslims are described as vultures for 'our' largesse and are damned when 'we lose them' to communism, or to their unregenerate Oriental instincts: the difference is scarcely significant.
>
> These contemporary Orientalist attitudes flood the press and the popular mind. Arabs, for example, are thought of as camel-riding, terroristic, hook-nosed, venal lechers whose undeserved wealth is an affront to real civilization. Always there lurks the assumption that although the Western consumer belongs to a numerical minority, he is entitled either to own or to expend (or both) the majority of the world resources. Why? Because he, unlike the Oriental, is a true human being. No better instance exists today of what Anwar Abdel Malek calls 'the hegemonism of possessing minorities' and anthropocentrism allied with Europocentrism: a white middle-class Westerner believes it his human prerogative not only to manage the nonwhite world but also to own it, just because by definition 'it' is not quite as human as 'we' are. There is no purer example than this of dehumanized thought.
>
> In a sense the limitations of Orientalism are, as I said earlier, the limitations that follow upon disregarding, essentializing, denuding the humanity of another culture, people, or geographical region.
>
> (from *Orientalism* by Edward Said 1976 Penguin)

There are numerous examples of how colonial discourses are presented in literary text. One particularly transparent case is that of Joseph Conrad's *Heart of Darkness*, a novel which specifically addresses itself to the intersection of European and non-European cultures in the context of colonial encounters. Here is an extract from a part of the novel in which the narrator reports an initial contact with the indigenous peoples of the country (at that time the Belgium Congo) but specifically from the point of view of the European narrator:

> We were wanderers on prehistoric earth, on an earth that wore the aspect of an unknown planet. We could have fancied ourselves the first of men taking

possession of an accursed inheritance, to be subdued at the cost of profound anguish and of excessive toil. But suddenly, as we struggled round a bend, there would be a glimpse of rush walls, of peaked grass-roofs, a burst of yells, a whirl of black limbs, a mass of hands clapping, of feet stamping, of bodies swaying, of eyes rolling, under the droop of heavy and motionless foliage. The steamer toiled along slowly on the edge of a black and incomprehensible frenzy. The prehistoric man was cursing us, praying to us, welcoming us – who could tell? We were cut off from the comprehension of our surroundings: we glided past like phantoms, wondering and secretly appalled, as sane men would be before an enthusiastic outbreak in a madhouse. We could not understand because we were too far and could not remember because we were travelling in the night of first ages, of those ages that are gone, leaving hardly a sign – and no memories.

The earth seemed unearthly. We are accustomed to look upon the shackled form of a conquered monster, but there – there you could look at a thing monstrous and free. It was unearthly, and the men were – No, they were not inhuman. Well, you know, that was the worst of it – this suspicion of their not being inhuman. It would come slowly to one. They howled and leaped, and spun, and made horrid faces; but what thrilled you was just the thought of their humanity – like yours – the thought of your remote kinship with this wild and passionate uproar. Ugly. Yes, it was ugly enough; but if you were man enough you would admit to yourself that there was in you just the faintest trace of a response to the terrible frankness of that noise, a dim suspicion of there being a meaning in it which you – you so remote from the night of first ages – could comprehend.

The view taken of the indigenous peoples corresponds to certain preconceived stereotypes of blacks as uncivilised savages. Such people are described as barely human and always a source of mystery, capable of producing barely decipherable meanings. Their 'monstrous' actions can only be equated with madness ('an enthusiastic outbreak in a madhouse') and the only available sanity is invested in the 'civilised' outsider seeking to comprehend and to control, and who presumes the 'we' he refers to includes in his audience substantial numbers of people with the same presuppositions and viewpoints. More particularly, too, a view of history is presented which has white Europeans at its centre and which allows of no history independent of or outside a European history. It is, of course, a narrator who transmits this version of reality and it would be naive to equate such views with those of Conrad, the author of the novel. But the mediation of viewpoint is more subtle and correspondingly less transparent than the views (along not dissimilar lines) conveyed directly by this character, a British woman, in the novel *Scorpion Orchid* by the Malaysian writer Lloyd Fernando:

"Thank God the British are here. The Malays are in their *kampungs*, the Chinese own all the business, and the Indians are in the rubber estates. And the Eurasians — not half-castes, Roger, or mulattoes, unless you want to lose friends and influence people — the Eurasians sit in their cricket club and imitate us, rather poorly, actually. You see, they have nothing in common. If we left tomorrow, there'd be such a lovely bit of mayhem that we'd have to come back to keep the peace. No. I'm afraid we have to grin and bear it — the white man's burden. I mean," she added lightly.

(from *Scorpion Orchid* by Lloyd Fernando 1968 H.E.B. Heinemann)

As we have seen in 7.4, there has been in recent years a rapid growth of literature in English in post-colonial contexts. In countries such as India, Nigeria, Kenya, Malaysia and the Phillipines a rich literature exists which is characterised by its own national identity and which represents a challenge to Western colonial discourses. These are second-language literatures in so far as the writers are not writing in their mother tongue (which may be Igbo, Tagalog, Hindi, Malay or whatever); instead English is chosen as a creative medium. This does not mean, however, that British English or American English – the language of the colonial occupiers – is the model according to which these literatures are produced. Instead the defining characteristics are more likely to be the local Englishes of the different nations, and it is thus a particular expressive use of Kenyan English or Malay English or Indian English in which literary texts are written within these cultures.

Such literatures also have different ideological inflections. One objective is to seek ways of rewriting history from local perspectives. Another is to fashion themes which are specific to the realities of developing countries and to create characters who represent particular perspectives on life in those countries. Yet another is to explore national identities in the context of newly emerging nationhoods:

> The classical culture of this region [i.e. Southeast Asia] has remained dormant through not being drawn upon during more than two centuries of colonial occupation . . . Why shouldn't local writers in English re-examine this deep and varied past and put it to fresh purposes? . . . If mythic power is lacking in Malaysian literature in English as yet, it is not for want of traditions or history apart from the colonial . . . [The present is] profoundly complicated by western norms . . . [so the aim is not the] restoration of a bygone, relatively homogeneous Asian cultural order, but rather to retrieve and recast items of a great and neglected heritage in the light of the complexities of the second half of the twentieth century.''

> Lloyd Fernando

Questions for discussion

1 The following passage is an extract from a short story by the American writer Charlotte Perkins Gilman (1869–1935) and entitled *The Yellow Wallpaper*. The story recounts the experiences of a woman who is suffering a nervous breakdown. Read the following extract and consider, in particular, the possible significance of the room and the wallpaper both in the life of the 'narrator' and for a general meaning of the story as a whole: (John is the woman's husband)

> I get unreasonably angry with John sometimes. I'm sure I never used to be sensitive. I think it is due to this nervous condition.
>
> But John says if I feel so I shall neglect proper self-control; so I take plans to control myself—before him, at least, and that makes me very tired.
>
> I don't like our room a bit. I wanted one downstairs that opened onto the piazza and had roses all over the window, and such pretty old-fashioned chintz hangings! But John would not hear of it.
>
> He said there was only one window and not room for two beds, and no near room for him if he took another.

He is very careful and loving, and hardly lets me stir without special direction.

I have a schedule prescription for each hour in the day; he takes all care from me, and so I feel basely ungrateful not to value it more.

He said he came here solely on my account, that I was to have perfect rest and all the air I could get. "Your exercise depends on your strength, my dear," said he, "and your food somewhat on your appetite: but air you absorb all the time." So we took the nursery at the top of the house.

It is a big, airy room, the whole floor nearly, with windows that look all ways, and air and sunshine galore. It was nursery first, and then playroom and gymnasium, I should judge, for the windows are barred for little children, and there are rings and things on the walls.

The paint and paper look as if a boys' school had used it. It is stripped off—the paper—in great patches all around the head of my bed, about as far as I can reach, and in a great place on the other side of the room low down. I never saw a worse paper in my life. One of these sprawling, flamboyant patterns committing every artistic sin.

It is dull enough to confuse the eye in following, pronounced enough constantly to irritate and provoke study, and when you follow the lame uncertain curves for a little distance they suddenly commit suicide—plunge off at outrageous angles, destroy themselves in unheard-of contradictions.

The colour is repellent, almost revolting: a smouldering unclean yellow, strangely faded by the slow-turning sunlight. It is a dull yet lurid orange in some places, a sickly sulphur tint in others.

No wonder the children hated it! I should hate it myself if I had to live in this room long.

There comes John, and I must put this away—he hates to have me write a word.

Do you think your male and female students would reach different interpretations of

a) the reactions and behaviour of the woman?

b) the significance of the room and the wallpaper?

Does this seem to you to be the kind of story you could teach to an exclusively male class? If yes, why? If not, why not? What balance do you try to establish in your classes between

a) texts which are narrated from a woman's point of view?

b) texts which are narrated from a man's point of view?

c) texts by women writers?

d) texts by men writers?

2 From the above extract it is hard to disentangle whether the woman is confined or believes herself to be confined to the room, whether the confinement is more properly a symbol for the restrictions of a marriage, or whether everything can be reduced to a particularly neurotic state of mind. (Much will probably depend here on whether you are reading the text as a man or as a woman.)

In the poem 'Song' by Thomas Carew (see p.187) the actual form of the poem is a tightly regulated one of aa/bb. How many of those poems you teach which are love poems written by a man to a woman enshrine the women in such confined patterns? Is this practice as disabling as that of only describing a woman in terms of physical bodily parts? Would you draw attention to such matters in your teaching or do you consider such interpretations of confinement of women by men to be unreasonable and invalid?

3   The following is a cloze exercise (see p.80). On this occasion, however, the exercise is specifically targeted to assist students to understand how women are positioned in society, both in general and in the particular case of the nineteenth century novel *Middlemarch* from which it is extracted. In the example the following items are deleted: *pronouns; reflexives* (e.g. himself/ herself); *names;* key gender-marking words such as *Mr/Mrs, boy/girl*, etc. Ask your students and/or try yourself to insert the appropriate items. What does the exercise tell you?

Two hours later, _____ was seated in an inner room or boudoir of a handsome apartment in the Via Sistina.

I am sorry to add that _____ was sobbing bitterly, with such abandonment to this relief of an oppressed heart as a _____ habitually controlled by pride on _____ own account and thoughtfulness for others will sometimes allow _____ when _____ feels securely alone. And _____ Casaubon was certain to remain away for some time at the Vatican.

Yet _____ had no distinctly shapen grievance that _____ could state even to _____ and in the midst of _____ confused thought and passion, the mental act that was struggling forth into clearness was a self-accusing cry that _____ feeling of desolation was the fault of _____ own spiritual poverty.

_____ had married the _____ of _____ choice, and with the advantage over most that had contemplated _____ marriage chiefly as the beginning of new duties: from the very first _____ had thought of _____ Casaubon as having a mind so much above _____ own, that _____ must often be claimed by studies which _____ could not entirely share; moreover, after the brief narrow experience of _____ girlhood _____ was beholding Rome, the city of visible history, where the past of a whole hemisphere seems moving in funeral procession with strange ancestral images and trophies gathered from afar.

But this stupendous fragmentariness heightened the dreamlike strangeness of _____ bridal life. _____ had now been five weeks in Rome, and in the kindly mornings when autumn and winter seemed to go hand in hand like a happy aged couple one of whom would presently survive in chiller loneliness, _____ had driven about at first with Casaubon, but of late chiefly with Tantripp and their experienced courier. _____ had been led through the best galleries, had been taken to the chief points of view, had been shown the greatest ruins and the most glorious churches, and _____ had ended by oftenest choosing to drive out to the Campana where _____ could feel alone with the earth and sky, away from the oppressive masquerade of ages, in which _____ own life too seemed to become a masque with enigmatical costumes.

| she/he | boy/girl | Dorothea/David |
| her/his | Mr/Mrs | herself/himself |

8.6 Summary and future developments

It is difficult to draw firm conclusions from recent work in literary and critical theory or to evaluate the likely impact of such work on future developments in literature and language teaching. Our view is a generally positive one, however. Although to date most of the theoretical investigations have taken place on the plane of 'theory' and although the precise nature of their relevance to pedagogy has yet to be fully explored, it is clear that there are important implications for the teaching of literature in a second or foreign language context. For example, the consistent exposure of the cultural relativity of liberal humanism and Eurocentrism inherent in much critical practice is especially valuable in such a context. Above all, however, recent work in literary theory remains challenging to the ways in which interpretations are made and the socio-cultural positions from which they are constructed. The claim that there is a universally valid reading of a text is shown to be suspect.

Our position in this book is that recent developments in literary theory cannot be dismissed and that ways need to be found of sensitising students to the issues raised and the changes in critical practice prompted by such issues. Our strong view is, however, that it would be a mistake if such issues were to distract attention from the textuality of texts. This is paramount in the teaching of literature with students for whom the language of the texts is not their first language.

In this respect we do not see interest in the linguistic organisation of text diminishing, and continue to see it as a major responsibility of teachers of literature to assist students to respond to the uses of language in literature. This interest will need to be modified in the light of insights generated by literary theory and it is vital to pay more than token lip-service to theories of literature; but language-based approaches will, as we argue throughout the book, continue to generate practical, creative and systematic 'ways in' to literature and continue to constitute an important strand in genuinely integrated language and literature teaching. Necessarily, too, as we have again argued in many places, these approaches need to feed from and into the personal experience of students and awake their active engagement with texts. This remains *central* whatever the gender of the student, whatever the culture in which they are situated, whatever socio-historical positions they occupy and whatever the ideologies by which they are embraced.

Select bibliography on literature and language teaching

This bibliography is a *select* bibliography. The items have been selected according to some specific principles, but exhaustive treatment of the field was not one of them and must await the work of future bibliographers. The guiding organisational principles of this bibliography are as follows:

1 It aims to be an introductory guide to the field of literature and language teaching, mainly with reference to the second or foreign-language learner.

2 In keeping with the chapters in this book there is coverage of work which is mainly methodological and classroom-based in orientation. Reference to books on stylistics is to those designed as student textbooks.

3 References to articles appearing in journals are normally to those journals which are widely read and used by language teachers.

4 The terms 'literature and 'reading' are interpreted quite widely and the bibliography includes material devoted to structural readers. The reason for this is that learners regularly encounter such texts in the course of their literary studies.

5 The period covered is 1970–1989.

6 Classroom anthologies are not included unless heavily annotated as student textbooks.

7 A short *annotated* bibliography is also provided giving information about the main textbooks published at the interface of literature and language teaching during the past five years – years which have seen a rapid growth of published material in this area.

We alone are responsible for the subjectivities which inevitably govern selections. Any omissions, whether by design or by default, are also our responsibility.

Ronald Carter and Michael Long

Bibliography   Adeyanju, T K 1978 'Teaching literature and Human Values in ESL'. In *ELT Journal* 32/2

Allen, V F 1976 'Some Insights from Linguistics for the Teaching of Literature'. In *English Teaching Forum* 14/4

Barker, M E 1985 'Using Children's Literature to Teach ESL to Young Learners'. In *English Teaching Forum* 23/1

Boardman, R and Holden, S (eds.) 1987 *Teaching Literature* MEP

Bouman, L 1985 'Who's Afraid of Reading (Part 1)'. In *Modern English Teacher* 12/3

Bouman, L 1985 'Who's Afraid of Reading (Part 2)'. In *Modern English Teacher* 12/4

Brazil, D 1983 'Kinds of English: Spoken, Written and Literary'. In *Readings on Language Schools and Classrooms,* Stubbs, M and Hillier, H (eds.) Methuen

Brumfit, C J 1979 *Readers for Foreign Learners of English* Information Guide 7, British Council

Brumfit, C J 1981 'Reading Skills and the Study of Literature in a Foreign Language' *System* 9/1

Brumfit, C J (ed.) 1983 *Teaching Literature Overseas: Language Based Approaches. ELT Documents 114* Pergamon Press/British Council

Brumfit, C J 1985 *Language and Literature Teaching* Pergamon

Brumfit, C J and Carter R A (eds.) 1986 *Literature and Language Teaching* Oxford University Press

Campbell, N 1987 'Adapted Literary Texts and the EFL Reading Programme'. In *ELT Journal* 41/2

Carter, R A (ed.) 1982 *Language and Literature* Allen & Unwin PN 203.C2

Carter, R A and Burton, D (eds.) 1982 *Literary Text and Language Study* Edward Arnold

Carter, R A 1987 'Reading Literature in a Foreign Language: Language-Based Approaches'. In *Praxis* 11/3

Carter, R A and Long, M N 1987 *The Web of Words: Exploring Literature Through Language* Cambridge University Press

Carter, R A, Walker, R J and Brumfit, C J (eds.) 1989 *Literature and the Language Learner: Methodological Approaches ELT Docs 130* MEP/Macmillan, The British Council

Collie, J and Slater, S 1987 *Literature in the Language Classroom* Cambridge University Press

Cummings, M and Simmons, R 1983 *The Language of Literature* Pergamon Press

D'haen, T (ed.) 1986 *Linguistics and the Study of Literature* Rodopi, Amsterdam

Dillon, G 1978 *Language Processing and the Reading of Literature* Indiana University Press, Indiana

Duff, A and Maley, A (forthcoming) *Literature* Teachers' Resource Book Series Oxford University Press

Ferrar, M 1984 'Linguistics and the Literary Text'. In *The Use of English* 35/2

Fish, S 1980 *Is There a Text in this Class? The Authority of Interpretive Communities* Harvard University Press, Harvard

Fowler, R 1971 *The Languages of Literature* Routledge and Kegan Paul

Fowler, R 1981 *Literature as Social Discourse* Batsford

Gower, R 1986 'Can Stylistic Analysis Help the EFL Learner to Read Literature?' In *ELT Journal* 40/2

Gower, R and Pearson, M 1986 *Reading Literature* Longman ~~PE 1128.G6~~

Greenwood, J M 1989 *Classroom Readers* Teachers' Resource Book Series Oxford University Press

Hedge, T 1985 *Using Readers in Language Teaching* Macmillan

Holden, S (ed.) 1988 *Language and Literature* MEP

Jones, R T 1986 *Studying Poetry* Edward Arnold

Knight, R 1982 'Literature and the Language of Linguists'. In *The Use of English* 33/3

Leech, G N and Short, M H 1981 *Style in Fiction* Longman

Littlewood, W T 1976 'Literary and Informational Texts in Language Teaching'. In *Praxis* 1/1

Lott, B 1986 *A Course in English Language and Literature* Edward Arnold

Maher, J C 1982 'Poetry for Instructional Purposes'. In *English Teaching Forum* 20/1

Maley, A and Moulding, S 1986 *Poem into Poem* Cambridge University Press

Markwardt, A H 1978 *The Place of Literature in the Teaching of ELT as a Second or Foreign Language* East-West Centre, Hawaii

Markwardt, A H 1981 'What Literature to Teach: Principles of Selection and Class Treatment'. In *English Teaching Forum* 19/1

Marshall, M 1979 'Love and Death in Eden' : Teaching English Literature to ESL Students'. In *TESOL Quarterly* 13/1

McConachie, J and Sage, H 'Since Feeling is First: Thoughts on Sharing Poetry in the ESOL Classroom'. In *English Teaching Forum* 23/1

McKay, S and Pettit, D 1982 *At the Door* Prentice Hall, New York

McRae, J 1985 *Using Drama in the Language Classroom* Pergamon ELT

Melville, M (et al.) 1980 *Towards the Creative Teaching of English* Allen and Unwin

Moody, H L B 1971 *The Teaching of Literature* Longman

Morgan, J and Rinvolucri, M 1983 *Once Upon a Time: Using Stories in the Language Classroom* Cambridge University Press

Muyskens, J A 1983 'Teaching Second Language Literature: Past, Present and Future'. In *Modern Languages Journal* 67/4

O'Brien, V 1985 *Teaching Poetry in the Secondary School,* Edward Arnold

Page, N (ed.) 1984 *The Language of Literature* Macmillan

Pickett, D (ed.) 1982 *Literature in Foreign Language Teaching* British Council Seminar Proceedings

Power, H W 1981 'Literature for Language Students: the Question of Value and Valuable Questions'. In *English Teaching Forum* 19/1

Prodromou, L 1985 'All Coherence Gone: Literature in EFL'. In *English Teaching Forum* 23/1

Protherough, R 1986 *Teaching Literature for Examinations* Open University Press

Quirk, R and Widdowson, H G (eds.) *English in the World: Teaching and Learning the Language and Literatures* Cambridge University Press/British Council

Ramsaran, S 1983 'Poetry in the Language Classroom'. In *ELT Journal* 37/1

Shackleton, M (ed.) 1985 *Double Act* Edward Arnold
Short, M H (ed.) 1988 *Reading, Analyzing and Teaching Literature* Longman
Sopher, H 1981 'Discourse Analysis as an Aid to Literary Interpretation'. In *ELT Journal* 35/3

Tomlinson, B 1986 'Using Poetry with Mixed Ability Language Classes' *ELT Journal* 40/1 pp.33–41
Tomlinson, B 1987 *Openings* Lingual House
Traugott, E C and Pratt, M L 1980 *Linguistics for Students of Literature* Harcourt Brace Jovanovich, New York

Walker, R 1983 *Language for Literature* Collins
Widdowson, H G 1975 *Stylistics and the Teaching of Literature* Longman
Widdowson, H G 1983 'Talking Shop: Literature and ELT'. In *ELT Journal* 37/1
Widdowson, H G 1985 *Explorations in Applied Linguistics 2* (esp. Section 4) Oxford University Press
Wiley, G and Dunk, M 1986 *Integrated English* Cambridge University Press

Yorke, F 1986 'Interpretive Tasks Applied to Short Stories'. In *ELT Journal* 40/4

Annotated bibliography: textbooks

All books annotated here are targeted at upper-intermediate/advanced students of English.

Boardman, R and McRae, J 1984 *Reading Between the Lines* Cambridge University Press. Students' Book and Teacher's Book. Ten thematically-organised units. Mixture of canonical and non-canonical texts, plus extracts from newspapers, magazines, etc. Very detailed Teacher's Book encourages 'open' responses.

Carter, R and Long, M N 1987 *The Web of Words: Exploring Literature Through Language* Cambridge University Press. Students' Book and Teacher's Book. Ten units organised according to language-based approaches (e.g. prediction; cloze; reading aloud; ranking; role play, etc.) Activity-centred, communicative approach.
Clarke, D 1989 *Talk About Literature* Arnold/Hodder and Stoughton. Five theme-based sections combining comprehension with activity and task and linking language and literature.

Durant, A and Fabb, N 1989 *Literary Studies in Action* Routledge. A unique activity-based introduction to literary studies containing over 100 tasks covering literary history, literary theory, interpretation, literatures in English, etc.

Gower, R and Pearson M 1986 *Reading Literature* Longman. Students' Book. Ten units focused on developing responses to theme and dominant literary forms and structures. Wide selection of texts thoroughly glossed and annotated.

Lott, B 1986 *A Coursebook in English Language and Literature* Edward Arnold. Students' and Teacher's Book. Traditional textbook concentrating on comprehension. Teacher-centred (compared with other books on this list). Language sections devoted to language forms rather than to functions. Twenty units each devoted to the study of extracts from a wide range of texts, including Indian and African literature in English.

Tomlinson, B 1987 *Openings* Lingual House. Students' Book. Forty extracts organised in eight thematic sections and chosen on the principle of English as an international language. Numerous suggested activities leading to communicative exercises.

Walker, R 1983 *Language for Literature* Collins. Balanced mix of comprehension and exploratory language activities on a range of texts. Ten texts taken for close study including African writers and a spectrum of different literary forms.

Wiley, G and Dunk, M 1985 *Integrated English* Cambridge University Press. Students' Book. Aimed at mother-tongue school students but usable in EFL/ESL classrooms. Thematically organised. Eighteen units containing linked language and literary activities. Mainly comprehension-based.